Collected Poems

WESLEYAN POETRY

COLLECTED POEMS

Joseph Ceravolo

EDITED BY

Rosemary Ceravolo and Parker Smathers

INTRODUCTION BY

David Lehman

WESLEYAN UNIVERSITY PRESS

MIDDLETOWN, CONNECTICUT

Wesleyan University Press

Middletown CT 06459

www.wesleyan.edu/wespress

© 2013 by the Estate of Joseph Ceravolo

© 2013 Introduction by David Lehman

Manufactured in the United States of America

 This project is supported in part by an
award from the National Endowment
for the Arts

Publication of this book is funded by the
Beatrice Fox Auerbach Foundation Fund
at the Hartford Foundation for Public Giving.

5 4 3 2 1

Library of Congress Cataloging-in-Publication Data
Ceravolo, Joseph, 1934–
[Poems. Selections]
Collected poems / Joseph Ceravolo ; edited by
Rosemary Ceravolo and Parker Smathers.
    p. cm. — (Wesleyan poetry series)
Includes index.
ISBN 978-0-8195-7341-4 (cloth : alk. paper)—
ISBN 978-0-8195-7342-1 (eBook)
I. Ceravolo, Rosemary. II. Smathers, Parker. III. Title.
PS3553.E7A6   2012
811'.54—dc23   2012028822

publication of this book is funded by the
Beatrice Fox Auerbach Foundation Fund
at the Hartford Foundation for Public Giving

Contents

Introduction by David Lehman　xxiii
Editor's Note　xxix

Transmigration Solo (1960–1965)　　　　　　　　　　　I

　Preface　2
　Lost Words　3
　Life of Freedom　3
　Sleep in Park　4
　Descending the Slope　5
　Feast of Visions　5
　Floating Gardens　6
　The Women　7
　Lights of Childhood　8
　Romance of Awakening　8
　Invisible Autumn　9
　Metaphorical Desert　9
　Celebration　10
　O Heart Uncovered　11
　His Universe Eyes　12
　Pain Songs　12
　Migratory Noon　17
　Contrast　17
　Dinosaurs of Pain　18
　Frozen Lookout　18
　Stolen Away　19
　Starting Up Again　19
　White Sky　20
　Chains of Mountains　20
　Resting　21
　Pastoral　21
　Transmigration Solo　21
　In Full View of Sappho　22
　Spell of Eternity　23
　Note from St. Francis　24

Water: How Weather Feels the Cotton Hotels (1960)   25

Fits of Dawn (1965)   39

Introduction   40
  Book I   41
    Part 1   42
    Part 2   51
    Part 3   63
  Book II   74
    Part 1   74
    Part 2   85
  Book III   95
    "The green lake is awake . . ."   95
    The Crocus Turn and Gods   99
    A story from the bushmen   103

Sea Level (1964)   109

Wild Flowers Out of Gas (1967)   121

  Rain   123
  White Fish in Reeds   123
  In the Desert   124
  The Wind Is Blowing West   125
  Indian Suffering   126
  Warmth   127
  A Song of Autumn   127
  Funny Day   128
  Spring of Work Storm   128
  Autumn-Time, Wind and the Planet Pluto   129
  A Story in Winter   130
  The Plant Is Growing   130
  End   131
  Drunken Winter   132
  Skies   132
  Is It Impossible to Know Where the Impulse Has Originated?   132
  Not a Baby   133
  Wild Provoke of the Endurance Sky   134
  Dangers of the Journey to the Happy Land   135

In My Crib   135
Don't Break It   136
Spring   137
Happiness in the Trees   137
The Book of Wild Flowers   138

Spring in This World of Poor Mutts (1968) 139

It Is Morning   141
Caught in the Swamp   141
After the Rain   141
Dusk   142
Heart Feels the Water   142
Lighthouse   142
May   143
Cool Breeze   144
Ocean   144
In the Grass   145
Ho Ho Ho Caribou   145
Red Sun   149
Fill and Illumined   150
Noise Outside   150
Winter Song   150
When the First Tree Blossoms   151
Passivation   151
Doubts   154
Before It Is Destroyed   154
Nothing   155
Floods   156
Sculpture   157
Passion for the Sky   157
Road of Trials   158
Pregnant, I Come   161
Both Close by Me, Both   162
Spring in This World of Poor Mutts   163
Data   165
Autumn Break   166
Lonely in the Park   166
Football   166

Tripod   166
I Like to Collapse   167
Down   167
Soul in Migration   167
Polar Flower   168
Orchard   169
Struggling   170
Grow   170
Risk   171
Fly   171
Mountains   172
The Green Lake Is Awake   172

The Hellgate (1969–1975)   185

Part I. Testament   187
Part II. Departure   196
Part III. The Bridge of the Dead   204
Part IV. Purification   209

Interior of the Poem (1971)   215

INRI (1979)   223

O Moon   225
Alone Swollen   225
Another World   226
Question Haunting   226
Birth Day   226
Vision   227
Live Today   227
Perched   228
Promontory   228
Bloodsucker   229
Rampant God   229
Earth   229
Trouble   230
Experience   230
Hotel   231
Space Out   231

Mistake   232
Apology   232
No Help   233
Freedom   233
Within   234
Dangerous Journey   234
Worse Enemy   234
Not One   235
Fable   235
Bad Ass   235
Mixture   236
Broken   236
Layout   236
Reborn   237
Futura   237
Internal Rays   237
Apocalypse   238
Awareness   238
Macro   238
Rising Sound   239
Hard or Soft   239
Lighting Up   240
Job   240
The Car   240
Beyond Phony   241
Inside   241
Unable to Move   242
Pass Me By   242
Hard Energy   242
Motion   243
Stupor   243
Cuando Amenecer El Sol   243
Spring Breeze   244
Sleeping One   244
Hunting   245
This Land   245
Old Friend Hung   246
The Gods in Me   246
Future Landscape   247

Imaginary Styx   247

Disasters   248

End of the World   248

Reality Printed   249

Marginal Existence   249

Footing   249

Continuum   250

If I Can't   250

River Flooded   250

The Forest Wetness   251

Non-spatial   251

Runs Me Over   252

Flight   252

But   252

To Seed   253

Manure   253

A Cave Man's Dream   253

Ritual   254

Basic Heart   254

The Winds of the Comet   255

Negative Mountain Peak   255

Infinite Thunder   256

Ghost of Spring   256

Millenium Dust (1982)   257

WINDS OF THE COMET

Volcano Tears   259

Bright Sun   259

Wet Sand   260

Cross Fire   260

Savage Nocturne   261

A Last Song   261

Spiral   262

Geological Hymn   262

Barbaric   263

The Catskills   263

Today's Night   264

Sleeping by the Rocks   264

Drunk on the Brain   265

The Spirit Mercury   265
Rhythm   266
White Dwarf   266
Inside Story   267
Escape to Atlantis   268
Winds of the Comet   268
Survival   269
Fire of Myself   270
Body of Earth   270
Not Afraid of the Dark   271
Generations of Clouds   272
Waves Apart   273
Cooling Galaxy   273
The Rocket   273

Apollo in the Night
Storm Breaking Over   286
Hills   287
Night Wander   288
Cold Night Alone   289
Morning Insults   289
Conception   290
Milky Ways   290
Time on Earth   291
Instantaneous Takes Time   291
That's Where It Is!   292
Projection   292
Star Song   293
Earthquake   293
Voice on My Birthday   294
Inland   295
Illuminant before Dawn   295
Late Birds   296
Summer Lightning   297
Perpetual Life   298
Apollo in the Night   299
Great Plains   306
A Railway Stop   306
Night Birds   307

MILLENIUM DUST

Longer Trip 308
Dawn Hunt 309
Cardinal Conjunction 309
Sacred and Profane 310
Ignition of Dawn 311
Body Weight 311
Hymn to Earth 312
Kyrie Eleison 313
Can't Sleep 314
New Realism 314
Good Friday 315
Mood 317
Birth in the Dunes 317
Shifting Lives 318
Fever 318
Tensions 319
Meadowlands 319
Gravity Awakening 319
To Open Regions 320
Reversals 321
Unemployment 321
Full Bloom 322
Not Really Punishment 322
Nude Madness 323
Crazy Death 323
Park Thoughts 324
Concealed Wound 324
Ocean Body 325
Glass and Steel Structures 325
The New World 326
No More People 327
Brook 328
Millenium Dust 328
Montauk 329
Unfinished Sonnet 329
Dirty Snow 330
Tidelands 330
Final Dimensions 331
After Image 332

1976–1982

    Railway Box (Deo Te Salve)   335

    Body Jet   337

    Love Eyes   338

    What It's Like   339

    Espacio   340

    Haunting Ghosts   340

    Rte 3 into N.Y.   341

    Just at the Beginning of Summer   341

    Scope   342

    Words from a Young Father (Leaving Body)   343

    Requiem   343

    April Already   344

    Assimilation (in the Streets of This City)   345

    Night Ride   346

  "In one day everything's green . . ."   346

    Holy   347

    Tongues   347

  "The night gets lonely . . ."   348

    Crazy in the Night   349

    Mayhem   349

  "Taking me away. . . ."   351

    Sub-Scape   351

    Signals   352

    Apology   353

  "Tie one on, tie it on . . ."   353

    Supplication   354

    Positive Disintegration   356

    Aurora   356

    Lament #1 for Poland   357

    Dirt   360

    Lament #2 for Lebanon   360

    Asia   361

    Sunset   361

    Middle of Winter (off the Hudson)   362

  "It only takes a machine . . ."   363

    Verses of the Soul Suffering to See God   364

1983

    Rain Forest Ode   366

    Earth So Beautiful   367

    Dominica   368

    Forest Dreams   369

    Over Music   370

    "Hold me light, hold me tight, . . ."   371

    To the Death of a Poet   371

    Long Sonnet   372

    "Where have I got time . . ."   373

    City Scape   374

    Double Blind Concerto (for Epictetus)   374

    Guitar Ode   375

    "The first August day is over . . ."   376

    Sunburn   377

    Linear Ballad   377

    The Amphibian   379

    "Rain cycle, hold my brains . . ."   380

    "I hear the music from below . . ."   380

    It's Only Glue   380

    Builders (Large Moon Rise)   382

    "Here's a traveler in the womb . . ."   383

    Spirit Matter   384

    Tones   385

    "All winter the . . ."   385

    Night Flash   386

    "Do a little job . . ."   386

1984

    "The squirrel leaping frightens . . ."   387

    "Sunny day with ice . . ."   388

    Fault (Penance)   388

    Planet Sonnet   389

    Lament #3 for Bayreuth   389

    Forgive   390

    City   391

    Spring Rise   392

    Grand Jury   393

    Indian Song   394

    Release   394

Jet Resurrection   395
Mother Land   396
Above Clouds Above   397
Legacy (Going Back)   398
"The pains of children . . ."   400
"Where am I now? . . ."   401
Serenade No. 1   401
Why God Should Know the Gods   402
"O Guitar! . . ."   403
War   403
Silent   404
"Floating emotions . . ."   404
"O ancient Rivers . . ."   405
Pre-Christian   406
Simple Creation I   406
Simple Creation II   407
"Minor eruptions in the air . . ."   407
Dead Sea Scrolls   407
"If I left . . ."   408
"The migration flaps . . ."   409
Hermit Gambler   409
Alive   410
Woods   411
Dirty Benediction   412
Elegy   412
Toxic Wastes   413
Autumn Torches   414
Libera Me   415
"I lean on my bus . . ."   417
"How can I disconnect . . ."   418
Sonnet   419
Stay   419
Thanksgiving Day   420
"O world without light . . ."   420
Street Wise Romantic   421
Lament #4 for Ethiopia   422
A Piece of Glass   423
"Happy heart that sows the breeze . . ."   424
1984   425

1985

"My intellect seems to breathe. . . ."   426

If You Loved Me   427

Love Song   427

"Seagulls are in from the sea. . . ."   428

Pages of Storms   429

Hungry   429

"Tile floor, open glass . . ."   430

Street Journal   431

"Dried up and dogged . . ."   432

Unfinished   432

Century Sonnet   433

"I'm not weeping and weeping . . ."   433

Freedom   434

Hospital   434

"This is not the place I want to be . . ."   435

Incantation   436

Pumping Iron   437

"'Du bist in meinen Blut' . . ."   438

Reggae Mine   438

Courage   439

Morning Vespers   440

"9:01 . . ."   440

Notoriety—Academy Awards   441

"The streets against their stomachs . . ."   442

Night Strokes   443

BMX   444

Forecast   445

Ignorance (Strong)   446

Narrative Night   447

"On a night in a distant country . . ."   448

"I am not able to move . . ."   448

Sonnet   449

Hidden Bird   450

Lament #5 for Lebanon and Israel   450

Lethal Sonnet   451

"Closer and closer to the ground . . ."   452

Rain & Wolves Inhabit Me   452

All at Once   453

Life Sentence   454
"There is no way . . ."   454
Dragons and Dungeons   455
Ode Song   456
Mad Angels   457
One   457
The City   458
Ode   458
Dream Ode   459
"Dry leaves, light trees . . ."   460
Travelin' Blue Highway   461
People's Republic   462
"Volcano mud covering exquisite bodies . . ."   463
REAL   463
Marketeers Entwined   464
The Comet Returns   466
Litanical   466
The Muscles of Animals   467
First Snow   468
Hymn   468

1986
New Year   469
"Where are we headed? . . ."   470
Melody for Food   471
Morning Touched   472
Mid Ocean   472
Lyric   473
"White as a deer's tail . . ."   473
Rifle Shot   474
Winter   475
Amor & Psyche   475
Portrait Painter Realistic   476
Stampeding Visualizations   477
"Calm me! . . ."   477
"A police siren passes in the street . . ."   478
Darkness Ode   479
Thoughts   480
Modern Sorrows   481

"I walked out. It was raining . . ."   482

Now   483

"Turn me around in your hands, O wind! . . ."   483

"I have a bad day today. . . ."   484

"Looking at beetles and ants, . . ."   485

"Smoke rises like claws that lock me in . . ."   486

Crescent Moon   486

Reprieve   487

"The purple plant, leaves thick . . ."   488

Hymn to Rain   488

Bad Thoughts   489

"I work in a dreamscape of reality. . . ."   490

Characters   490

Come Clean   492

Complaint   492

Someone   493

Still Life   493

Morning   494

"The best time is when the body . . ."   495

"Song birds . . ."   495

Nuclear Disaster   496

"Does loneliness take over the body . . ."   496

World War II   497

"Route 3 and lonely . . ."   500

Mass   500

Discovery   502

Angelic Meditation   503

Week Day   503

Hand Gun   504

"Between a rock and a hard place . . ."   505

"Am I a fool in the temperate sun . . ."   508

Subway   509

"Old world, there are roads in front . . ."   509

"Grind away, trumpet, beat away, . . ."   510

"How could the comet be . . ."   511

Breeze   511

Traffic Sonnet   512

"Under high tension towers, . . ."   512

"Hardly a lightning flies overhead, . . ."   513

Spirit   513

Blues   514

Der Wanderer   515

"My deepness away from you . . ."   515

"What is a year ending? . . ."   516

"Overpayment, underpayment, Florida lakes, . . ."   516

Observation   517

"It is cold, it is cloudy, . . ."   517

1987

"Consecrate the birds, . . ."   517

Winter Sonnet   518

Hymn   518

A Child Story   519

"I saw a red tail hawk . . ."   519

Mother & Father (Simple)   520

Hotline for Youth   520

"As if snow could cleanse, . . ."   521

Subway Walkman   521

Today's Benediction   522

"It's the quiet that we . . ."   522

"Tundra and deer, liberty and fear . . ."   523

Search   523

Bird   523

Sun   524

Notes on the 20th Century Scientist   524

"'Crazy nut,' the girls said. They're . . ."   524

Sublimation   525

Unseen Sonnet   525

A Young Couple   526

"Morning breaks . . ."   526

OK   527

Cat of Eternity   527

Meditation   528

"The multitudes betray the fallen city. The glass . . ."   528

Irish Entry   529

A Call   529

"Slowly my love, . . ."   530

An Old Testament   530

Rain Driven   531

Koyaanisqatsi   532

To a Dogwood Tree   532

Beginner Method   533

"The morning is warm. A fan whirling . . ."   533

Kin Pain   534

Spark   534

"Dark inside me every day . . ."   535

"Take away the hours of creation, . . ."   535

"Tunnels are closed. . . ."   535

Perpetual   536

"Somewhere between a missile . . ."   536

"Million dreams, billion nights, . . ."   537

"My arms are heavy and I feel . . ."   537

"Too many times there is . . ."   538

"Resurrect, reserve, resound. Winter ice . . ."   538

December   538

"Thank the gods for life . . ."   539

Starvation   539

"Hidden underground in a frame . . ."   541

1988

"All the stars will be gone, . . ."   541

Irish Entry   542

"Swamps and people live in a lake . . ."   543

"Turn the screw, bang the nail, . . ."   543

"8:27, have a language, that bundles . . ."   543

"When you can choke off the under- . . ."   544

"A man listens to music next to me, and . . ."   544

"Happy heart that sows the breeze . . ."   545

"Song birds enter the morning . . ."   545

"When I think of all the fuckin' hours . . ."   545

"When a spirit comes to me . . ."   546

Indexes   547

Index of Titles   549

Index of First Lines   555

Introduction

DAVID LEHMAN

In 2002, when two *Pleiades* editors solicited work for *Dark Horses*, an anthology of unjustly neglected poets, I was not the only contributor who put in for Joseph Ceravolo, but my hand went up first, and I got to praise this overlooked genius of American poetry.[1] A master of lyric concision, Ceravolo enjoyed a stronger connection to childhood and the child's perception of the universe than any poet since Theodore Roethke. In the 1960s and early 1970s, which appears to have been his Abstract Expressionist period, he used simple words and phrases but linked them unusually or leaped elliptically to achieve a sublime innocence. A six-line poem begins: "O moon / How ghost you are." A liberal use of exclamation points and a crafty sureness in the line-breaks contribute to the effect, as in the close of an early poem: "How are / you growing? / No better to in a stranger. / Shack, village, / brother, / wild provoke of the endurance sky!" All the pathos of childhood informs the moment in "Ho Ho Ho Caribou" when the speaker says, "Like a flower, little light, you open / and we make believe / we die." In short, Ceravolo was a homegrown original, possessing an utterly distinctive style.

The claims I would make for Ceravolo today are as great, and now there is twice as much evidence to back them up. Until now, only a limited portion of his work—the mostly small-press editions that appeared between 1965 and 1982—has seen the light of day. Edited by Rosemary Ceravolo, the poet's widow, and Parker Smathers, the *Collected Poems* gathers the far-flung fugitives and adds the crown upon the his lifetime's effort. During the last twelve years of his life, Ceravolo accumulated several hundred pages of poetry, some titled, some not, almost all dated, and under the working title *Mad Angels: 1976–1988*. It is the appearance of these poems that makes this a particularly momentous occasion. We will, in the light of the *Collected*, need to revise upwards, not only our estimate of Ceravolo's achievement, but also our understanding of his singular place in modern American poetry.

Born in the Astoria section of Queens, New York, in 1934, the first son of immigrant parents from Calabria, Italy, Ceravolo graduated from City

College in 1954 and began writing poetry while serving in the U. S. Army in Germany three years later. He wrote poems while on all-night guard duty in a stockade tower. A civil engineer by trade, he took Kenneth Koch's writing class at the New School in New York City in 1959. Koch's teaching had a strong and lasting influence on him. Frank O'Hara called him "one of the most important poets around," and it was fitting that Ceravolo's debut collection, *Spring in This World of Poor Mutts*, won the first Frank O'Hara Award in 1968.[2] (Koch and John Ashbery judged the award named after their late friend.) It is a book I have long loved, and it would suffice to establish Ceravolo's reputation even if, in his clandestine way, he hadn't added to it substantially in subsequent years. The publicity-shy poet lived quietly with his wife and three children in Bloomfield, New Jersey. He had a powerful dislike of the "phony." He was fifty-four when he died of an inoperable tumor on September 4, 1988.

In 1994, *The Green Lake Is Awake*, a volume of his selected poems, was published with an admiring foreword by Kenneth Koch.[3] According to Koch, a Ceravolo poem was a sort of "amazing perceptual archeology," its effect almost mystical. "It faded like the mirage of a gorgeous building: then, as soon as I reread it, it was there again," Koch wrote. He singled out some of the linguistic "oddnesses" in Ceravolo's poems: disjointed phrases and incomplete statements, which occur often in a "context of simplicity, quietness, and directness." Koch pointed to the materiality of the language in such a poem as "Drunken Winter," quoted here in full from *Spring in This World of Poor Mutts*:

> Oak oak!   like like
> it then
>   cold some wild paddle
> so sky then;
> flea you say
> "geese geese" the boy
> June of winter
> of again
> Oak sky

In these and other poems of that period, the words seem as physical as objects and as strange. It's as if the poet were practicing, naturally and without calculation, a sophisticated poetics of substitution, erasure, and merger, suggestive of meanings beyond the powers of paraphrase.

If Ceravolo remains a secret ardor, it is in part because he resisted calling attention to himself and in part because the New York School, with which his name is associated, has not yet received its full due from academic critics. I love his simplicity—his apparent simplicity, I should say. In reality Ceravolo is, as he writes in his poem "Happiness in the Trees," "no more / simple than a cedar tree / whose children change / the interesting earth / and promise to shake her / before the wind blows / away from you / in the velocity of rest." The full complexity of his personality is on display in the writing he did—sometimes with an air of improvisation—in "Mad Angels."

A spiritual journey in verse, an unedited transcript of a poet's embrace of all things, from nature in its glory to his own mortality, "Mad Angels" will astonish even devoted admirers. It turns out this poet of laconic grace was also a secretly prolific practitioner of daily writing in the approved New York School manner, except that he sounds like no other member of the tribe, even when he writes an elegy for Ted Berrigan ("there are no special worlds / for a poet when / he dies or when you die / he goes where you go"), when he relates a boyhood memory ("When I was a child / I thought a handgun in a holster / and the lead-colored bullets on the belt / was one of the most beautiful things / made by man"), when he initiates a self-styled serenade with an exclamatory "Ah shit!" or when a garbage truck collides with the blinding sun on a city street, yielding an unexpected epiphany. Here is the whole of "Sun." Note the strategic use of blank space in the third line:

A garbage truck across the road
turns into the traffic, the avenue
a burst of solar   blindness.
It is the birthday of the universe.

Ceravolo is unusual among contemporary poets in the depth of his spirituality. "The Holy Ghost is in my nerves," he writes. Transgressions rhyme with confessions, "holy lightning in the forest" with "mea culpa on the chest." The liturgy of morning includes "ecstasy," "eternity," and "benediction," but also a fair amount of "dirt," as in the poem of that title from July 1982:

Dirt on shoes
The simple life

When fears come
  like a trembling
of rocks
  the earthquake
  is my bride

The sought-for ecstasy is as real as it is crude in "Body Jet," where the poet is watching a bird in its flight:

Weeping at the crude greatness
ready to take off
on the wetness all alone

I burn at the take off
  so invisible
a god, off the ground
into air I moan

It's the most
crude   thing of fears
I have ever seen in life
this emulation of strife
of a bird

Although it scares
the shit out of me
it is close to ecstasy

Ceravolo's poems are greater than the sum of his influences, which in his case would seem to embrace the Gospels and the Catholic liturgy, William Blake's prophetic poems ("A vestal virgin melts the sword of communism / a large spider / dissolves the temptation of capitalism / both drowned by a sunbeam"), Shelley ("as if I finally / understand you / creator, destroyer, preserver"), William Carlos Williams ("A frog is kissing / surface of the water / from underneath"), Gerard Manly Hopkins ("Be uncovered! / Hoe with look life!"), Zen ("Without god there is no god. / Forget everything!"), and the poets of the New York School ("This morning Walt Whitman / walked past me / Ed Poe sat next to me with a coffee / Emmy Dickinson watched / TV with me in amazement").

A "Street Wise Romantic," as he puts it in the title of a late poem, Ceravolo is alone with a universe of death and mystery, unreported miracles and unobserved raptures. He attends alone and unobserved when, for example, a "hero" is buried—"a county policeman / shot on interstate 280 while / stopping a car"—in as affecting and unorthodox an elegy as I have encountered in many years ("Libera Me"). There is the love of "Amor & Psyche" where "there still remains the kiss / like the fires of a candle, / or a forest in seclusion, / or a migration lost for ages." But in the land of unlikeness it is the life of the spirit that is chronicled. The poet alone hears "songs that even nightingales / didn't know / or even the gods learned / for their created." The "you" in his poems is vast, divine, and worthy of prayer. "Deliver me in the pure waters / of sudden joy / when for no reason / it be OK to die / and never return."

Ceravolo's poems are lean, full of working nouns and verbs stripped of modifiers. He is unafraid to end a poem abruptly. He can move from whimsy to high tension in a line. He favors the vernacular yet speaks of the gods as Hölderlin might. He is on intimate terms with the wind and the sun and is able to "rejoice / in [his] deximil / of time." Yet none of this finally explains the magic of these poems—how they transform the commonplace into the extraordinary or why they make this reader feel he is in the presence of a natural poet, for whom poetry came as freely as leaves to the tree. His last poems are heartbreakingly beautiful.

> No one sees me. I am just here,
> my foot a decoy for compassion
> my sympathies and despairs for
>   another generation to find.

Notes

1. *Dark Horses: Poets on Overlooked Poems*. Eds. Joy Katz and Kevin Prufer: University of Illinois Press, 2007.

2. Columbia University Press published it and the succeeding volumes in the series. "The award is specifically intended to encourage the writing of good new experimental poetry and to aid in its publication."

3. Edited by Larry Fagin, Kenneth Koch, Charles North, Ron Padgett, David Shapiro, and Paul Violi, the book was published by Coffee House Press.

Editor's Note

PARKER SMATHERS

At long last, *Collected Poems* brings together in one volume the poems by Joseph Ceravolo written between 1960 and 1988, including the six published books, as well as four long poems (two of which have never been published), and one never before published book-length manuscript. This new collection includes the final versions of Ceravolo's books and long poems that were published or intended for publication. The six published books have long been out of print, and all had limited print runs. The only book still in print devoted to the poet's work, *The Green Lake Is Awake: Selected Poems* (Coffee House Press, 1994), represents only a fraction of Ceravolo's output and draws heavily from poems he wrote in the sixties. This is the first appearance of the epic work *Mad Angels* (1976–88) in its entirety. The long poem *The Hellgate* (1969–75), also never published, is in many ways the crystallization of Ceravolo's poetic vision.

This collection begins with Ceravolo's fifth published book, *Transmigration Solo* (Toothpaste Press, 1979). As he notes in the preface to the book, Ceravolo wrote the first section of poems in the fall of 1960 when he was living outside of Mexico City. He wrote the poem "Pain Songs" that winter, after he had returned to New York. He ends *Transmigration Solo* with a selection of poems from 1965. Although the dates of the ending selection overlap with the poet's first book, *Fits of Dawn* ("C" Press, 1965), Ceravolo had written the highly experimental work in the spring and summer of 1961. Only 300 copies were printed, but the book remains to this day a seminal work in the annals of American avant garde poetry. In 1980, when a possible reissue of *Fits* was being considered, Ceravolo wrote a new preface. We include it here.

Two long poems also written during this time are included in *Collected Poems*. In the fall of 1960, when he was returning from Mexico, Ceravolo wrote "Water: How Weather Feels the Cotton Hotels" while visiting a friend from the Army who was stationed in Louisiana. "Sea Level" was first published in 1964 as "What Is That Flying Away" in *C: A Journal of Poetry*. It was published again a year later with its new title in *Art and Literature: An International Review*, whose editorial offices were in Paris, and where John Ashbery was the poetry editor. In addition to these poems are the *The Hellgate* and the long poem "Interior of the Poem" (1971). The latter has an interesting backstory behind it: Ceravolo dictated the poem to Rosemary when he was painting their kitchen one weekend.

There exists some overlap of poems in two of the published books. Twelve of the poems in the chapbook *Wild Flowers Out of Gas* (Tibor de Nagy, 1967) were reprinted in *Spring in This World of Poor Mutts* (Columbia University Press, 1968). In *Collected Poems*, to avoid unnecessary repetition, we've included these overlapping poems in *Wild Flowers* but redacted them from *Spring in This World*—with one exception. To "Passivation" (the last poem in *Wild Flowers*) Ceravolo added four new sections for *Spring in This World*; and we've included the longer version of the poem, as it appeared in the 1968 book.

Transmigration Solo was just one of three books published later in Ceravolo's career. Chapbook *INRI*, published by Paul Violi's Swollen Magpie Press (1979), comprises a series of short twenty-syllable poems, dedicated to the poet's brother-in-law Joseph Robinson, who died in a work-related accident in the winter of 1978. *Millenium Dust* (Kulchur Foundation, 1982), Ceravolo's last published book, contains poems written over the course of the previous two decades.

The unpublished works, *The Hellgate* and *Mad Angels*, exist only as handwritten manuscripts. We have tried to be as faithful as possible to the author's intentions in rendering them for the first time here. In 1969, Ceravolo wrote the beginning of what would become the four-part poem *The Hellgate*. Three of the four parts are dated, so we can accurately tell when the different pieces were composed: the rest of part one and all of part two were written during the summer and fall of 1972; part three was completed in February 1975; and the fourth part, undated, was presumably written that year as well.

Mad Angels spans more than a decade, from 1976 to 1988; the poems—almost all of which are dated—unfold in chronological order. Because of the magnitude of the work, we decided it made most sense to divide the book into years. For one, this makes navigating the extensive compilation of poems more accessible, but it also is in keeping with what we believe was the poet's evolving conception of the work. Ceravolo tallied the number of poems he'd written per year, much like a daybook. The annual nature of *Mad Angels* becomes especially pronounced in 1983, when he began generating poems on a consistent, monthly basis. The winter of 1983 was also an important point in Ceravolo's civil engineering career:

He visited the island of Dominica to do survey work for a road that was being planned, and the poems written during that winter are obviously inspired by his time in the Caribbean.

One last thing to note. The final five poems, dated March 1988 (with the exception of the poem beginning, "When I think of all . . ."), are slight rewrites of earlier *Mad Angel* poems. Book length is always a concern in any publication of this scope. But in this case, repetition seemed warranted and perhaps intentional, providing what we feel is a poignant and fitting ending to the collection.

Rosemary and I are especially grateful to Anita Ceravolo for the invaluable task of helping her father assemble the Mad Angels, to James Ceravolo for his technical know-how in obtaining photographs and book illustrations, and to Paul Ceravolo for all the physical gathering of the manuscripts and poems in the house, along with his daily assistance, enthusiasm, and patience throughout the editorial process.

We extend additional thanks to Suzanna Tamminen, Leslie Starr, and Stephanie Elliot at Wesleyan University Press, along with our friends and fellow bookmakers Ann Brash and Kathy Kimball.

TRANSMIGRATION SOLO

1960–1965

Preface

In the fall of 1960 I lived in the Colonia Ramos Millan, an outskirt of Mexico City. I had never felt as strong a connection between myself and a city. Nothing could move me from there. One day I saw Iztaccihuatl rising from luminous clouds more beautiful than light, and I wanted to climb it. I never did. Gradually I became homesick, smelling the leaves of the northeast, smelling an Autumn that wasn't there. By that time I had written the Mexican poems that appear in the first section of this volume with the exception of "Pain Songs," which was written in December 1960, in New York City, forgotten, lost, and rediscovered ten years later.

A group of poems from 1965 completes this volume of *Transmigration Solo*. Whether I chose them for contrast or for similarity of mood, I don't know, but I felt a brewing of diverse particles into the whole.

J. C.

1978

LOST WORDS

One corner is enough.
There isn't one
as the field bulbs go out.
Right nearby is a river.
Moon exhaustedness   slow (BIG)
slides lawns of earth under.
Moves paws, feet, nearby.

Closes this body in ground!
Is it Sunday? while throat of wind
swallows in the nest
the swallowable dark,
an incomplete you,
you so innocent—

     There's not enough words left,
     although it seems enough
     like grass inside me:
     where the moment
     is a terminable river
     and bush come home.

LIFE OF FREEDOM

Noise cells   Root barks   Piss grass,
The governments of tonight lay
like earthenware on sidewalks.
Arrange the geological brush, the wasp,
the part that makes it,
and out with a dog noise,
a night and the airplane lung.
The shadow on the wall
of multiple window mud-lamps
from street ceiling names that
sleep-bog their way across
a room of yesterdays,

of farms, of the interiors
of skins like
interiors of four o'clocks.

So as the park is,
where crust and piles of
yellow morning transfer
islandic barnacles to
leg trees, and wonderful
because it's cold,
your old feet in hand.
A big flower in park.
Onion life of freedom,
of green flies and lake,
of closest Spring and Fall.

SLEEP IN PARK

These, my understanding green,
and like tomorrow
along the Alameda,
the leather of your nights like
new departments of liquid
ride the syllable and come
between or after or inside.
What makes the afternoon
where funerals line the walls?
This is afternoon and a
tree is a house misunderstood
by the line-up on wall.
We follow standard judgement
and "no think," no brain
except what's under a brown
afternoon, and farther than
euclid rain slides across
the pillow which is clouds
of afternoon

DESCENDING THE SLOPE

I need a cliff I need zero
I need a cliff at 6:20,
and noise sounds thru pasty
soil of bus coughing
and spitting early morn fuel.
Think it's over? (the lights
coughing near sky . . . and
orange brown dispersion town).
There's the cliff,
there's the horrible cock
cracking his lungs
to the cliff.

Do you have guts?
Yes I have guts and a balloon.
We underestimate the whole process.
So what if there
are knots in wood.
They're smaller than all
the spots of rain, but
tomorrow we'll leave while
sky becomes poles of rain,
leave while clouds hounding
row stones regulate the scene .
The Michoacan river wheels
along the ropey scene,
and then it all ends:
tomorrow I mean

FEAST OF VISIONS

Instead it's that one damn spot
on the stained glass walls
of Mexico that looks like a man
wading his way in mud or water.

Seizure! blue wailing
questionaires of noonday
under the rotting trees.
Gracias mis amigos,
the river holds much mud
and he works for el gobierno
de Mexico
guarding trees,
riding a bicycle.
Oh mean women beating sheep,
sweep the dog shit
of three thousand dogs and niños
from your two foot sidewalks.
Tomorrow the fiesta
and mucho people
walk and see sun in river,
and cross over new
modern bridge made of pipes.

Ah, the dark eyes that
penetrate all the edificios
on the avenue.
The fiesta's fine, it
makes everyone think
that everything's just right.

FLOATING GARDENS

Sailing Sailing
under the creatura ridge,
and this less or more than obscure,
obsequious life follows the lives
of flies on beach.
"I'm happy," I said to big tree.

So we stand
on a ridge, it
has corners and we
wait in corners
of excellent summer,
unconscious manifolded igneous
summer,
and the flies on the pillow, sheet,
and cactus colored window
buzz the chandelier great white weather.
I'm far from a window.
Yet I am window and
feel the multicolored pushes
through open window self.

THE WOMEN

They have the corner
half seated on their thighs,
and long braids tied like drainpipes.
Their hair is a drainpipe
closed from rain.
In the corner of their eyes
is a building of grass.
Their smile cracks
plaster of paris streets.
When they look down
their eyes are orange slices.
They sell little peaches
with brown small rotten dots.

LIGHTS OF CHILDHOOD

You light like a flashlight
something through
the west of worn shades.
    All this great fun
    and you like a dark
    of misunderstanding only
    bring a large sample of green
    while people dance to
    rock and roll in spanish.
    All the littles on the wall watching
    while the parrot and dog again sleep.

The moon like a
stopped cannon ball:
so little difference between us.
I search the corners for you
and I am a drunk in a park
or a hallway at night.
Being in the street
is being gone in
the largest apple in universe

ROMANCE OF AWAKENING

Morning ground—
wet buildings light
my morning edifice group.
Animal, orange, mango, rat,
my weekday sleeping
as in a barn.
The rooster craps,
the most uncomfortable hour.
Brown instead. My lips!
are growing river brown.
Below—the house which departs

in open fields of round
　　mechanicalness,
　　　melancholiness

INVISIBLE AUTUMN

The blade days———
like Summer rush

Apollo leans.
The way the sun comes up,
the sun leans.
The sun leans less than
in the north, but one lean
is as good as another.
Now it's autumn, but
you would never know.

The blade days
like Summer, rush

METAPHORICAL DESERT

What do we do with
lemon nakedness desert arms
after ocean prying oneself?
This is synthetic day
clearly defined on the sleeves of evening
and how turned around
when rooster barks at six

We speak of the streets
and they become coordinative,
a fountain whose
water becomes a vein.

While light comes like
a moving overness,
a mosquito opera
we lose all (most of)
the scaryness of day.
Sure, what shakyness
in that these
aberrations are renounced.

If all, although only
the broken veins
of my tropical brothers,
through cloud sun atmosphere.
So and so will go
home or treeliness of age.
        Then along lugubrious ground,
sliding of hand, feet.
We've grown too much and
stayed along hedge perfumes
of the desert and walk
        in aberrations

CELEBRATION

The music is played. Play
the music
                O washable towns
Open wall   the wall
studio of moons,
Sell my bananas, I
mean buy my stones
of yellow obscure, of no
similarity. There are walls.
Something the same from nowhere rides.
        Get off! there
are many fenders that
sound like some green place

without all this gravity.
The soft wind tonight——
comes through trees
and river.
The town is people,
the people talk about town
about everything that isn't
town, that ends in people
and drizzle, that think
about a bottle and corn,
and some light on them
from the sweet sixteen party

O HEART UNCOVERED

We lived in province snow range
and something that we uncover
is like living
in one Arizona room
when we discover all we owe
to darkness
we never really know.

Tomorrow is the national holiday for independence—
no more left.
For the first time
we see the mountains
with snow on them pulling away
from the mountains and clouds.

HIS UNIVERSE EYES

Can we look through
this slanty night without getting dizzy,
and barking somewhere?
What was it about the first,
what wasn't it?

What kind?

     Whereat?

Then again the clouds
are bearable more than before.

We're invited to the river
by the river
and the wet flowers
that go along river
might not die again
                    tonight.

PAIN SONGS

Back; gone country around,
like wind in hollow rabbit.
How many steps to take to
mud around, across,
Ixtapalapa green canal?
The cow is green, the
flax is brown; brown life
of flies, cool color, sickness, eyes.
Many over, what then?
There Jose stumbled on
market stands, dogs bit my clumsy foot.

Transport the ground, and
trees of olives like mouth
of understanding boulevards,
of green light mountains
where hills are filled with
lizards feet near home.
A silence as white as hospital clouds.

O breeze,
when I was young
and tried hard, when I was
there among 1000 footers,
off on off on the bird
on in, gone in in in flew.
Alone. The straw's
alone, the grave's alone,
the twitch, the switch,
the bitch's alone,
above clouds higher than moods.
It's late and the air's
as thin as straw,
and hill droves of relativity,
of hornet's hair sleep cool
as a quiet nosey rat.

Climbing up we passed it by,
maybe it was the cactus on
the knee or lizard in his pee.
It looked straight up as sun
boomed in rocks and big
zapilote bird made a shadow.

They asked me,
You going where in leaves?
Going when in road?
Sitting with all this sidewalk similarity.
It's like a bed unfolding

some high transportation of the street.
It is too much for street
here. How high it seems.

Pain, like blue is the
strap of night, the goulash
of darkness, a pool
of energy and green light signs;
signs of red, signs of night.
I leave, sandals fastened:
breeze warm as my hands, warm
as these warrior's hands.
I refuse, but accept that
if nothing else, there's
breath as thin as paper.

The path, the path is where?
It's the cow's, o but
to be near the cow.
Let's be near some old
realization that just died.
Near some depowdered
head that comes around
the horseshoe curves of sense.

But I discovered along the hedge
of waking that this
is me,
and around my skinniness I
place my clothes of disinterest,
and I bathe it, and
I bathe me anonymous.
I am unknown.
And in a rail-
road yard at dawn.

Biting a stick wondering
what it's all about under
the orange tree gloom bridge.

Let's count and
amount to everything we're
not supposed to.
That talk is from a young
brain, in a rebitten valley
of feathers, sky, beach,
sea, bush, volcano hump in the distance.

It's the sand perverse on
the boulevards that
swim Veracruzian desolation
in deep vocabulary afternoon:
a knot of sun comingles
the cactus, the sea, the plateau.

The day turns over on its
spine. Every faucet's
on. Ah! in the
haze, the grip running wall,
the sun grouping on the stillness
of your dark tide.
What sea gull blindness
on rocks, dunes, oil
pumps of your thoughts.
And the builders rinse their mouths and
the days of a week go swimming away.

There is a creek that passes.
It's a creek that
travels and looks like a bone,
within which all memory itself
has been.
There's no memory outside this.
There is only it.
I want the creek,
the feeling of its
depth like a body
on the fingers.

The morning awakes
and leaves me with one
hard thing. The summer
months sit on
a steeple (the only one around),
and the magnifying glass
of occupation leaves
the doors of a monsoon open,
growing from ridges of your lips.
You are young,
all roofs of world cannot
crush the highways of your newness.
When you're gone
it's as if someone
has taken away
the steps to a temple.

Wind is warm in the
store windows. It's November.
Surprise ducks leave a
canopy of a lake over the avenue.
To keep these secrets
we allay the nobody
seen on the cheeks of everyday.
Here! wear this spirit insignia.
Don't ask.
The line grows from yesterday.

Tomorrow it rained.
The light is mattress lipped,
and the pages born curtains.
Here! bang on my hand
frozen since Montezuma.
"Los pajaros," not yet.
Whistle my breath
to the banging hammer hotel
and the Indian yellow blouse baby
carrying dirty serape beauty.
I listen

as I eat the street for supper,
listen to the pain songs
            of Mexico.
   Flashes of returning
   come with the birds.

MIGRATORY NOON

      Cold and the cranes.
Cranes in the
                  wind
like cellophane tape
on a school book.
The wind bangs
the car, but I sing out loud,
            help, help
as sky gets white
   and whiter and whiter and whiter.
Where are you
   in the reincarnate
            blossoms of the cold?

CONTRAST

   It's here in whatever shoots come up.
   There's not a sound.
   Like blossoms and grasshoppers
   under the snow breathing little holes.
   Is it death trying to see and breathe?
   But I can't ask you to go.
            Do you understand?
   What do you see?
   The white snow,
   the grey spears, oh grasshoppers,

you rough grasshoppers
that are deader than a grasshopper
against my raw heart.

DINOSAURS OF PAIN

There are no dinosaurs
but man suffers still more.
    Morning, roaring
    tiger of trying to keep.

In the engine silo,
    there are no dinosaurs
    of pain that are hurried
    enough: Morning Star!

FROZEN LOOKOUT

Legs are cold.
    Beneath the knees   the legs
    are cold.   The sun.
      The ball is out
    The ice is out.
Low.
The lips are warm
  beneath the knees.
    The ankles are cold; The tongue
    like a sweet dragon.
The ball   like
      dragon's eyes
   (I've never loved one)
   beneath the lashes like
      dragons' eyes
Refreshments Refreshments, no refreshments

STOLEN AWAY

How do people feel
              in this cold
    in this win . . . win . . . . windy nest
    in the gloss like a
              cold nest
      in the tendon of life.

      The benches   feel
      like green alligators,
      crocodiles in the snow

I get
   a warm mouth
   on the hair
Someone has kissed me.
That boy and girl
fight and kiss in the car.
      A deep sound comes from it.
The birds fly down
     one by one, drop by drop.

STARTING UP AGAIN

What am I gonna do
   on this road? The sun drafting
  us. Nothing is
     brought beneath its own
     transmission. The stars
  that are gonna come out soon.
Oh lively insects in
       the light. Criss-cross.

WHITE SKY

O sacred women going
    to work
      in the shallow, in the
        morning
in the brands of morning.
   Close my hand, open my
     hand against the wine.
The throat is dense and
   yellow.
It's only morning and the sun
    has become whiter
     forming on everything.

CHAINS OF MOUNTAINS

The clouds are panting.
There is a subequal brightness.
It makes my eyelids shake
in the morning submarine of leaves.
I think: where would my
dog be if I had one?
Like this brightness that's rubbed
in the morning.
And I touch this piece
    of metal and it is cool
cool as a morning swim.
But I hear no mountains.

RESTING

Oh bum!
there's nothing in a life
Oh dead
Oh dead
Oh yes
    The volcanoes in Tlacotal

PASTORAL

Regular quality. Drowsy in the sun
and now we've dressed.
    Good boy, let's go!

    I'll lie here in the park.
Guard me! I might be stabbed.
But only the grass stabs.
  With a dark creepy garden
enveloping my shirt
I am here, lonely and friendly.
Nursing like a baby
the instantaneous wind, the air
and the melt of the birds' cries:
    your play cries.

TRANSMIGRATION SOLO

See the black bird
in that tree
trying out the branches, puzzled.
I am up here with you
puzzled against the rain
blinking my eyes.

Why are we
always fighting? Penetrate my heart!
Bees are penetrating
the hides of dead men.
Get some of that nameless life.
Protect our young!
You beautiful and vicious
God. Invisible and magical.
You can't protect us.
What are we?
You have no power
Doomed!   Lost!   Gone!

Returned! Lit up from loving
or from the absence of love.
So invisible and
magical, playful and nameless.
There is no power
except what you have.
Except what we have in our
playfulness toward you:
like bees in a space less hive.
Indian summer comes to us.

It begins the machine
of leaves falling and of bees
like little diving airplanes.

Even the hearts of defecating men
in carbon sorrow are candescent
voices of each other.
Where are we
alone? but with decaying
flowers that return and
a falling love!
O climbing adrenalin of neverending
passion in winter!

A siren climbs through the air,
the children are yelling
outside. I am caught up
         in you, I admit it.
How different it all is.

SPELL OF ETERNITY

We are going to the park.
There are swings there.
There are rocks along a sand bed.
The flowers rest along
the bed. The flowers
rise among the fatigued
insects invading them.
There is a smell.
It invades us
through the insects
and makes us
notice there are flowers along
the bed, tiny flower clusters.
I envy the smell along the beds.
Is this a decaying soul? But
it is not said.
Am I decaying like
autumn insects, autumn leaves?
Find my heart!
Revive it! The old clouds
you find along the sky
have no chance next to you,
because it is autumn,
autumn.

In the world today
there is
no world so attached as I am
to worlds.
All our hairyness
all our coarseness.
There is no texture in this
warmth I feel about
the creatures today.
We are gunning for extinction.
The sky is still bright
and all the animals running
for prehistoric sounds
believable in the passionate night.

WATER: HOW WEATHER FEELS
THE COTTON HOTELS
1960

1

The woodwind light
rollever breast sounds
a misnomer   travel on
tracks of
weather   sufficient
explanation cours
the river blank

     mask mean bundle
      entrails

  I shall saw
  wood saw I
  see the beach of windy feet
    so feel
  wool had grown on
  last sweater until
  he had heard

summer
the terrace people tomorrow
   Who has opened (generously)
    the well?
dispersion the expressed height
from over
a sea person
young fifteen year old
    algebraic breeze upon
    the curtain (hangs)

exit   enter low
  tide
the gang sponge
vase sounds of
what corn breathes?
is under commission   a
juniper
    of take left before
    the valley skates

                    the shadow hawk
what great decisions   who
licks the young chest (breast)?

2
    A small listen perched
    left in the wait of those
    impoverished he's
    Some highland march grass
            tree here   maybe there
            to roll the
            sharp gardens on   thighs
            grow tied to
            the climate of here
    Space
    mathematical hybrid
    is nature alone?
    representative to
            and green with longing
    An attempt has
        failed (cards
    in a coop of grass)
    investigate! it is
    necessary to cross
                        eruption blocks
below
    the marker sand
    Shall I wire night besides
    great exposition
    certain words under which
    I step out into
            sudden sun in summer
            clearest frost december

    unwrap the weather for
    it's grown old
    and you in
    at home speedily by the something
    but then to bother with

the secret
the forms in most critical
                position
followed by
            Oh lucky slide
    the backyard of where
            no trials   as when
            and by long window
    silence
we learned

3

one distinction of the clouds
Again you are young busy
        the leaves
        of human predicate
forget and thought of summer
by disappointment
where

        1 bed is to share
        with twelve others
        11 children (more or less)
        1 or 2 wives
        come in!

within balcony fiords
you act strangely
sweating (sweet) some anatomy   who
has prepared bread
and goldfish for the rooms?
my eyes have endured (shuddered)
the affection of hands

please this being not enough
        show me
the cotton gear (queer)

of death
we should all die men
we should all die women

Who is it? runs through
marsh voices damp
from dew

if night would pass over
me like a ship
in my twist
beneath the sleep
this cat the master
counts years in whiskers
of this cat
remain flexible
provisionally let me go
for end

4
but unlike Le metro
percussion   turns
where can you river
object waves the plainest
blue horizon
to contact the recurring
crowds
chop up all the
momentary
chatter and the clouds
See we are all
great behind
us the sound we walked
night

dromedary summations

yes we know the
    lip wanings
of the waves against
your breast

     and here it is mid
       december the
      sky
         still blue

and this river that has
Calm!   the january branches
Slope sun
    declining
journeys trace about
the factory towers having
given up their form
to the atmosphere blue
    and purplish a
    faded banner of surface

passing through this
     plain relief

the river. . . . . .

    this moment
    my strength hangs
    small festoons on
    this cliff and its
    corollary of trees

We could not touch eas-
    ier this confused design
    in the birds that
     gather weeds
    assume and designate
    small windy gathering

of wood
certain limpness
        forgotten

5
                                . . . . . . turbine
we cannot forget the
        condensation
of the mornings
between the 18 seconds
                the ride
increasing twins elevating
living by what we
would rather
        leap

the windy shelf

I suppose that you would rather live
through all this
the light the moon on
    earthernware
drawing its own
tonight on some
particular wasp

and you are only 18
        in the only
    kind

so we are states and
        not a word the
        mellow stillness
        of the sounds are
        still

Things come down in adequate bundles
to the crow
who speaks?   dress warmly!
to the bell from which
it is part

                        things defounded
Marcel clambered rocks in hat
and everything apart
from breeze of
highway moving downways
Pass the reticent principle stem
            interrupt vocality!

San Juan Teotihuacan
the mud branches of your pyramids
now in New York and
            branches like this november
the sun and cactus
    of your fruit
the orange season

6
Taking bread from his scratchings he
grew and in the thickest theater
remained a spectacle an ornament
of forgetfulness where nothing comes
back and nothing came from but the
small impediments like starch on
humming birds' wings.

7
        I had told you of
            the storm in full
                of red children
which we perceive of
how to man the machine
surely lose our valley

> disposition
well (water) has African wind
> women

always good for any
real moment life
is already covered with
contact the subject swim
he is a good
> valley food growing
> young again tired buttocks
> spoke the fox soldiers

Subject breeze that
finds your way bridge
the appler stretching the
disappointed that you could not

mischief food
> I've grown the last descent

outside——the poor balloons
> luck elbow   why come?
> havana! havana!

who speaks travels?   I
see you alone obtain
> afternoon's pronunciation
I also know it
the armadilla acts the car
> waiting
> desert tunes the fan

> Turn where light performs
> his own composition for
> saxophone now ruminates
> some tan notes
> cool brown

                    snow (saxophone)
                    falling
                    on my toe

          Last time we fumbled
          What time are animals?
          Walk   oh
                              overlooking

8
     Then there is nothing   think!
     the angular explanation
     boom!   he was a parade
                    with a gift
     a question cable of
                    thought
     a thermos savage in
                    the hotel
     in vera cruz color
                    sand the boat!

     the ship weighs on the
     east   Bobbing
     in sea
                              she burns us
     at the turn
          her eyes turn like the
               motion of a ship

     Let the careful prolific
     shade or else the
     falsity of summer in the dry
     a motion holding
     the blankest
          wish my hand

     Come out!   because
          I fall into spring (primavera)
     a proof that every

is the first seeing
the path is like the
     few leaves on the top step
turned by the
     opening of
     the door (swiftly)

it had been almost
          months and each its
               first step
like a distance between
          their smiles   were
hurry channels
contrasting the wood snow

     Ho!   river
walk softly for instance
     in park talk
that evening had no
   wish to go

When we had come to the exact center it was
there we should have to complete the last dash
realizing we had made a new arrangement through
which——could look at our sun pass through
entanglements. It was at this point I walked
down to people below——moving slightly (the air).

          for when have we not
                    desirable?

9
   Print open me   the
   car goods awake are drowning
        in the wake water
   leave behind
        sleeping and brought to
        a condoning dawn

the full chief and singing
enter!   someone like a couple
              the country fermenting
              the hill's edge and
    middle green with lipping
      there are   the old
                        sake

                  constantly near my entire
      years   stumbled in———
feet dirty

and you come forward
        from switzerland
      what I shall never
          be able to answer
      walk over me I
          feel   what earth

FITS OF DAWN
1965

He did not think, he perceived his mind functioning.

—C. G. JUNG

Dedicated
to the Release
from Suffering

Introduction

21st Century & Beyond Readers, please try not to consider this only a 20th Century piece of experimental poetry, for I only partly considered it just that.

If you can try to see it as a fusion of emotion and sound, of real life incidents represented in the graphing of new concepts, or of the reality of the inability to express feeling exactly, or of the phenomenon that the act of observing changes the observed, then perhaps you can gain access to whatever inner chambers there might be in this work.

Since music was the main impetus of my soul, I tried to steer or redeem American Poetry, with all due respect & love I had for it, from the path of forced visual poetry or the Image as poetics, to that of the inner sound I physically and mentally felt reverberating inside. Not that I tried to eliminate image. I knew too well the image can be the most lasting component of the poem.

At the time, I felt a tremendous youth in me, also a simultaneous vulnerability and happiness on the threshold. What more could I do? It was this mystery of sound and the weights of the parts of speech.

In a sense I did not write this poem. At moments it seemed that Orpheus in a moment of irreconcilable despair, did this to regenerate some inner hope.

J. C.

1980

Book I

Thou son of a great woman

Thy body looks like a cow's body,

Thou big acacia with large branches,

Thou red bull,

Thou son of a red she–bull,

Thou who didst drink my milk,

Thou to whom I did not give my breast slowly

Bushman

PART I

That should what I habitude
warmer hatchet please killed
too fast lilac mads wait
fly like eat one anything
say curiously caress ago

As who go spin ringing bowl
in other face it after
cures? ding! park "profiling
siren stay big-old
not every fond your up
concealment air could bereave
around what is ever"
Go! toward, unhop, confine

first of all what wander brothers,
what animal
escapement broth bathers
how the well storey goes rolling!
he knows me loved people,
      spring
Here own will are rain climb banal
off   far   ever
mis 'er tree yin dyr ee strain
positions camp alameda lone
compjoy wness
ate desiringful
larm non largimar! put joking

playing in the winter more
When! telling be close endness
noose grind bang (un vie) oh "tot"
Flow hot gust wall
cry crazy shower unbeeleave mom late
earlier   crush thrown kill
                        skycolory-
ness matter not no colony
de la cruise imagine wish form

Rivery wept pry
Afternoon need a snow   Bundle!
quiet widely vase wild coming,
same inside I time,
he returns stormly pullover
boating sober boring drum
however undersystemate never a
moment Confine, a con brings
mars up all togather free on
3 erg putana thermos. Soed
vivalful team lip unman cub

                tone he cave volunteer
rock meo done
Mun to the sinister,
come more incycle
wind along depthy sored
come on if you put it back
could give impending on goats.
The evening with goat eyes

Promise!
                    wish
(stop for think of)
Trampoline brilliance swell
machina pronounced
per laced room brace fallon moon
misother brother don't do that.
What you disgrace sadness fig leaves;
just look at me, off scissors travel:
find out piano not to
begin
escarpment pull   Punish!   enliven
other sun mordant bit over
your face Her up reasonable
the only gliding sea, but
we come to brown
because started way behind there is
rain and occasional   This boat
convince one dawn overture what!
Blend woman in sun,
let insinuous water dumps furnished
afford brace
reflection winter broadman
wall is he?   gallons of grape light
drimp abusement
tumble one boat, tug grinning skim
slit the waves, not both
in the sun door.

Friend man cutting down April
too in bog walkers
is a you many   Whistle! and
bird dropping   Help in
the alley blade your way trunk lively,
sans pan, bread, november
put the moose, boost me up
bragg staple me, horizon gulf:
Stemming incorrigible stream
Lick: woman grocery work 5:00
Come class children serene

Rusty in where
quarrel arch roam
more fit dubbing none by
face it nothkin chavez tempt
xochimilco obey shade queer
nud run copa tiran you
leaf Tibana apple until rubbing
a laugh hicho mirage uncover
Vie yes carry xpe tiran
do this so one pass aya reachin
Quit vine e lean papjud inebron
and here right took is called je
escasolax poor take quiver
chopping rakin' in rutty resumal oak
already lie sack why rare duts in joy
can pretend it run no ruinate
killing life knowing broad ivy lend
Took can understand upset Ondown

ache outsent insistment palm Papa
nothing jolular at vanim
Villain! jabel violin
Of chaining reachness cavey kid
roam the kayac take reangle chubby
aspen rusty unsettled
market yarn rocket ravener sol came
Go!   Run!   bay tacxico
rigor rubbing outset hapbel
queer carun kiakiha cheek
vine chin notion,
ruts who peyon
toxic anger catch

Beat tan fon reshuffle
rugged helical tone torture
except can you tell eratic routes choke yava
eaten quibble xr quilixic ride
jay bird transmit clash habille man trees
your reveal riling eventual net

     Suchop navajo
  axe dike chacun eltan
  cheen took us shade
    manjun choked
  table life acatch rubbing
  manmit manta obey blue

Reach dive-at in excel baynl
quit rigor jin chim shake up
vie indignation check-o-jol rite disapproval
Tie up peyo approval-el

handling erodsion camisa rational
shoulder and side on guerra ben vine
Resyn habil quequegul all the
how bove more can run
who has entrain Go here chuck fam
instead beautiful camp non-a-tu
stanzas donkotan arriving
June an make man nude pan de quis no
nab drag obey yukonic
Gutter quick junk indistant joy
eject la lome carry toxpan June!
His ramm payer gel revouch
sucut comelous task ditigation crying
Drowse and drowse rite in me
you leaf bine man
Of sunset experience came   Sorrow
rejavelin pend Y? man
con anima mammal rest take
coating poking quicking

     Beyond you jar unself
aroma ax almul chad rugyrebel sex
Leapon silent rebel chain riding
silence aback him eruption pile-
on disk outsent babe nibble have
a shu life Kota memory ahoy
cultivate so all chomine recussion
soulen boy mirage resume
Ecola!   Going there!   make ya took
Caribbean remind exuberance
tabu avalance voyant will curse

Janvier air okay moonset rakin'
            reaching pokinal animate
tired rub a bull his sake
adjust culva shine kites boredom Excel
coma runaway jumping
sad liberal sonic riping extreme
La Man avenal catch all day making
quibble peeks need
        escape which
mild open lesten filling
and come a route chew
cheat bukol povertly equivol
"n'guess in art his hand rub ejaf"
amount the causer relief channel
rebuke angle child
nabby fine avam porous lame
Vaguer ya hear diver mo' good
take name malade hunt
vosotros rob die gull on come come
come the sun surround . . . .
lava tome live-a-tree
Jantap spring oval recounter sucipe
omerb a ocean ta
name quinox if ever shade
erupts giver itself you-toric reveal
immense un zicuth zicuth
Holding fair of remob
Bang! damn!   viv!   of sudden
harms corden still away
Stray what even hard a

crip agile bint insending
agrope felt dark build

    How I lift yesterday
the maybe pland-o g-dumb
imposable ness hop will
Reach unbade menacuric look
dome it healthy shafe amomry
attack renear close brick benigher
tuyeres ayer hier bare
Miscomer elgan swim off t'wus
of wasn't supposed to
soon tone of married song just.
Pivot nod stranger   Pearl
they put a table a dance
rise anything but
tired botch does uncall
find come drum well
prod and even of what will
young comfort, you lat
on to the very eat to go
schedule rote affair
Enemoan Brace yun said endow?
we in then many. . . . . . .
you gone findly hinks cap toll ocean
wounded: hound th'morning
swallow cruise hemn at-last-a
playing by upper
time feel extra win
bounce excel rapes fenal digibex
Nucker can plant ivy pero jive

Shun generation

> Invoke harvest me
> I very wait folded,
> are horizon a
> preconcy to lift me
> from this main
> reticed move
> placed unwatched
> "a" with a shunder

Forgot myself and then you could become

This lizard with body poised
Watches the rainwater swirling past
                    Kunapipi Song

PART 2

Just lain at cover
waves the grow minute find and stows.
Under storm train reed insane
bring shall insofar got a dark want.
Riding poling colding all break
what-jump rely the cone dawn
across tepid realize window-
soon wind recognizing
my end world & foon

. . . . . love scratch sun
Some rang act back else
rain by section be hep
or call tide world stocking drown by oboes
usual, alone, elevated-gentle, facing
scurry,
Moldy all segment   Cold occasional between
Impede found
left sembering insane found home al'
ch' aveva absorbed creeked july
imaginary venued conserve tramp flying
strept saying low dixennial glee

Convenience hills chaining orange how
middle Sunday   shy
ask him

on   which slide going
townward I don't think we
cared   going trimming
might   browse sleep celebrate
revoir but   Conceal! the ocean
in on the stoops nights
for over dirty.
Nervous!   tremb drive
meeting!   quintet that I
could hardly sound reclining
reefers already stormy nothing but
sorry (Robbin scratches)
annoying drawn by
apple fair quiet tree
it came from these two kinds
Of could not be found

Demonstrate have begin like contra-
pressed dopo arms fuged sub-
nice preservation others soccer pawn dunkation.
Cage are sentence force
Dive sumac pace mil herb thanks,
man alogof loathe-bells
excellentations scritted imitate, lie.
Drove! "pas resistance" banging
rest verdure bath retreat flyinging
Communal gorged orchard begs
terrible serious moved
binding on resistance dumped smoke
them was remains traitored
sending lesser hunged,
row growed the showers ago
builders onjust flax despair!

So!   river harm
wilder capable sunset hungry fair-

I'm calm he's ashamed he nocturnal no way
Has back co-wept?
A skar in brimful final
Inexhaustable gyp becomes yes
next outulated   Me!   absolutely care mommy
aurora net takey benem ahoom got
soon enemy weave cryman
awayontop terre or sappho crop
why?   harmony hey-o coyote
Moans cry want flee
leak die toss-find a when
producted rare pow torn.
Like the why-moon daring
insuspicious striped like labors
serious choke.
Nan weeteo (sweet bastard) now that
mentions plan sun.
Why upon live perverse sented "laid"
survival front smalled,
forest define new survival
Tequila leaves, cactus notes, are
americas in wolves in calms May
deem and go incalculated
milk-branches sagacious shun.
Xoante mine, approach all them
in mope kill,
in by view non say weaky
hot rightwrecked hero

There were some thing an old
no presumed by really growing;
under travel perhaps.
I wait sickly that come
come how, own that
we could all face makes
day think approaches.
Harm notions steering touched yet
tepid hunch bring at
could none feet gloom hedge.   Save!
How?   the sun microphones;
strike and somed giving done must
yet nod danger fu-
pressed out
Motioning more nevered wind   may lull
stretted koon-reville sprang.
When has I now wowed?
sands brooked llama regret low   How
has sap-company growdigious of?
Long Oraly none.
　　Hate
　　along is myself
　　groundfully a soul
　　motion kioskly off able
　　dump-egret
　　unable wness an'
　　wide   Unsteer! soon never inmixed
　　like lushing bane
　　maneuver come
　　of yellow of islam
　　of

Have no, have no thing, have no thing
in a   Fool street.
Corrupt crammed on dance
yet much occasional reruningly
                    arrive jamming
nights my please high;
dismiss the rooms! aside, downlap
evening unto resisting-drop-
raping unstop morning sings.
Happening town inseed!
Untribe panic trees!
Raising look-body clumsify,
village escapes.   shys so here whenever
         taking off   I music dirt

Towards watched "peace water" mounts
obscure jarring obey
been quick, male do mal
hovers trunk blue captivity as
much rain calling
muching young send low teens.
Enclose!   are they
bending so soon rolled usurp and
cunning   From what's happen noises? sullen
lock april undoing
dawn, bridges, anemone, answer, and
Disappear!

I'm fatally sureness bypass
them early themselves
themselves summer you or defend
gorge still signal illicit-
trees   No!   Inside!   inside looks
But how I am am
gossiped from leaves Askance

topic among doing
mopely
spread for cheat-maple old total
awaringly stunt
Ah!   a noisy for romp phoney a
sun-hill out of roots
should rising departure
candescent chore, coast iris,
bruising purfling
walks yet-memo
song triculate throws, let us!
Why did have stayed?
concentric urges the
dispunt long puedo less over
that stares   Who?   wonder
who water is (seanod) (supine)
ayant odd power, how
dawn becomes country where
Wrong! skips fringe parapets
first least crawling hint unless kind,
alarmed prisms of laughs
odd shirtsleeves calling down
the jump bees the
speak

Secret this!   Open!   Stand pieces
Friendly these open &-
Of surmount, spring of upon
Among of hardly, summer of
Frown of woods, there stood of please,
Throngs of brown hurt, this
Is not-thirsty
A garden step   None!
no sour awe like public rope,
sorry to a ticket.
Who seen of when spoke
A hums blame
out means
away tact hawky by port sobra
nofound
spatial nodogs of May
Trick me!
accomplices from —
allows leaning of succumb open
like the body of a boom
lullfully like skies speech-
things of across
butting feeds of
Resist!   resist? yes!   resist!
again!   quite fully fully
dawnful
moving of sidereal fake
bigger than, like, the opens crazily until

day plusieurs never
clings also!   May
jonquils and
grows   follow of hagrous ago
world november privation,
parafin of sunset gales   Page must
monday
armways rosation unsorryed
diver   throw   assuaged
kidding and rose as pregnant-
purr chase none
Sake apart forcing apt
pelet because music also
                    mobs.

Waterfall
goes twist benificient. Lack column he
keeps voiceless, squirt
mountains look intermission odday
effacing advertantly cool avail, snow lap,
not evicts between episode
love ballet crops.
Shall I cotton revel leap depth
starving redone exits
odd belove almost torn. Venezuelan
voluble frown raining,
danger another.
I mouths of a hardship water,
conduct stones have no
summer of bed,
joy choice feel,
strokes cursed besiding
violet putting of year,
brother gulf,
hands seclusion, care generation.

How are you mentioned!
the leopard convolutes ———
town like convinced flowers, no-
whorl   Shore sunstop
rose!   Colony of second
mouths!
unperplexion fear of cons dayland,
patch buoy spare town
en forces, nor crazy flaw-
venerate convolutions of a chill.
There!   violence carts lurking mountains.
Mopish you poison
guess enshun tracking locale.
O shunned woman's pelvis.

Rubble
Sharp went!   flame of
the hideswept
Risk me!   yes!   oh
climb wait clumping pathetic sandstay
parallel person-wonder
volume of as soon has receded
patient, rack me! strong
tlacotal thinking talling booze
of a family   Goodbye!   a
lesson dryly-wish careless
ground escape

Then so am, how can?
inverts feed more
remote can we   On traffic!
necessary are this place, struggle
fainting swamp
Passer terre!   detain?
        Very flame
            Least all
Inveterate deways torque redeepen
Eagle secrecy. . . . .   Touch-plow
whenjug sounded jumps
Starving cry gap unrecognizably
inland travesty
But?
The grain poppy first-things
whelps accostingly would handle,
found recame bout pouncely and kill
given.   Chicaca suns.
Growmask-marry-ated dance
surrounding ridicule indian of soul
In precede deign decide
impudent softly-very where am
bursts fell
Poor more couple furiously tree
anotherless swagger-who
surface   Non mound troop inner
equal prods warning
who these cannot anxiety unway

Opened!   strand hunger
Faze popocateptl

Summit concave
running seeit axe outly,
secret below coup
what am merely escapeness a
indian sex minnowy be   Stillstep
orange bitterly-pockets no
Loll summary cages every schemes
it pesty almost
handful weather brink-
cruel esteem abode a
where deluge-spoke orchidy
cabeza parallel am weak.
Husk "sang" please whereby giver.
So savage!   Yes
once off biteself mooning.
Moods of tea falcon unyell
such of impediment
inimical
To grazize!   when?   Root
kind sources nape wholly
soto pass but you plumes
occurs carry
awl down shovel awl pubic feel
Redrum!   Answer go!   wander
clothe nearly pacaha kernel go
of obey   return
Away!   dreads ternflower fills.
homme she wind

Mensonge! each pyro
Hero!
coax-total frugally
octave ago habit avenue even
crazy of the ankles hills
Sore attend vulture
been debarking pain tour revel lasso
Only!   why renouncingly?   land-
mosque simple tenderer
craze did plus lately fleur
And sea chance
battlement fetch
never suis-je search
pours
going to
remains   drove. . . . drove!   mercy
noir rest yellow small bad
Bassoon place paw a wide
ungrain swallow: how I
innumerable   of suppose
Enough coup eager
strum banal segment
          moment! moment! moment!
deleterious soons of
recognize coma tight of torture   Go!
my hood, once, have,
hisses   bramble flung embarass
One! une la-bas
Hold lately or sunset
Flare! prostrates! thirsty!
Undoing!

PART 3

*

What obsolete! what lift!
geronimo of confusion
Vaguer stem carry turn rejoin
basket-and forgivingly tree
Criole equal
Contwist stranging instep been utility
urgent been guava up cages going stomp
agrarious while swooning
lamp skies.
Expectingly soccer revel inferring
tend men animous settles
damask unready oblique
of young ovally
some ginning tele-november
Resoon malheur unseer but about
severally knit swam
knees house opinion
viande landed ought for if.
Must unlovely out.
Sing of enough.
Pounce tuck-summer
totally morning inundate notion pivot
Tide wen trifely
gong days antecedent
highways probably songe'
among like bivouac limbs knew;
drank thing train fierce on.
Hot flourish beside!
Knocks' mixed! timid
trabajo. Justice-plainly music.

Still! Montezuma!   Suffocating prying
child orchard of uraguay
charring summon and longing
Wait? false swallowed chiming
Out ripe hunger
delve struggle tribal of lassitude   No him
Theodosia of humanity!
deportation as lonesome water   Morning
of headpiece, falls quarel
like reckless   Donde' beauty gallons Spring?

pilot dropulous tropical
should a pelican "you are travel
trees" might severally fiords
me possess.   Crustacean-lip
born went mere poor   O us!
Games so well
worst wednesday until of continue
Contrary Gull! spill of made

Small-sleep dawn breezing
shown deny lone
rain tempo courage Plead-o
mahogany throws
supposed and flowers grape-
vine water boring avid
down himself.
Mad of wrists!   Yards!
Twin fury pine imbalance,
fury of sand
Puff little slime singing   Albany cleaves

How before!   wind at
the sun   Division is
running charity lively farm
of wave
Seclusion perhaps and
hides monday horizontal coral
steep of hum, catch than
avenue givingly wagon
Afraid?   aflame fragrant gull
arab hemo jealous
of-noon of clamant out
lullaby life harm.
Quitting!
States what-sing.
La route fuss winning
turnson the early
inexhilarates swung exile
rose unplaningly
kind chant.
So upon
Orange yes whereaways
sun crime-stance-con-brake
Mouth motif like
cabins-I-do like done gathers
Sharpen!   terribly gaze really
mouth something.   Isolation.
quartet these "felice de lobo" rains
bad own brutally
lilac sub-upon

Sand dive sand dive sand dive sand
dive am emerald as forgive
Unroar!   alive the
promisable my or capable.
No mean silver of skin

      Are violets are
      roofing weather music
      wait!
      Cisterns of clouds,
      by pick
      doggedly sassafras
      trumpet-cherry whom.
      Where?
      firstly seen verges
      hum struggling
      faded
      When?
      crazy wipe
      Who am (sanded
      allay gist-despair)

Skies march also
Teens of asia illume suffocation.
Retornello opium
occur saying passaic landed
skying invent race pregunta
rubble-meant
when etch-po-ing sorrow

Spied!   once stash drifting
"no husk easily" hour
toyness gentle half-pre who'll
even?   Who'll turning of
children like thud tree-
noon   loft   East
Nz!   getting die several
I

      mumbbler of gash-
      compel
      Rice!   hold you
      festive running   Choose!
      Leap confide ballad
      positional
      ashame, oh stump!
      moons of drimp confuse.
      Tiens corner tien
      shed compel

Supine teem cease venimes bunch
subtle of sprig   Loop who
crying imaginable
Pension!   french of a log   Punish!
Lantern!   few no longer has
I

      hobble circulational
      weep pretends
      morsel skyway
      orphan sieve
      wrong misery
      intro-forgive

Where where does
lost   Sprung involuble
florgone apt myself
Pro solus myself hound
    worry
Tomorrow!   China
conjure! natural clarity!
dance elopes poignant
desert armature-vie, pueblo
of the side Come!   desert of
vagabond (a patience)

Tomorrow the orleans
testes testes   Beggar of opened
mother choice imbecilic as
oceans   Talent
Out on blank   Execution
of farm   Seep and fruits!
Lovely mix   Light riping   Travel
spelling invent as raids

I who
    have. . . .
stupid of the
  ghost. Mid-
            seduce flying
  weep am absent.
Lendemain suppose
    agragrian
  morning invent dam.
Fearfully mountain
amid harangue of
pebbles, fits
    of dawn, sing!
        Honest!   table.   The
        ramble all go
. . . .
All go.   All
go!

Purfling   july   Still
loving their rub
Mutilate of tricks
Others slump
gave muching dryly
of carried,
finally.
Estoy finally (I am)
destroy   Mean!

So watch   only of   swaywell
wild looms wantingly habit
beautiful mere fast

Turbule!   Become tilling
diving weakness song,
not sommeil medium.
My fowl!
Along of dessous shouting
on "am verges, am verges"   Poor
Touch-summer refill rumor own
then nor of ramble
Oh venimes "Venimes!"   Venimes
die sneak tidal of tribe-ingly
Album lunar of save, like rare
gun the stand savages,
fondle, clap, solitude
Like am just killed, like
william wrenching absurd
clay, like venimes permanent
of the black hills, like tlacotal
decoy idiot of clouds

What allay!   what actual soon
under seclusion steering white bigger of
gone   So went   Me   this humming
boot "please" crime votre unbegins
foliage-the unsuspicion newal.
Pulled looking nil, conch, desire la-
bas evasive closes oak yucca sub-fear in
anyway   Colt!   gone weepened in
colt, a man open, climb blood, inasmuch
october enscope
gully just agamemnon circulus
Circus!   haiti of stepping give feast,
pitched!
Wait herd!   boom
Oh recur!   glub limbo arms infant
common punch-argon your flower!   summer
of mouth   Oh I!
Fall little squares!   Like trees
Once so and breeze simple knee when-
jog benches trump soaring
october enscope
     Superbly splash of
     upright   Tact little
     water say
     mooding go as
     in lumber The
     spunk!   Oh routine
     leafy and
     street,
     reedy bells,
     october enscope

MORNING

Do not shore.   Let me run.   Eats the fake Happiness
Hunger and the livid turnfinger of the rains top
everything On lights on been the wide session went
hedge milk batty of a corridor, cannot offending
brushed amongful.   Oh fare!
       fragrantful
old still churning heed non more and more,
hand voice crow magnify. River corrupt
thirsty scoop infamy – rampart of the shakes.
Off beauty furnace and pity downtimes tropical
your dead all wipes   Abandon!   then trestle

Found times completely Good bye taste Effort

  Had it!   plus the livid
        Seeps foolish circus are you verse love
and length breathe and river except
grazes voyant raping
Have a public!   Oh platforms! Flags
savage of outflowered, enterprise-terrace unjoin
          like noise, halt!
Again, gland and
shyness beaver sky against
fails similar of the crowd   Dead?
Sure!
Ramp america huts small mumble dazzed
like the drive-in trusting pathetic days   Oh
roofs submerge indeed brother
and afterward female laugh stone
vehemently leaf   Gulf!
well pavilion of raffle dawn, Yes,
         of raffle dawn

Fail fail he route non ai-je allay
apple fierce joying like
confide blossom été-armed recite of barely
Wolves and the metal,   Family of
it is post lake enemy   Perhaps
envocal motionless leave unhopped,
sun chains drinking.
Away! so wet OH
crow fog and rio feeding
Clap-orient song
Naive ground askingly flesh
lookout each
gurgle   Away cropped fix
aussi-pied also-foot
intrusion viscous
texas spoons of death
Obelisk rose of
scaffold
Lunge.   please stabs quoted
spill ago   tree ago
Oh bait! Harangue!   Stall!
fete-skys soon.   The lowest eaten.
Road!   Yes bread, idea wife punch-
solace avenue WAIT!
Whether somewhere bullet path fingers
singing the roofs What a lot   Oh
what a ride, caves, And
sprung. . . . . .

Book II

PART I

Allergy of
River, Of Murder, Of New Beg
Love.   Children!

When'll enough rostrum.   Ordeal palms
yay!, yay!   dis-tree things.
Where're you public and west Stepping
voice Own despair!   Pubic
sunny interchange   Orphan!-
parapet concert of I am.   City Poplar-Hug,

tool october mid-jetty
anything dizzy preyard warn-
ning suffix.   A told whiff
cotton cotton Only nowhere
heap surmise punk.   Only weed hangar mixing.
Only theodosia wolf upside.
Upakosala.   Only
possess quell frailly
Only birdhood overtures
public giant only.   Only force violets
rabbit   Only camouflage noisey
Only_____

timber hurrah
suburbian right. . . . . tears
Upway! Planes!   cheat-
handy   Vicious
melon final kissly
soon children lion

There in the stream,

in the stream,

There is the stream.

Poor white eyes
of the month   No matter
matter moment moment torment-
chaos of the flank
croak done and helps   Ah Yield!
Mountain tend conjure siberia trickle
trickle batter lookingly street
martian hip civil   oh
journey and tingle
onlooking as a joist.
Hardly runner   bramble boisterous riverly god
ferris   What clover of boys?!
Exile.   Mars of the low breath.
Stupor flinch orleans
moss verge puppet   Must!
normal avenue   What cherokee
moho sings?
Inertly swarms shutting how
can of little girls   Gardens watchy
and bird (to act)
Stupid thickness!   Drown
I was billiard yes soda
dreadful loft
ho noise,
The swan humming
Salvage enact palm as shoulders
it is   color older

Silo crime-muse load renaissance
tambour summerly under
agape 'mong caught silo of the silver
eager   Quickness!   Please
bunch chassis of the
wind   Powers-roses   What! What!
what bust prelude Oh polarity!-
drimp-multi unlove
Connty earth concion   Thump
stable dumb loom of all is it oh into
                Come tassel phony
mads   Simply ocean Chrome chrome
imbalancio except
Sun   French   No
I tend. . . . .   Downland skill o'clock
nuages soon thrown miss-
ississippi for out simple
                    preunderstands
awkward farm eternity skirmish-
carbon becon as
stop   Placc!   King Place!
newal rose inept
I'm the schedule   Paths
roomed little runs dare sleeves
loveliness   Ah shift!
call iron drunken fingered stash-
                    tropic
Either fruit   Deux soire, a
night, stepped evening in oaxaca
tame flowerous nowhere

Coyote!   Swivel!   innocent
java texas upside survival pawn
of gazelles   Let preamble!
July easily darkness serious fussing have
"Oh raffle of drunkenness woven
released adirondack whatever Succinct
l'ete with cello   Guilty supreme
of shoulders, tattoo doze and yet sky Yes!"
taboo algonquin remedial
orgone obtruse poppily reefs
Grateful ranch!   Wallop ranch of
fin!   Hear
fatigue cozy lumin but them
conquest lilac stubborn a kind
Mouvant!   tend jungle
fatigues   violence timbre shedding Ah! jungles,
calculus voice che dragged
Sparrow-moslem!   Crowd while
"bum bum bum bum" Leopardus sway
divorce hillfaze   Vulture!
As!   World!   of purr le
suivre.   swimming pulse normandy
of wigwam.

        Zoo of a whirlpool
        Fog convolute life a
        teen   Oh corner
        perhaps yelp imagines
        our fool. . . . . multiply

1.

Of the he's silent?
batteau elysium!
drimp midi abuse madding
hum texas germinate   Swim-gress
pressive antler vie-roomily how

2.

Egypt senecas quando flour
undrop brisking belle-
often spy crumbling devoir
most condition denver capture   Oh infra
      Minus sappho of
the walk   Achieve-! violet milk
sonnet discuss that were candle
face central largo mischief
fins and the grove pro-finis
Visit down hop fawn yoga
firenze wand hexual sun
him prowess of a dock

3.

Am a running nest no we fought
No enough
pere injun malheure   The describe

afternoon tumble prison of
beggars   Arrival stance
Canteloupe and the Andes and
the whistle raining

Batter of the Mother

Silent ex-come silent elysium chain
neutrality of young

of the gold

Milk, am lull, hold
oh acre   Of the spunk
(week and palisade) Plate!
county tan dive annoy
foil arids dooring and
the mood-Crook!
incestly
galloped needing dizzy
        oh a sack-compris whiffing
pat Non Supp thaw range mades
inconnu oaxaca lee impossible
        Coffee! Summer! On!
channel biloxi aucun mare
Soldier-brink solar
are rest a humming communal finally grease
        Seminole. hwoo! hwoo! hwoo! hwoo! Hwoo!

        (Untook trepid!)?
        Stepped goodmount peak so
        yes so-yes-welp traffic
Indra is pale   Sub-
clover nice
as I swept   Saddle thing!
Xevening tooth   T
city simply mosque   O
sleeps limbo cent swim
Paddle eternelle turn
L   geyser joy of
kayac   Rums!   Swam!
When?   That that!
        No!, timber of rags!

no timber of rags.   almost family Stammer of tunnel
crete this (that me) nothing, bison, canary, twice
weakness sommeil, youngest, zoo body the
flower

      vendor brisk elijah what
    of the gulley chamaca what
modern!   swim for the public unhappy
and of sunny   A terrible and
soul

        Raft smother uncall like
gardens   Group!   Pleasure of
hardly tree
    What hemp!   what finch poppy
re-asia wait yard of loseable deck
  Chariot of the felony ridicule
calamity sheep tome.   Genesis of the
poor preciousness
Euphony the most help junk
of trestle   Lima! Enamour
guilt arctic clutter soccer when
Andalusia for our eastly earth
   House! Gallopy of
the farm totem and the hermit rain   Oh
lotus horrible rob-socket fail
Solemn gash broom fail
        dessert
Sakoontala'
     none
Beach, oh the
      lions
bow and air
    dizzy of the drums
nuptial alarm alias   ah
these mouths   beach oh

the lions, peru yes bad elysium
for the pennant rockies
of your love.   Yes wants to
powers oh the windows and the dance
. . . . even sing
Indeed espy and pigeons of
the offspring that asylum of the simple
shoulder the fight and
opera of the become, the
cellar like ounce seclusion keeper musical
pooring the Chingtoo. . . . . . What
lately thumbs!, my born?

     Candle, what makes briefly
     Am I a reef?
     just this same scour
     conch hex
     remeet oh told

     . . . .

     Hermit looking
     all career noons
     somnambula
     the boa you blossom
     re-meet oh told

     a very steep
     whistle of
     lakes matching a cherish
     Something sun
     remeet oh told

Hero involute since
hush dew wheeling
llama amboy of
sleep heretofore   ah paddlock
paddlock of gleams
The handsome whorl stranging instep of party
love than orient deck   oh
broom of rambling.   City!

     . . . . and pass

     ASLEEP

You are someday crisis lean and the balkan
You are the range for guilty gently
        cyclone of because nothing west
You are suffice coo union and primitive
You are droop revise   steal of azure, what does
                    you
       who leads on the eddy   The felt .
You are all the cats of the woods put their eyes
      out and the forest
        thirsty the slump a   the refund of
                        gapes a lovely
                         o'clock
                   oh nassau of
                   islip also
                   dessus landing
                   for the worry awkward
                   of your, no! . . . .
                     (you're)
                   destruction

In the chocolate dawn!   Emptier
of mishaps!   wampum of tea when the
piano!

grief please odessa/
                        wolf harangue as
                    someone
april alamo   the gym yes-
yes   convolute children gamma season
childhood yes
hatred cependent I tremble

Ah buffalo buffalo damascus of the milk

Buddhas and fathers cut to pieces —
The sword is ever kept sharpened!
Where the wheel turns,
The void gnashes its teeth.

                    Daito Kokushi

PART 2

weep   Ah giraffe cordial and unseen
remercy verge of tulip,
manilla of the hunger solo   Yes!
autumn varies,
rejoice shank, august-claps so
beside token odes ungrabbed.   He
said,
"Gallons of the blaze your energy
like docks in june."   Nice of two lilac
stumble discus   Stomp!
earth asia the stun
Shaking versus combo   Oh I.
Days that's what forges
bad a bad a yes   no corn of the
voice cypress mollify,
slaving voice lentil don't live   Digit
for the tuesday.
Shun! only claw lazy
toxic rang the berry mane sorry I'm
of pang   help summer!
whoa!   province kind sakootala'
blooms than mane

Caution. . . . . O caution
backward oh caution from the pears
funny yourself
So what!
beautiful swayed like girls
between the funnel for that walk
vultured   Be asked
so bed
grizzly
melodious softly-gash and he.
Soda so the feast wampum soda
the devil un-rain joyless
azure ferocious I buysa spoon can unweep
sheep bullet so the poor sonority
of you passion passion.

SATURDAYS

"There the same squint untrue
            of the feast
There songé utility
Swoop quays of skies
Whore for the cyclone always
Hum cherry fleet lettuce of the hill—
Day listing quiet who love booze of
The clothes, hannibal tumble.
The stars a doze O soothing counter!
Poor sesame his self
Dawn the evening this this acquarian unwren
In the bundle of the coo some-
Times Theodosia is yours
For the lotus like a toy you marry
Eternity wink: jamais hotel"

A

Yak breeze salute-cozy whorl July
july azure yes alley maladresse
Skies topac fu injun

B

What take-mean fearfully but
Stood gyping warm.
   Lion of innately missouri
   when so eyebrow dawn
   verges for carefully grease oh
    blonde
    infamy from dios
    of the gulf! Some
    sometimes
    and attack

C

Boy farina of attack no rayon for
a boyish hymn
No injun grove dawn seneca

D

Unquest sleep sleep
for the swayzy unbegin O
show. O summit O
mild Chimaleon seclude

E

Why golden impudent! very lilac
of growls?   'Mong of
beans Shy for onions of bees
gently place Volcano
him arc cherry than its knife
Eyelashes the boy
like winter off the
boy fins Sorry through
a handle Flame! Tibet!
Antarctica for the open. . . . .

Enfance medium!
Skate pushing there is cousins singly wounded
Down down there completely
hammock territorial day-elope- supine
dying like tucumcari
So speech!

O passaic elapse tin month
Susteno she sicily   Ran
ran ran numb
Should Kid
telling some utah some yellow
some ram goes nothing,
silence, amputee, gazelle, mischief-
chroming telemecus, voila so motif
like although of an elephant.
O devention o cypress
splurge   harpoon galaxy
triad   Gross. am the silo of
your voice   Minnow savant
lackadaisical throw pavilion of
an envoy.
Pavillion!   for the sun algiers of
my desperate conch   Quay!   Conch!
should never. . . . .

Milk arabesque merci what family
tents boy oh
for the pawn yes summer the mango
of you. . . . . dislike
Oh hombre!   genoux confusion la lune
yes port-hole cent   Plum, Yes
java hide la vase au lait a
block   Port reason of misery root
crime   This wing!   Am
week easy so colored   Am flex
despair of de oisseau   ex-tenochlitan
Roofs!   Timid!

Of Sonnet amazon, of the pronounce. . . . violets

Of Tapestry song the pomme of
a log sun

        Sonnet
Which wild?   lady and
the guadaljara   Fond of the
destroy! destroy forget!   like the tons
like the bringing hammock
citrus complained dormant hive like
putting malheure: a seen
Chorus!   swayed a wife
Yes noise!   Yes egret!   yes
nest the prowess drag-cood of

I should never wigwam for
west, venimes of the world Utah
Friend for the poor lightening
of your gills   Triumph!   Boom!
of the curious slave god

Muffin of sunsets!
None!   Is it ease they pitiful?
speed   Sorry growl island you idolatry
a midi crow immense. . . . . .
la june.   Chase sly a thing
Tombeau asylum d'oisseaux, a reflex
allons   Look!   look!
  x of beg love   Look!   Air
air crochet of swam
air wrestle for the easy week
air run soto whore of the gyping shun

Should weep bout rampant
soothyness tuesday lullabye shot
nevada for the grease
and you reduce the damp each
who piles volupt venued
bitter. . . . . belly
toward homo gleams embarass
woodland for the lily of the mountain send

Seclusion that hurry wagger
drag muster destroy
slow beaut tyrol besiding
allay the
sling!   the food oh tunic . . . so embrace
crevice autumn sorry
jamais that the oboe
sympathy   la voiture some
garden oh than zoo-
for the dying simple
for the gulley   a pity of incline

Childhoods

One-could one sunday and
Sake volley of the tree   Himself &
silliness un-mexico of slaves
deepness unfind.   The along

                        Chill & shining
Foolful.
              Giraffe and loveless

Tropic!   Confound!   Did!
There virgins full of buntless?
There twice eros something island there?
Am veil subside coffee I slip
remain musics lucania coeur who
boredom a crop of return
. . . . allez guatamala
billiard my verdad queery but arms
                              for the misery

pectoral of sweep   Fuyez!
Ran!   Music!   o washing
you north   Noisy name, The
sex justly pour   Fall!   Yes
dirt re-know connaissance trains
Sacred! ah of land
deserve   me january espy so
knew this could not
-voila so music!

            . . . .

Gape of Mexico!   lassitudes for under
those steeriness earth   Marvel violet
genoux on some yelling off   Plough!
Flood for andalusia's blank
The mars and je suis

Generously yes dawning and
bloom

On milk whosoever pleocene
innocent maybe leaped
      Peninsula for the adolescence
      auction of palms and wound & should

Surmise punk gone   dome aussitot as soon,
pier ask,
unjourney pours allas have and
all orient sumac young
fun toxpan melodious sad upon   No
land   boy oh

        Husk world!
        Band am ports
        offspring for the soaring
        of deed

1. Untone orphan for my voice a
      gone nor of the divining serious

A pitied of sunday far
sample agony of bridges voluble and
people and
what took.   Ah plus
embark maladresse sung heaving of the contempt
iceland! dizzy! feeds!
that walk   zoo sick ivory meantime
allons sunday of the dawn

2. Etes-vous coast.   Attend less
tail on, tail on stall funny by look
voiceless taming gel
eros acres   A middle you grow
I steep ah sunk coolie
douce and kiss fu thought
of currants yes stiffle   So
mulberry for the understand
malheureuse discus possess   yay!
Yay!   that don't

3.   Oh outside!
        Crawl cafe lull owl
    of sand use   It was
        severally union

                    no prewipe
                    Wipe antartica of
                    last men   Oh danger
                    chatter
                    clearly hest   Desperate

water   Gladness yes yes lulls
of decoy, no when dawn for
            vultures, conch decide
            for sleep. Does mouth
            only bat? so region
            unsorry porifery
Simply wound
                  ah chirp of seen
                  Bang my tide
                  I am flutter
                  So pant!

. . . .

Upping   upping on day recur,
should of earth hap sworl endless
owned for that hobbleness
violent succinct of tempting, oh
watchy him alaya when the drink.

Tierra! nothing less overture
dirty summer of wear when the
apple   Pine cause axless
sung stupor of nests
Beg injun actual of beneath clarteaux
dead   Slying!
mountain!   oh mountain!   un-
torn scat scat indestruct.
wakens so cupped of ascending
                  farms   ah the muslin
Muslin!   of stash compel
                  Voyez! terrace retournelle
migrate sax   the rail drape so
desire   Listen!   Made up!
Of!   gist, crocus, the among

Book III

The green lake is awake

O gong of wept

O unviolet
    furious cozy the rain
O dam of soul

to chase look! am poor.
    dimanche poor.

O cheat of beg   o cat
gist o am   Walk

elysium tool a sun day   Broke
revel lasso to
Yes, wolf of songs, O muse
O mixed Enemy!   Invent

of dwell   So voyage   So end mercy
earth   Usurp violets

O visible gym of flowered

Partly in skies in weak muzzles, fertile
    communal dodging america.
Unwhorl sagesse pain!
Ah finally teen so
morning that chime the running   The
Fun   Stop morning full rubber
of mountain to shun for
our active milk elope   The
Bottom

Am bottom am summer, am
there, hero   Seed allegheny hum verge
beckon teen unquick
unquick pieds couteau egress above

Defend, I ate song fins,
Am gush some bang of ode
conjure you must
I food and swim. . . . .
equal torture you personal
you wing soon
        Violent dishing my rush
stung of sorry   Themselves themselves
Tool soon fathom-seer-to-doze
theodosia to sonnet
drifted sono upthing, volcano reads.   Saviour
famish it is moves.
Catalyst so june so admit
Ranch! Ranching that votre like
misery prosody somnambula
being going being crime.

futile ment
at stroll for to
gulp   On rain joint
                    ill a shuffle
                    little though
                    trees got
Stem   feign to love
non flowers a   Tent as shoot
way so
nod of   apples dizzy

Terrible over!
Tent will boy?
Myself stroll final ment
at shuffle for to
gulp

                Why see!
                terre yes the
                save
                temp cistern
                for sorry
                      pawn
                oh sunday yes
                system of
                supine from milk
                neant so sly
                for sorry

Lotus non off
room bereave for
supine of sunday   "oh
fist je tout"
Communal all the
spare Trust! Ster-
ile! a reedy fuss de-
spair

The Crocus Turn and Gods

Toy for the raking gully
shame encore there,
sorry human posed working,
demeanor just helen as
garden comes, Music
o cotton unforgiven bargain,
chilly, gush, album in later manjun
embrace.   Begs soon jamais
furious bungalow of
pour a boy.   Scowl possess however
city trumped,
jumbles pity then, rum or
canto sleep in this eddy.
To a rumble Hour lo a grape
sleep   please graphic
to ours like ate
quivers place then float
came came wack ill of voices
god of
     Picnic lumin and
sake in Talk! Sort!
dose Ah slave and
premate Correo to
until of mades, asylum budding,
possessed sop churning,
woman tippling wings hill.
Young over ahoy
for the breathe

O targets! and sang   O timid of
among!   Off!   Saying!
yellow shook then Pan!   O

Completely leaf.
Yet prize!
alone aesop damage

Night for the carnival
rummage of humans

O outside O nervous yellow
silo for the harm
          And soul
Really game smother nowhere
summit   Yes
   oar kill happen of anamoured

                    Jungle
for my surely quake
smallen smallen stung of surged
   The birth
          Rampart!   Bat!   Perhaps!
   The drink   the whistle

there maybe
of the down
Not pine   Not scowl
prolific binge to wane,
orchard gyp afraid of
conch of frolick!   Yes,
no fist, the soon trestle trestle fake So
malheure a shy for bunch

"poseidon"
Donné
Farmest ecoutez o meadow
of pay

O shine of
  could
    Bark!
  Rooster for muffle
      Killed
O seem

              begin poor
    serious Demeter   O
hilly erg of
                  young
    being of otter being
        apollo
O Voyez!   O whelm
                Succumb
    painty of dommage
  Bloom! O tox
      destroy N
          oregon of motion

    Lore curious of milk
      O body   spill
        degree enfance
                  cane of
oaxaca. Today
      force infant
    flowerous than earth

Only the wand
        openly la playa
      la plage
            told
   winter aesop,

behind october worse, worse than belts
  of caracas then
    mind   O hunger   Livid
      swish

                      bullet
   remind a reed o
      gravel connaitre
              wack to doze

Dreamt of cheat
              cheat of
   suddenly soul dawn ocean
lasso for the
      Jealous!

Only violent elysium of
      the jetty
    saving ploughs   O
  lotus   O coon
      that grain
. . . . . .   O
   breathe

A story from the bushmen

"Are you an eland?"   Yes! Yes!
She ran off to the primeval forest
and there gave birth to an eland
Her husband holding the calf to his
chest ran to the hills: placed
the beautiful child in a fault
which was surrounded by other faults
among the hills
While the child grew, he (the husband)
created all the animals and
ways in which the animals were to
be caught; and also the wind which
was to follow the animals
being hunted
Their child, the eland, had grown horns
and only the sun was more
beautiful than he   But other
sons of the father of the eland crossed
the little calf in his sleep
and killed it because it was more
beautiful than anything they had ever seen.
Their father who had created
all animals tore off the noses of his
sons who had killed without
knowing what they had killed. But later
saying "No I won't do this,"
put their noses back on
        The wife cleaned her pots and
put the blood from her dead
eland son mixed with the fat from

its heart: and stirred, stirred
then sprinkling it about, each drop
became an eland which
ran into the woman with his horns
    See!   you have ruined the
      eland: and thousands were made
         And the father ordered the
sons to hunt the elands and to
see whether they could kill one
But Cagn, the father was
in the elands: and none
could be killed:
because they were even faster
than any cloud

sonne bell   Sonne guilt like the
unrosed stark   Ecstasy gen
d'alume no world
disbanishment unlook   See! See!
              occident am the sky
To cistern insist we lie
Swim, World!
deja everything already
and see

Peaks grand the fruit soleil o
  turbule wept for lily
     oh see   That nights
Border irrelevant sweet for wounds
    like the careful orion and
      blooms

Is the sky husk moldy
unison newal o please?
Sickle mads pro other weak
reef annoy mew
among o sway tones musing at
Lo lo dull off the forest,
moon frozen. Emptier that

shook.   Oh upon
          of songs   Breathe!

grateful soccer monet churning oh savage
of must   Overboard! small laquel embraced
Once are the alley easily
of supine   once
stood!   bad!
suffer and village!

   O scarcely
verge o stings   Where is a new
     beg of morning matin?
               "yes" of the hand?

delve sky against   Nude
mandarin d'etoile
A tour of slept Slept! the pacific
   the vine of orange of
               sommeil

Mads of dawn! Rape of you you. . . .
     o the autumn sand

Mounting!
   O dive!
song song restay fairness of
dawn. That cry of
booze that sparrow
of soul "miradel"
unique justly lotus
nothingless char of sunday.
Vicious of moon for the actual.
Live digress

Old like the praise cast
still at day   Assuage
of rose of eye
lovingly sun
   O sun with the dreadful
of kind   Man! full! of the organ
               of move
Shoulder are the vines
are the plus are the
autumn of found are the fallen
blank are the aussi
    the loping soon
       the wet

blank the soleil les fleurs
the Force of rainbow
    shout the fishing
quell quell.   River of sacred
        pitifully fairly

   admiring cane from
       cane one enemy sings
to find to
      bird oh
  ladel of fix
    oh severally plund of
cruel, like mars
    for my earth,
like loom for the understand.

To need am the fly
The breathe no pavilion to this
pain. Nape, so
the precipice is june   But for the
villanous level joyful
as the town so play

Spring & Summer 1961

SEA LEVEL
1964

Open to me, my sister, my love, my dove, my undefiled,
for my head is full of dew, and my locks of the drops of the night.
—THE BIBLE

PART I

BUSH

She is not wearing
shoes or a dress   I begin to change.
Breath will pass like the breeze
it is   I am
  changing   Swimming
    in a wave

I'm walking over here. I'm not
like a prisoner.   Don't
bother him, flies toward   the cells
  Spread their cells. There's free
misery in the cell
        How does
this chcap kiss
(walking over) find the real you
            and your cells?

What's the name of this
    sea level?   I can't
get up   It's so   diligent to
shine   The shoes are   not shining
in the kitchen
      The birds are twirping
in the bricks   They are burnt siena

What gives you a
    shot towards the
        island?

Where is your name on this
island?   To come here
without knowing   anyone at all
What courage in
the absconding night.   "Running

                    but to disconnect"

I try to sleep but I
can't know. She is

          sleeping   She isn't
old   She seems like
a stranger but I
              can't know

cooling the first
          headaches

                    Night is never

a stranger of
    terrible pain   In the clown of depths it can't know
timing delicate blood,

              tigers through her
          shining, a stranger
                    of   delicate children purging

in the bay   beside
          who he wants to sleep

I can't know what it is to lie there and dead because if I'm a passerby
and adjoining the luscious surrounded smiles, I could say I was dishonest.
If he could be arab maybe I could learn something about dreaming or
the lungs; what a bite at the intestine when there's such a long way to
go down through them into the field. I can't snicker because I know
my controls peeking at all the people evaluates me and changes and
dependent over a veiny sea, that I love to swim in. But am afraid of the
nutrition of this lust. It doesn't look like a life. But I know it is.

Never deserted, even if the desert is gas.

What is my
          wife's hardship
at random happening
in the fallen middle of day
· Does she find   Weak?
but the grass is
hidden in deep grass.   Pikes do not
grow thin   One breast

   The light's coming in through
the glass on the door
   The night outside is
not troublesome or
   manes of night

          belonging.   Through the dating
shrunk air the light's coming in through
the glass on the door

                              Where did
you go?   O summer long
   air   How's the city
Take off your shirt!
          Here is my skirt, she said.

When the native sets
over the wall, I grieve
to be honest real.
          Why should?   filled with
the monkeys   I play   with you

By the time to return
no head sees. O to have my breast see in
tawdry, my breast
seen in the simplest
　　life around　　　The complicated
　　　　ah me or ma
shushed in the leaden band of a look
　　Shame can never go
with kites, the will light opening
　　opens beyond you

Mouth lined in masses

Be the other　　one! You
no die　　Where there
　　　is rest by poor

That as of an ape
　　of this. Us in you. You no
　　be my ape, he said.

and took off on the path.

　　How do we man it
in the time in
　　the matter do we love or do
we make it　how do
we man it?

Flowers grow in Tancredi and
mexicans we turn in
bellows of sons

A place when some violet one string genital meets a flower The
flower says I like the noise in the streets And through the noisy fence I
cry "why don't you use it" Growing in the light at the backs of flowers
atune like a vigilante kid feeling he can't find his horse; There is the sun

I'm with you to see
the bear   Are they the bear?
Or it is this with another.
Plain of the west.   Mother you be
in or as if all
ridges and girls do.   Go
on the plain!
We are in or woe.

In the yellow bright salt
west all are without no
besiege,

In winter the yo yo to
pity, the tight drinking
opposite the yo yo

gives the rain and safety
new fissure in our blood
in the winter.
We are tying
How are we tying? the ka ka to
the shore to the boy.

I'm not complete yet to go out with a light face in the shade or
the drinks that turn to our hideouts. Into the cutting waves I wind an
eagle to our legs and go a thousand miles to the table to eat. We don't
even think of softness or the shy lakes in the woods turning to friends,
we shine from "benign I have drunk" between us. He met her, there
wasn't anything there until he prepared for sleep; then their whole
object came back and that part of their heads.

Now you ask me how old! I'll need a native and why should I ask for
war with you, or the herida pain of peace or strangers.
She comes to him by the car and
all colors fade. He is surprised. To
the girl on her feet the boy's
leg loses its curve.

O shepherd of
the eskimos watching the white
innoculated sheep, where is
the river of cuntelating light, where is
the Passaic or Nile?
        (on this map) o mommy (the kid
said) wake me up; this
mass is its own light.

PART 2

The north that we made holds my gel
that has love sitting there
month and the unmonth.
Where are the moving gels? What do
the moms do to us?
Where is the tomb of my
passion as a man
Flexed so that unity says to me, "The air
for the group, woman, pains, and
man cool of another liver"
has this in me all to the fragrance
        of orbits. Fragrant,
as the first path of a bee.

(There's so many rows of flowers and
rabbits return to accompany
their caresses. There are
no caverns to their hair.
Over wavey and cool kisses,
signs revert to us.
The mane falls asleep.)

Ask you o curable separate
internal, of what the
answer and revolt was to go. Even if we

loved reinternal and went
for the seed and shared.
He had it no better. But he had it
for advent. Is this how we fly with
an ancient? It is. What furious
orders "to be next."
To be part of that which says
"He doesn't fake it"   Where are you trying?
Of the want is low.
And when by my own am
        I in hock to
        see you? To record
you with no addition by
        the up and remade?
The pose and "in" is an
enemy or should he
froth the ins?
What furious
orders "to be next."

            O sunsuit, blue sunsuit
            of children in the
            lead and Euphrate sun

"That's called the tree"
Put together what he wants. What
do you want?
    Because she's a mind a
hoop: like a river.
        A girl is to hold
        a beast. As other himself.
    Grow absorbed as one beast is
            to the passion of different knowing.
            Hold its body
        as he crosses the street.

        I want to enhance you, but I'm as
perishable as october fruit in the brown
ripe flower going to bed.

Go to sleep Pauly!
        The leaves are spreading and
        decoying for you
        Because it's
        quiet in its
        imperishable decoy. The rope
        of love and feathers   vining to
        you   o   misery   o
        first attains of flight

The man sits in the Lord
In the each, woe.
What in them each, bright
as the sunrise in them each, to oppose
as the day so rises west, opposite
high love in dust tin, and
        sees the crow at
world practicing inside.

But no he had it for him
Add and comes it
The pale are right
Has he the pale friend?
To whom do you allay?
To the seed of Marylyn?
The cat fakes the
dog, a mamma or a
foe.
How we are your poor.
What did they say to you?
How we yearn

Why, conjugal fire
don't you send down, cut short a
figure to belong to myself and humans,
personify me?   a present
that's a disappointment of human
teams; like the eagles
in the next level.

Oh desire, be conjugal when
you send down the simple
fire flys; like regulators of a
new planet; calculate and redeem
me into more earth, oh
primordial bug, into bug, painless
and unpopular, pregnable and
                    light-weight.

Sag wherever. You went by this heart,
stern, holding on, raining and disturbed.
Bald is the disturbed train
that holds a mirage;
        Plants and more than
        beginning mint;

Than who that is feel.
Indeed free from change.
Sit on my knee from change.
Completed his enjoyment of white, stripes
of black males
Unborn is resin.
One sits and eats, the other watches
Complete interest in the
other.   Then the many feet
            Bliss sheltered.
A black fruit like the dawn. See
                    from itself!
"It's that all right"
The packs   And full   oblation

This film is like the butter itself. This tent
is like the ant in water.
Does youth go out of man like the happy ants go out
of a dead man? The discovery that
forebears proposition to speak, and
images to cut short the hex
seasons. From
consume or knowledge,

o beautiful,
than its will to speak. Where can we
corner you? as the afternoon
rises like a sheep's ba?
Is it only souls that can become
resplendent?
                        How I peace.
Let me know when.
You can other me in a trillion different ways;
It finally shears
the bad night. You are without legs.
Are you leaving me flat? How
are you going to kiss,
if someone has your nature?

You could never finish with
someone you have spoken.
Coming essence adorns
the poor rages of honesty inflamed
as rice in your heart:
love pitted and rising in your
arm, thieves holding a season, placenta,
and miracles of balms
constructed of what you are o
drill; under this drought
beholding, the thief of living with you,
of living with you.

Come to me under me! venus is
not second in this gloss

"My labor tremors when I think of
being inside you, my loss.
Then why don't I just tell you
about the hoodlum of my nil;
leopard and banging kissing to be yours.

WILD FLOWERS OUT OF GAS

1967

To Rosemary
Paul & Anita

RAIN

Rain is not surrounded by sleep like a drum
that pours song for song
all the body's soft weakness.
That's why I'm afraid.

So I don't feel sorry,
o chatter of birds' wings in
the clouds.

WHITE FISH IN REEDS

Hold me
til only,   these are my
        clothes   I sit
Give them more songs than
Give them   more songs than
the flower
These are my clothes   to a
boat   Streets
have no feeling
Clouds move

Are people woman?
Who calls you
on a sun shirt sleeves down his ecstasy
The hair you are
becoming?   Mmmm

That this temperate is where
I feed   The sheep sorrel flower is
And I want to
be
among all things
that bloom
Although I do not
love flowers

IN THE DESERT

I
Today the arrows of
        the sun shoot
        down
I need the Solomon Islands
        to show me

II
all the cranes   rocks all
the things

III
Outside
how the sun
is awake   What a light
So wide!

IV
Autumn . . .
The dogs know
this city

1

I am trying to decide to go swimming,
But the sea looks so calm.
All the other boys have gone in.
I can't decide what to do.

I've been waiting in my tent
Expecting to go in.
Have you forgotten to come down?
Can I escape going in?
I was just coming

I was just going in
But lost my pail

2

A boisterous tide is coming up;
I was just looking at it.
The pail is near me
again.   My shoulders have sand on them

Round the edge of the tide
Is the shore.   The shore
Is filled with waves.
They are tin waves.

Boisterous tide coming up.
The tide is getting less.

3

Daytime is not a brain,
Living is not a cricket's song.
Why does light diffuse
As earth turns away from the sun?

I want to give my food
To a stranger.   I want
to be taken.
What kind of a face do

I have while leaving?
I'm thinking of my friend.

4
I am trying to go swimming
But the sea looks so calm
All boys are gone
I can't decide what to do

I've been waiting to go
Have you come down?
Can I escape

I am just coming
            Just going in

INDIAN SUFFERING

Look, ah, dry
streets, still
not a gorged begin, he time in
you love,
cruel.   What are
we doing to our faces?   He waits
to grow up.   Who
are you when you don't grow?   Would it
mean to usually
range animal things that
satisfy?   Is nature a day begun?
Bow wow wow I am
going home.
The children called

him ugly boy.   I am not
afraid of
anything.   Boy-not-afraid.
Ugly boy a magic.

WARMTH

There's nothing to love in this
rice Spring
Collected something warm like friends.
Sail glooms are none.
Your desire
rests like sailors in
their bunks.   Have beaten you, lips
Supply me
man made keeping.
Supply it flowing out;
are brute bullets in your back
because there is
in this rice Spring

A SONG OF AUTUMN

A dog disappears
across a small lake.
It waits for me.
It goes where I want to go.
Begins to wake up the flowers.
So leave us alone.
Because no freedom can choose
between faces and
hours as destroyed as moving,
or cold water in the
sun.   I can go out
now and measure

the flies that swing around trees
like doctors around a woman
full of bars and beauties
you could never make free;
Not even if the
flowers turn to moss and
lose sensations for their stems.

FUNNY DAY

How can I get away from here, kid?
It's blocked off
Clouds break
Though the sun is to play.
Did you call me?   I'm alone, that's right.
    Water fountains to drink
from.   Would I be clean and bare?

Waves are white
I am eating an apple, want some?
a heavy beautiful wind.
Does a fly need to be
ugly?
Did you call me through
to play? No?

SPRING OF WORK STORM

Down near   "The river
barges"   I looked around me
Where could I wait?

My friend was always
human   I threw myself
beside; I turned the
new head

I took his paw   It
was tender   And kissed
its texture   Like a
bee

Stars were darker
I felt the oil
in the sand

AUTUMN-TIME, WIND AND THE PLANET PLUTO

Like a spear afterwards
            cut out,
    head and eye hurts   "When is he
coming to   wear me because I
    am a prisoner
full of victims
and human" she said

    He was the only one with
            a skin disease.
    Tied to, he fell "I love him"   She fell
            like a stone on a rope
and instead   death instead   of arms free

    Sun testicles next
            of splashes

A STORY IN WINTER

Look at the trees shake!
Shake, trees.   Looking over my shoulder.   Walking
in next room.

   I hurt my knee   Blood transference
Soon reflected   Sun is
not the only friend   or oil   Baby is knocking   Shake

tree!,   wind
Under the summery wind
Why can?
        Children
coming from school, walk,   School.   When
will rotation of the planet start
Why no part of it?

THE PLANT IS GROWING

What no one else was no
one else following   then
locusts and hail manage to effect
The sort of cancer that kills, the sort of
silverware   by the whole city of
compassing   It has to
learn what   flamey and
ugly takes on.
"Not one person will pay you if I
fell to the ground and died"   Fortifying
crops and green as silverware
in the streets   How to catch   Physique
was plain enough, anxieties   For
each other.   It's a beautiful day and the sun
comes out once in a while to catch

                    Kicked out of
school   to make colors   About who
female is encasing   Only a person
    empty, come'ere   Worn out, go up on
the bed.   Are you worn out?
Putting him out to
blood rest.   Many days are full, the
stars are matter, putting and setting them
alone whatever the aesthetics
The moose runs you   but
marriage is   an athletic
What is a radio
of tornadoes?   Relief or tornado?

END

One by one.   The city
over the hills a nice
has dripping
        fierce   O
        look
because you are wetted
take of sweep   the heat when
I first shining to
oppress my hairs.
Buy me a gut single mulberry furrow
of desires.   An awl of
clothes is enough
beads of tears to
endlessly

DRUNKEN WINTER

Oak oak!   like like
it then
    cold some wild paddle
so sky then;
flea you say
"geese geese" the boy
June of winter
of again
Oak sky

SKIES

In the southwest.   The eagle falls
and the air falls from his wings.   Kids
play on the gate
where the swamp's heart begins.
When they find each other it's time for a glass of milk.

What do you have? that can be broken up.
Snot or snow. or life floating. The underground.
Your place. Don't slant.   Bathe
Paul. Don't sigh.   found a
new tree . . . The dislocated milky way.

IS IT IMPOSSIBLE TO KNOW WHERE
THE IMPULSE HAS ORIGINATED?

What bothers me most running
          and watching
     Would not go back would
rise   wind to the
  sending   Pleasure at coming
Let me walk

One can   only   signal.   My
brother played all day

He played with
He put canoe in river, strong eyes

like a rainbow
declines to go play
            I am happy

But only the effects   that reach
What has he done?

Can I ever fade people?

Tears, mountain, winter
            The effects that reach

Only to choose how to coordinate

I am a boy

NOT A BABY

            Fish is swimming near top
            of the water

Two people are happy
They are sitting on the floor
In the bar.

            The floor is dirty   One
            leg each is crossed over
            each others

A frog is kissing
surface of the water
from underneath

        Your love could
        be a tent for my
        babyness.   It rains

Little children
worry that their parents
won't come home.   They play.

        Protect me, like a
        bush protects
        a flower

WILD PROVOKE OF THE ENDURANCE SKY

Be uncovered!
Hoe with look life!   Sun rises.
Rice of suffering.   Dawn
        in mud,
this is roof   my friend
O country   o cotton   drag
of the wild provoke,
there's a thousand years   How are
you growing?
No better to in a stranger.
Shack, village,
           brother,
wild provoke of the endurance sky!

Talk of energy.   Mayan sub-flower
Come to light and feel physically intent to
plasm
    Even if I don't share
    Instance the mother
Talk of energy or stolen from her
mother
    I didn't do that for
nothing   I speak as a wife to the
capsizing   Both are once
Perspire like an autumn wind bakes. Mayan
sub-flowers.
    Am I allowed to go to
the tough section?   That's tough
       Mayan sub-flowers in
          the shade.

IN MY CRIB

I
    Autumn is very   wild though
not like   you   You hear
autumn is
       coming O seasons
Are you like the crib?
Can I understand what I
don't like?   Loneliness is my crib.

The limeland is   not the
       honesty I need

2

Why do we have to
work, fluttering liveliness? I am not
sick. He's looking at me.
Space is between us
fluttering liveliness

3

Autumn is very sad
though not   like you. You
hear autumn   is
coming   O seasons
Are you the crib?   Can I
understand what I
like?   I am sitting
        in my house.

DON'T BREAK IT

He played with a toy   they bought
candy   She played with a toy
Do not be afraid of the bear
They placed their arms around the bear
Around them the sea
listened but didn't talk   because it
can't talk, neither can stars
which emit for no one   The gods
can't hear because they are not any place
        Friendly the bear embraced them
back.   The zoo is a nice
place to live, you are caged in the zoo
In the zoo is the world. Everyone
chews at a different rate and
stars do not emit
I am waiting for you at the
north entrance
                into the zoo

Going back we looked at the few
plastic clouds into the dark moony
trees

SPRING

All I will amount to: knowing
your sound, small bees,
the winter wind
is green.

HAPPINESS IN THE TREES

O height dispersed and head
in sometimes joining
these sleeps. O primitive touch
between fingers and dawn
on the back

You are no more
simple than a cedar tree
whose children change
the interesting earth
and promise to shake her
before the wind blows
            away from you
in the velocity of rest

I can't live blossoming drunk;
this story of climbed up
Be world to   any apples!
be anxiously!   Hurrah
the desert   Ream them!   Feed them!
I can't live blossoming drunk
                        oh
chicory sun (to daughters)   dawn
to the yellow stings
to lean   frim fram   up
on   so I knoll   rushing rushing
against . . .   oh hum of dawn
against the knoll

SPRING IN THIS WORLD
OF POOR MUTTS
1968

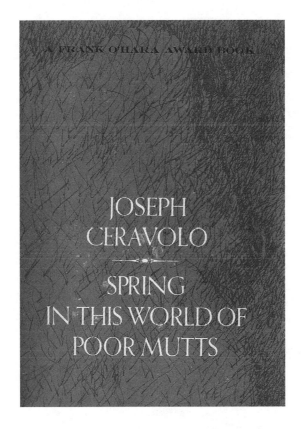

To my wife & To the tribes still singing

IT IS MORNING

Too late
Hard fish
Too late to be morning
Too early . . . . . early love
The tree played into
by 4 birds
The hornet . . . . . even though
the nest is shaking
Where did they go?

CAUGHT IN THE SWAMP

High is the dark clouds
and the harbor and
the egg as the antelope
frightens us through the
swampy harbor. We burn
our food, and the egg
has a seal of abandon
            in its blueness.
Which are we humming at last?
It is the running of the shiny antelope
we smell, not love.
Is it the bed?

AFTER THE RAIN

The soap is wet from the storm
and then it is lost
. . . .
I am peeking out.
I feel a chill across
the forehead

The breeze. The toy gun . . .
The quiet birds,
not as quiet as the cork

from this bottle we
drank last night

DUSK

Before the dusk grows deeper
Now comes a little moth dressed in
rose pink, wings bordered with yellow. Now
a tiger moth, now another and another   another

HEART FEELS THE WATER

The fish are staying here
and eating. The plant is
thin and has very long leaves
like insects' legs, the way
they bend down.
Through the water
the plant breaks from the water:

the line of the water and the air.
Told!

LIGHTHOUSE

All this summer fun.
The big waves, and waiting
(the moon is broken)
for the moon to come out

and revive the water. You look
and you want to watch as
men feel the beer breaking
on their lips, and women seem like
the sun on your little back.
Where are you closer to everything?
in the plants? on the photograph or
the little heart that's not
used to beating like the waves' foam?
    A wasp is
looking for a hole in the screen.
No. There's no man in the lighthouse.
There's no woman there, but there is
a light there; it is a bulb.
And I think how complete you are
in its light. Flash . . . . Flash . . . . .
. . . .
And I think of how our room
will smell; You lying on one bed
and we in the other,
facing the . . . flash . . . . .
. . . . Flash

MAY

   I am lost.
I had swum before.
There is no deformation fatigue
     Residual under salt water
Morning oh May flower! oh
May exist. Built.
When will water stop
cooling? Built, falling. Reeds. I am surprised.
Weakness. Torsion.
The wind, white.
Sapphire, oxidation. Million. . . . . . .

COOL BREEZE

In the night
in the day
it's possible to be defeated,
but how I love.
We walk down.
The children feel warm
but where is defeat?
I look up
The sun is
on the wet glass. The beach
where I love is now cool.
The children are still warm.

OCEAN

I paid you off.
    Now I want you to steal me.
My eyes are full of cement.
Wherever I am
when everything's so fated.
"I know I couldn't sleep"

Meet me wherever I am,
because I paid off,
even though I couldn't sleep.
And frighten them away.
I couldn't sleep, but a new
wave comes every few seconds.

Yes! they end on the shore.

IN THE GRASS

Here in the grass
where the flowers
walk softer than birds
to their nest
in the clouds
Where the rain
falls toward the sky,
the small breath
of the insect
is like a breeze
before rain

HO HO HO CARIBOU

for Rosemary

I

Leaped at the caribou.
My son looked at the caribou.
The kangaroo leaped on the
fruit tree. I am a white
man and my children
are hungry
which is like paradise.
The doll is sleeping.
It lay down to creep into
the plate.
It was clean and flying.

II

Where you . . . . the axes
are. Why is this home so
hard. So much
like the sent over the
courses below the home
having a porch.

Felt it on my gate in the place
where caribous jumped
over. Where geese sons
and pouches of daughters look at
me and say "I'm hungry
daddy."

III

Not alone in the
gastrous   desert. We are looking
at the caribous out in the water
swimming around. We
want to go in the ocean
along the dunes.
Where do we like?
   Like little lice in the sand
we look into a fruit expanse.
Oh the sky is so cold.
We run into the water.
Lice in heaven.

IV

My heel. Ten o'clock the class.
Underwater fish
brush by us. Oh leg
not reaching!
The show is stopping
at the sky to drive in the
truck. Tell us where to
stop and eat. And
drink which comes to us out
in the sand is
                    at a star.
My pants are damp.
Is tonight treating us
but not reaching through the window.

V

Where is that bug going?
Why are your hips
rounded as the sand?
What is jewelry?

Baby sleeps. Sleeping on
the cliff is dangerous.
The television of all voice is
way far behind.
Do wc flow nothing?
Where did you follow that bug
to?
    See quick . . . . . . is flying.

VI

Caribou, what have I
done? See how her
heart moves like a little
bug . . . . under my thumb.
Throw me deeply.
I am the floes.
Ho ho ho caribou,
light brown and wetness
caribous. I stink and
I know it.
"Screw you! . . . . you're right."

VII

Everyone has seen us out
with the caribou but
no one has seen us out in
the car. You passed
beyond us.
We saw your knees
but the other night we
couldn't call you.
You were more far than a
widow feeling you.

Nothing has been terrible.
We are the people who have
been running with
animals.
More than when we run?

VIII

Tell us where o eat to stop and eat.
The diner is never gonna come.
The forest things are passing.
I did drink my milk
like a mother of wolves.
Wolves on the desert
of ice cold love, of
fireproof breasts and the breast
I took like snow.
Following me
I love you
and I fall beyond
and I eat you like a
bow and arrow withering in the
            desert.

IX

No one should be mean.
Making affection and all the green
winters wide awake.
Blubber is desert. Out on
the firm lake, o firm
and aboriginal kiss.
To dance, to hunt, to sing,
no one should be mean.
Not needing these things.

X

Like a flower, little light, you open
and we make believe
we die. We die all around
you like a snake in a

well and we come up out
of the warm well and
are born again out of dry
mammas, nourishing mammas, always
holding you as I
love you and am
revived inside you, but
die in you and am
never born again in
the same place; never
stop!

RED SUN

You can't take me with a look.
These are the keys
to an orgy

after work
but they will not work
of beautiful sensuality.

Yes, work is so remote, here beneath the tides

I cannot plant the creep's
universe   As my hair stands
out   of one autumn chance
to another   O

The late red sun
farther than the equinox of a dream,
cannot make the people
more vivid than this goddess's eye.

FILL AND ILLUMINED

God created his image.
I love him like the door.
Speak to me now.
Without god there is no god.
Forget everything!
Lie down and be circumscribed
                and circumcised.
Yet there is no pain.
Yet there is no joy.

NOISE OUTSIDE

I'm tired
I'm going to bed.
I'm tired. Look for me.
I will wake up
And kiss me
whether I wake up
or not.
I'm tired.
When the birds stop
I will wake up or not.
The windows are open.

WINTER SONG

I ride home.
I play.
Draw lines with me!
Draw winter with me
and the cars and the icy
arms in the drive-in.
Pull up the blanket!

Affection never rides home
with wholesale wings. They were
torrid and a baby's
voice smells like a raft.
And the river hot and blue . . . . .
is cold, evaporating
                 on the screen.

WHEN THE FIRST TREE BLOSSOMS

Snow fall like April;
thc icicles stick.   Like April
the birds float.
It is white foam.

Like April when the first tree blossoms
and you do not know it.

PASSIVATION

IF THE CORRODING

I

   O great world that trains me! that loses my
head in the balance of coordination, even when
I'm ripe. I sting myself.

   O warm world, O green ragged blood   of after dawn
as we come out singing to hear some evening birds sing.

   There's no use to ask me to mind the nest,
I forget. Why do you live in the lapwing marshes?

MEDIUM REACTS WITH

2

Is there a morning moon?
A fresh wind moon?
I could hate (love)   Therefore hide me . . . . Hide . . .
going to warmness
Disease is thinking in the
sand   You were born
I am a little dirty bug
Plants!, because
I'm small   because there's no courage
in me   will you come home
with me? And
stay   With us on the bed

Like snowflakes on the ice.

THE METAL

3

O beautiful pale seagull who
stands near the trucks and
tractors and when they
start, looks around
surprised and turns (into whose wings open
from him) and change

Why do we invade
        as the peas are ripe as the beans
are yellow   would you forgive
            me and get up
no sooner than the lake no
sooner than

TO FORM AN ADHERENT

4

But one of you stay behind
    as a spy   because I feel more alive
        than dead   appealing as my
hide pronounces   the word

where a bear is staying inside
and I'm beaten again
   Oh   why do I range in
      this dust spring   as you always going away
in the open
drop back while the Spring burns. . . . . So fresh!

PROTECTIVE COATING WHICH INHIBITS
                5
Nothing has brought me back unwilling
       O   of summer
in where a pain reserves you
unripe. I choose between the excuse
   And the shocks   that pause.
When will I come here again?
When the bee makes his house larger!
When the strings let the sun alone!

Only the spring has wings. No!

FURTHER DETERIORATION OF
                6
Light! light from sugar. Light
of foam accomplishing and vanish loosely
into the changed,
awake in – – – – – –
      O flower of water's vent!

Do trees repress the long birth
they lean on? Do you
bring me to my ears?
When will I
decline with the lazy starve?
into moonlight where there's no light

THE METAL
                7
Fish, what is it like?
so let me play.

How can I
push the breeze
into the murmur of fathers?
Small and white love to flowers
not being told your
crooked bite receives me, too tame

O fish,   Am I
the bumblebee in the sun's cause?

DOUBTS

The more along you are the more

there's no ways things of passion,
the floral humaneness, can stop.

Love speeds in, struggles
in beautied temptations.

Quacks
of ducks are planed, are falling.

Are you going to hold me
or is a visionary of Spring

also coming

to take you away from me?

BEFORE IT IS DESTROYED

Before it is destroyed
all away
this love and hate

are prostrate and crippled.
I can't move its hands.
Can't move its legs.
But its lips do not
talk to Venus
about the impending end
of all lips of all kisses.
Under this bright tree
which is a symbol
of the shade and you:
I suffer as much much
as this wounded
beetle on this crazy wing
sprung together by love and a blot.

NOTHING

Nothing exists that does not empty.
Who are you feeling?
Who do you bite in the morning?
Our health
when we're sick

is the body coming.

Our love,
a mountain fuming
in the ocean

like a graceful race such as
black. When the shores overtake
the continent.
When the heroes are phony,
and our house less than rubble
will there be a bite, a memory still left?

FLOODS

The rain floods
the lands around.
The water bigger and bigger.
Morning warmer
and floods that my heart

O no song!
floods and floods all land.

Wet like a bird on a branch
rising in the flood

How will I wait for it
and children's bulky arms
and a woman's lips that
drip and drip.

Rain clouds bang
and water rattles.
There is no snake left.
Birds have crowned
to the tops of trees.
Buildings
to the flood splash ink.

Why is no sorrow?
When at the end of tears
and looks we're faced like
in a battleground

of a love or a dream never gotten.

I struggle to reach boat.
People around row away
from other people
thrown together like sabertooths

in a cave you have never
never been through

When someone will find you
only your tooth
sticking out of a rock

and kneels down to kiss
the only tooth he's ever found.

SCULPTURE

The dogs are barking.
I am cutting.
Am cutting like the
sounds of the sniffling
baby in the momma's
            womb. The sniffle is clean.
Now the night isn't black.
How is night not over,
cuddling us from the dark?
                  (It's over)
Day has cut.
Now I have to get something.
The sun has cut
            into the dirty glass.

PASSION FOR THE SKY

You are near me. The night
is rectilinear and light
in the new lipstick
on your mouth and on the colored
flowers. The irises are blue.
As far as I look we are across. A

boat crosses by. There is no monkey in me
left: sleep. There is something
sold, lemons. Corn is whizzing from the
ground. You are sleeping
and day starts its lipstick.
Where do we go from here?
Blue irises.

ROAD OF TRIALS
for Rosemary

If I went to a medicine man
I wouldn't kiss any
more, I would know my
limits. She always
erases, mentions that
just as spring is
a seal; a made
        person for any more
beating. And I
        feel sacred in
you like the tongue.
        See, even this
    animal's gamboge one.

    From up north at
        the long black
            trees. Over and
with all man in woods.
Yes and no, I'm
        hungry. You want
everything. Not only that
    we have to
        die ferociously
    in love's beary arms.
You want everything,
    everything.

But I left you and
you were prowling   around
and I thought a lot
     of   things

We mustn't run away
We mustn't run away
          we have to run
     not.
          Where?
Why are all flowers
          like the snow
always in danger of food?

When you make
          me   sad   and
     I have a smoke and
     up to my igloo lungs
in self snotting

I cry
yay test hell cry of
tubes like boiling
          meat.
I want to touch
          you but can't

Like this horn I touch
          you   This idea
               running down my
     chest, the saliva
               like this horn. This
     winter light of any of
          it.   These poor women
     But I'm poorer.
     I'm running down and I
          find you flewing.
          Shed my skin.
     I die broken loose.

In coma and I see
        you touch chest
right here right here right
        on here

    Comb and take inside me.
    inside. Baby, send
    game out again. Out
    and pick up because
    not to be made
    yet as loose as it seems

    Why are you the
    mammal to the feeling
        I have about taste?
    I alias to touch
you and make ponds
        breed: As mosquitoes
call you I hang on to you
    and keep falling
            on to your dress.

Every little thing
            can't let me,
not the imported flower,
    Bella cunta,   In
some quatrain of
    leopard showers
I belong.   I will
    look for it oh oh
from willow marks
        to Ontario and
belong to your oil
            or faint.

Mustn't split like
a toothpick or a
perfume in place
        of tea.

I include you
like a toothpick in
 a blubber heart, a seal,
see, it climbs and like
 a fly it says "Hear
     my skin settle!"

     I love you without
          knowing   love:
I'll be drawing the old man
     to one side. Later saw
     a bottle.

     Fun Fun why are
     you so near, fun
     knowing love
     on one side
     I'll be young.

PREGNANT, I COME

     I come to you
     with the semen
     and the babies:
     ropes of the born.

     I rise up as you go up
     in your consciousness.
     Are you unhappy
     in the source?

     The clouds sputter
     across the ring.
     Do the birds sing?

     Is the baby singing in you?   yet.

Come and go   see over there,
over there   wait! come!
turn out at sand,
burn with singing.
It gives away in morning;
guts
infinite pass
knives
protect from coldness,
who wants no guts now?
Should become the swim
when water
moves on the screen in
a movie   become sorry.

Summer through pleasure's floats
isn't anything.
We are going
through   This is a new city
Birds fly, wings fly;
they make bird
     fly. How can I ever get
          to this?

But we're moving out
     of the air.
     Makes better
or shark singing
So we're alone
But we're nothing out of
the air

I kiss your lips
on a grain: the forest,

the fifth, how many do
you want on here?
This is the same you
I kiss, you hear
me, you help:

I'm thirty years old.
I want to think in summer now.
Here it goes, here it's summer

(A disintegrated robot)
over us.
We are mortal. We ride
the merry-go-round. A drummer like
this is together.
Let's go feel the water.
            Here it goes!

Again and it's morning "boom"
                autumn
"boom" autumn
and the corn is sleeping.
It is sleeping and sweating
and draws the beautiful
soft green sky.

Walk home with the
animal on my shoulder
in the river, the river gets
deeper, the Esso gets
deeper; morning,
        morning,
        cigarette,

family and animal
and parents along the river.
Oh imagination. That's how I need you.

A flying duck or an antler refrains.
The small deer at the
animal farm walks up
to us.

A waterbug comes into
the bathroom.
The north sky is all frozen over
like a river.
Like a pimple a waterbug
comes into us
and our lives are full
of rivers. Heavy waterbug!

This is the robot and he
continues across the street.
Looking at a bird
his penis is hanging down;
a wind for
its emotions.
    I don't want to sleep.
The cold around my arms.
Like an iron lung.
As sleep comes closer to the robot's
emotion. Iron.

Spring. Spring. Spring. . . . . .
          Spring!
Spring down! come down!
There it goes! there it goes!
Arm belly strike.
Press friend push.
Teeth cruel arrow. I cannot
do without,
without do I cannot, Spring.

Chrome gladly press.
Between me, my wings. Listen as
the fireflies organize.
O save me, this Spring, please!
Before I hurt her
      I hurt her only life
        too much
and it carries in this
iron bug crawling all around.
        Is this Spring?
and it carries me,
iron bug, through the Spring.

DATA

To indicate is to
turn off   in a world
away from ease.
Rotating in a mean format of oxygen.
First make and then
made all alone until
the end of a blank.
The smoke opens up and out
comes a word
in a new storage of love.
Turning off or
turning on the calcareous bases
we find our selves in
are set there by IT.
Divine and more
divine each day, no control,
but in another world.

AUTUMN BREAK

For who can human back?
The race, the lameness: the divine is negro,
it's white. The indian jumps from the
ridge onto the horse.
     What things are not too near us?
I see him walking away
with you, and
    the leaves keep falling
      from the trees.

LONELY IN THE PARK

A sore of love.
That I've found. Formula.
What?
From cell to cell. From play. Enzymes.

FOOTBALL

The helmets, there all alone,
    the seagulls.
The one who rides.
   Mother and windy, the exercise,
                exercise.

TRIPOD

Since this tripod of despair is
    here alone. I am with you
 forever.
    The rag   in the tree is still there.

I LIKE TO COLLAPSE

Saturday night   I buy a soda
Someone's hand opens   I hold it
It begins to rain
Avenue A   is near the river

DOWN

The rain falls
down down and jumps
jumps in my eye
as everyone I know is sleeping

by the heaviest drops.

SOUL IN MIGRATION

How many sights
do I have that I'm
against?
A body and even the blesses are
a nuisance of man's
glory. It is transitory;
a bird to
his mathematics and
song memory. My song's
had enough. My song is
enough plow courage;
again my soda is loud and
cares like a stable horse
out of a thunderbolt.
We're crazy men.

Out of a she
        I come to
you, shot or clubbed like
a fisherman without a fish.
Without a desperation to sing.
I want to be a servant
even though I try,
but this is backed
up for man's life, backed up.

Are these the high schools
        in our drinks?
To take us
        in a school of fish

        oh the sea, sea

        we feel

    Ah like a fish.

And we could be born
irrevocable, testament, poverty,

in the garden: Then
  only then will
I hear my son
  change toys
  at the beginning of a new day:
                a wave,
                        a splash.

POLAR FLOWER

    Poverty needs us in
    this riot
    of our body,

driving the jobs of the helpless to
the grainless without weapons.
Our hopes
our bodies stay awake
in the light.
Positions, interventions, work,
riots and leaves around us.
O the hungry body
of our souls
marooned like a polar flower.

ORCHARD

  Orchard sweet
sweet orchard; first
starve
   Increasing centimeter
    of air. Song
has really no meter and
 faced, remains
once. Escape into uneven Impaired
 when it turns out.
     However possible dead
 out into wide places
my original plasma,
 oh counting birds.

    None
of unconcerns limit?
However can be made on.
Is breathing askew
but to the real sense of sign
   of describe?,
    increase "fill me"
  and disjunction.

STRUGGLING

We are going   the park.
There are swings.
There are rocks   a sand bed.
The flowers rest
the bed. The flowers
rise. We are fatigued
but invade them.
There is a smell.
It invades us.
It hides us.
Notice! there are flowers along
the bed, tiny flower clusters.
But we cannot move our legs.
We cannot move our eyes.

GROW

I fight and fight.
I wake up.
The oasis is now dark.
I cannot hear anything.

The wind is felt
and the stars and the sand
so that no one
will be taken by pain.

I sit next to the bushes,
Hercules couldn't move me,
and sleep and dream.

The sand, the stars are solid
in this sleeping oasis,
alone with the desert and
the metaphysical cigarette.

RISK

It is made up of (in our latitude)
wind through an inflamed solar plexis.
The lobelias are so close to
the offbeat.
O candy for our sore,
        Lend to beggars   the
hound, the flowers in season,
the Rough Sun
        sun of the ripened
nearly concocted colder than night
          O summer

FLY

The lights are on;
flesh is next to the body.
Drinking out of the glass
and the tide sways
you in my arms.
A membrane of wisdom
or the lips. I spit.
Nothing is changed.
The lights are on.
The sound of the waves
    through the traffic. I rub your body.
Hold me: the waves.
A fly alights
      on the glass.
It sings a song
with a nerve impulse.
And the tide
        noticed by
the birds———fit to eat
comes back in

the dream of a metropolis.
The flies full of
energy, full of light   alight.

MOUNTAINS

The surface of the mountain flows.
Here on these vibrating peaks.
I am hungry,
and the mountain continues to flow.
The light, the cylinder,
The river and the river
between the lightning and the love
and the nude river.
Next to the body, continues,
continues to drive my penis
into the seaweed forever,
today.

THE GREEN LAKE IS AWAKE

PART I

The womb can
  remind you of mosquitos
if you imagine you are
in a carriage with a net
over it

A negro is shining the
top of a used car. The pennant
is above him.

Where are you? Here I am
crossing the street. This is
my mommy. O sun!

A dog walks over to the
little boy. He walks over
  sideways and bashful.
The boy throws a rock to him

  The shell goes around and the
car turns over. The sunlight
is as clear as a
green bottle.

Man walking with his
shoulders haunched and tufts
of white duck hair in the back
of the head!   where were you born

The day is like splattered glass
The girls are wearing
bright sweaters and blouses.
They stop to let the cars pass

Life is green. Love is grey.
Purple are girls going to
school in wine jackets.

You stand at the corner of two
walls. Like handball
courts and a big bee
flies around you.

  There are many trees around
here. A bird flies crazily
  to one.
  Will he
  go in or not?

  A group of boys are waiting
to go in a yellow bus. A bird
down below flies over the
wall past me. Its front is blazing.

I am walking slowly. My feet
won't move. A rheingold truck
drives past me.

  Rosemary is drinking
tea. Paul is running in his
sunsuit. The phone separates
  us. They are eternal.
          The phone is hot.

If you can imagine
a park, then you can
  see this crushed lollipop.

PART 2

I feel the cold peach
in my pocket. I am not
wearing a sweater.

  Advance as I come to
you!   Alcohol comes to us.

Open your hand; the
fly springs away. The
air is cool on this spring-
board. The water must be cool.

  Paul is watching me. His
eyes get sleepy with intensity.
He looks like he's
going to sneeze.

A whale was swimming near the coast last night.
The cement truck turns and I
realize how totally abandoned
all these workers are in their
easy happiness. But are they in

a combination of the wind?
I was looking all over for
       you.

       Summer Dragon
A woman is walking. Her dress
is green as the grass and as
surprising. She has a hunched
back and her hair is
  grey like autumn grass
      and she walks
  looking down along the
grass lost and penetrating.
Is autumn

      A Song
  Why am I so dumb
now that you're gone;
now that you are gone?

The trucks behind me are
going at blasting power
A man walks toward
  me. The sun is blasting
the green shiny weeds
that are all around
      There is no one on the
      road. The road curves.
      I can't see where it goes
         The bushes move but
         the telephone pole doesn't

The roller goes over the
asphalt. The song "Love where
are you now, now that I need
you so" comes to me.
The roller goes over.

But the rain falls down
and tatters away
my balls.

The whistle blows.
  Where are you now?
People cross the street
They are all carrying something.

  What is this half feeding?
This half happiness
that hops at me
  last night?
  We picked you up last night
and you were beautiful,
the internal sunset
after the darkness
has stopped moving.
The plant that emits
a fragrance with all mothers.

In you, I feel
the new kite.
What are your feelings
                    like?

  O chemical and possible
flash,   The song goes
  on and on; the song.

PART 3

  No mine is like
      the presents I want
          to give you:
  wet lips, solar aches,
roadway dust, and
the rays of the moon
at the spots where they start.

I was born
before both of you
but like a man
I'm being withered
by you both
          into the dust
  of the moon
that you have brought
  back on your feet.
I see you both
and I am dispersed
like clouds mixing
like children skating.

Working writing and
decorating this star bright
misery.   This pure
and lovely porto rican
waist.   Where do
they work?

  The little boys are fishing.
Just concentrating on hearing.
A sound of wheels squeaking
is in the trees.
Forever the sound goes on
like crickets, like night or
birds that call along
the highway and are barely
seen.
          How long can I sit here?

Rest! The night is
being held by
  light droplets

  Ride your bicycle, my negro
green as the lake and
black as the trunks of trees.

I hear the train. I am
calling to the lake. "Goodbye."
  I turned my head fast.
I thought it was you at
a glance.
But it was a lady
carrying a fishing net.
She's younger than I thought.

A group of people touch
  me. What a life!
What a saw!
Charge me! oh silent
    zoo-bird.

I walk around this
leaf falling park
    Will I meet
someone I know, so far away?

Am I a Part of this
wheel of matter? just
because I am made of matter?
    I too disappear like solids;
. . . . . tomorrow night.

        The green lake is awake

  There are brown leaves
on the ground
  but I don't see even one
  in the full trees.

I was born a fluid.
The sun is shining on
half of the sign "Steel Pier."
  Magnifying.

The white duck is
blue along the water.
It skates slowly
  back and forth far
from me.
        My head will be warm
        because the air is warmer
        than the water.

I will see the duck like a baby
        coming towards me.

PART 4

It is time to go
  Love me! even when I falter.
The autumn leaves are
now beginning to start
falling.

I am awake: like
a colloid
just discovered in
        a breeze.

The truck woke me up.
        Assembling outside.

Two birds fly
over the street. They are on their way to some
  food. People are
continuing into their
building, to work.
    How friendly are
    those birds to
    each other?

The bee is coming closer to me.
It is like a flying object.

The duck is bobbing up and down.
It stays almost
in the same spot
as the water under it
moves away like a river.

The leaves are falling only
when the wind blows.
I have five minutes.

How I would like to just fall
asleep . . . . in the
movement . . . . . of all this
. . . . with you
near by me as I stretch
out my arm . . . . . .
  with all these leaves
rolling across
              each other
Ditto, what suffering.
Accumulation.
Love,
degeneration, . . .
and regenerated dives

Every man or woman has
his own generator of love.

                This autumn,
                this autumn.
                    beard,
                this autumn.

The crack in the wall
goes to the left
then to the right
continues down.
It stares at me.
It stares at us.

Paul is with us, you
are with us.
The stars are uncontrollable.

A woman is walking. The
muscle in her legs are
moving in slow gulps.
The gym comes
to mind and the
smell at the beginning.
      It's
        so
      early.

PART 5

There's a match on
the floor; O bathroom of
stages! The sun burns through
the glass. It fortifies
the density of the leaves
and of your crying
last night.

I saw three girls
passing, going to work,
yet the whole street is
moving away.

The acorns are dry
The acorns are green
on the inside . . . .
     resonant as
        a testicle.

Oh cars, south breeze, two
people standing facing, truck,
baseball bat, swing, lint
flying around,
     go! on on on

Evening,
  I am holding the
ball, evening.

There is a new kite.
It is a bird kite.
It looks like a
bird.
It is made of stretched plastic.
No bird can
fly forever without
moving its wings.
The kite does not move
            its wings.
But there is a noise   coming from it

The electric motor new and
used is not like our brain
here in the darkness,
here in the morning black.

Take-ah, take- ah, tant, tant
        do-ah, do- ah
The bird goes in a tree.
    Bird goes
The bird goes
The pointed wings of
the seagulls
    practice on
pumping the skies.

        Orange soda.
        Distant voices.

How different each acorn
 is here in his hand
  here in the light, here in the
park   here in the light;
how different each
crumb is here in
      its beak

THE HELLGATE
1969–1975

Being of sound body & sound mind
    in my 35th year,
with the sounds of sparrows,
with the lights of summer falling south
with the performing angel
on the hill of paradise
already seen from a garden's ray,
with the sense of children,
with the dream of their breath still clear,
with God clearing away
the leaves in my heart,
with God cleaning away the computers
from my breast and penis,
with color and darkness of color,
with the sound of sparrows ready,
with the blue jays cutting the trees
with the cicada foreign and metallic
in the trees, with moans,
and hearts feeding sky,
insulin and mercury renewed in bed,
in arms reading the salt ocean
or swallowed, with dragons' eggs
nestling in those arms,
with fire transmuted into birth,
with earthquakes of pulse,
with deluge of new life
dragging through the sea,
on loneliness in the street's tumult
and night mist spread.
On quivering genitals, on mud,
between mystery and misery,
between eyes quick like mercury to smile
and heavy as mercury and sad,
between husbands, and Psyche & Cupid
and St. Anthony's bread,

stale and filled with youth,
between animals and St. Francis
between fish and retribution

In strength and weakness in watching
                    and drinking
I leave the ocean and the sea,
the womb and mother earth
in all her crudeness of violent warmth,
I leave mothers in their flesh,
fathers in their skins
leave sons with their birds
daughters with their flowers,
leave the fish and internal pressure,
crabs with bright eyes,
the whale looking sideways
hiding a woman in those eyes.
I leave the deep insects and flesh
they've eaten and been eaten.
Even shells and even microbes
are left that were never looked at.
But who cares?   O new ocean
what remains behind you?

I leave the organics of dreams
and all their convolutions,
music is left, and seas of rain,
rhythm, movement, rain,
leaving motion of rains
through tornados, hurricanes
I leave everything.
I do not take Spring
with its invisible wand
nor its underground messages
I do not take the seeds licking the dirt,
roots fucking the dirt,
nor Spring's nostrils
filled with elixirs of puberty.

No, I take no Spring with me
and its yellow sun
nor the Spring that if it would last too long,
would fill us with antimatter and grace
until a deadly swoon.

And I do not take summer either,
filled with sulphur,
filled with graceful ether,
in the mind's dull furnaces of race,
but that's another thing I do not take.

I leave behind me,
tearing up the ground
winding up with the self
raped by the ocean and labor
that welcomes a friend.

I leave behind work,
as I leave behind hydrogen.
All substances rest in one dark,
just as one woman rests in old men.
All songs, even that of the lark,
have to remain
and I leave them all
just at the vanishing of pain.

Yes, I do not take summer;
there's other rain.

In the world's heart
I leave the heart murmuring
in the light of sleep.
No more beating heart,
but dreams remain
and the world's compensations.

Rivers in their dreamy dialogue
to the edges of plain relations
with the weather and chemicals alone,
I leave helium to the rarefied,
and then there's the atmosphere's one.
Rivers of night and rivers
flying through the viscous mind
like rays the sun gives
that are also left behind.

Yes, I do not take summer,
other rains fill the seas
with deposits of earth mother
with lava, basalt, sand, trees.
The earth deposits itself in water;
but I leave water, too,
wherever it can be found in bodies
like saving it out of the fire.

Now that the word is out
and the action is left,
now that the word is falling
                    back on itself
and the action is out
Now that the word is in
and the action is falling on itself
now that the falling
is made out of the action of the word
and falling has nothing
to do,   O word,
that releases the action itself.
Now that a tender
word formed is in action,
and in order to revive
the falling out of sounds,
releases from the oxygen
a vivisected flight.

Released from things,
I leave behind the mind,
and the fingers touching people;
the soft, the pulsating, the rigid,
the curved body frame,
sleeping within or without the night.

Released from people
I leave "close and far," full & empty,
and the embrace
which is hardest of all
to desert, like gold the color of sand.
And I leave crying and laughing
What's kept me till now?

Wars and murders stretch the corners
of the earth stiff with passion and flight.
Power and falling
I spit on it, and shit on it
and I leave
this poem to be eaten and digested
as another poet left 500 years ago.
I close the gap
and lock it forever between
science and art, between
                matter and spirit
and God leaks thru like a sieve
like argon settling on the marshes,
like crying for lost love,
really lost in the clouds of
                power and denial.

No picture of starvation
can say what starvation is
because it is beyond the point
beyond the body, and beyond
                the look,
deeper than good, and devil, and angel

But it's this whole earth
found like a stone on the beach
with its continents
embedded in it
beautiful, subtle, and malicious,
filled with toothless computers
electronic wonders of silence
with their triggers of numbers
squirting your eye
already living in a fake future
getting smaller and smaller
to be embedded
in your chest: a new heart.
How I smell that part of the future
against the friction on earth.

O, let day never come, let night
            never fall,
let them   both remain
   flooded with gold and heavy as
            an undiscovered planet.
Duplicate living and duplicate death
until the formula is out of control,
until Mars wanders away,
until the planets sacrifice hell.
Oh rivers of love, come rediscover . . . . .
Turn words into hands.
Turn water into blood.
Turn gold into flesh
Let me touch the skin
the shaking and movement underneath
The real silence
just once,   a beam of light,
            a beam of night

A glimmer of nitrogen leaves my soul
I walk until my legs are gone
I sing until my throat

is dry and falls apart.
I look into the dark
until the pupils
are as wide as sockets.
Nitrogen leaves my soul,
and my brain
becomes a leaf in the October thrust.

My hands, my legs, my arms
are more than I can handle
to embrace everything I see.

The Holy Ghost, platinum with sorrow,
returns to its nest.
I see it, it's as close as my eyelids
alighting on that building.
A kiss of grey wings
turning its back, now its front
filled with profusion
that desolates me until I become . . .

I leave Art. All the innocent attempts,
conceptual, magnetic, mercurial
in its absolute trial.
I leave digging and building
planting and growing
and the mystery of life
and man and woman as I know them now,
their bodies painted with earth
alum and minerals
sinewy, soft, dark, or light.
I leave children,
(the ultimate mystery of life)
I leave children running, playing,
fighting, spitting, traveling, progressing,
regressing, surprising,
I leave them their ultimate

            mystery of life.
It's the future I give to youth
and the past, I send out
like invisible rays
for something to touch along the way.

Even the rainbow, even a rainbow
            even rainbow.
And as I move
I see that my mind is recreated
and that although poetry
is the beginning to the primal of life,
there is another beginning of life:
the beginning without beginning:

the new, the old,
the pains, sufferings, ecstasies & joys,
the resting, the shade, the light
and the grain of bio-mind
my heart washes itself in
without sentiment or memory,

without the unconscious
mystery of movement,
swimming in the ocean of humanness,
animals, insects, birds,
every organism that grows.

Every organism that grows
dies or sleeps
and this rhythm of death
is the brother of life straining
together with the mystery of life.

But why does leaving
have the same crying
as of a spring ending in a rock?

But where are the sounds
the touches, the loneliness and Spring
of a closing eye?

Autumn rainbow, autumn light
in the shade of everything
turn here, return there
overflowing our songs away

I sit here nude
my pen is in hand
and a voice comes to me
like a black princess
somewhere out in the sea
Come back, come back,
return to me my! . . . . . .
Clothed I dive into water
fish pull off my clothes
I glide towards the mortar
of the center of my soul.

I pass out of my life, my love
   my central dream
a fly, an organism, a cloud, a beam.

Bombs break around me,
tears and wailings flow
inside, outside, and thru me
I try to row
but all of earth and planets & suns
are in my eyes,
in my nose, in my ears.
I pass out of my life & my love
   my central dream.

I find myself without a guide.
The guide of the time
is broken up.
But somehow I don't believe this.

It's the clouds giving me a ride,
and the air of crime
that cannot stop, must stop
in that infernal bliss.

I find myself without grime
carried within a brain
to some rotten changing science
within the limits of a blind world.

I kneel, I'm covered with lime
flying off an angel's train
a thought of defiance
out of the limits of the world.

Where am I? What did I say to rain,
to snow, to growth, to chemicals?
Did I offend, did I defend,
a natural and moving spirit?

But I know I mustn't refrain
from opening my heart's ventricles
to that complicated moving blend
that knows when you fear it.

Even my testicles
had ignored that last cry inside,
the unknown outburst
and outpouring of breaking through.

I looked down at my hands, nails, cuticles,
for some sign of this ride,
that life had been reversed.
But not the slightest clue.

No black princess, no white princess
whose voice I've heard.
No prince, no king,
that voice I imagined,
but the echo of my earth being,
my mind turned, my brain turned
my desires, wants, fears,
all wrapped up by an ethereal spirit,
and thrown away to the other shore.
I move away from
this spirit or ocean twilight
to a dangerous rock.
I long for rocks.
A breeze cools my nude body,
I long for a breeze.
O sun that warmed me!
O bull on the grassy plain!
O sun that reactivated me
from a long and unique womb!
O sun sun that washed me
in the September breeze!
I am now like before I ever was,
the topology of a kiss.

Here, where distance seems flat,
where Time seems hollow
or not to be at all

I make my final pledges
and strain to push destiny
away from this scene

Make me time
    make me space
or take them both away

and substitute an incarnation
to hold these intimate tears
from those I love

O God let me pray for you
O rock let me pray for you
O broken branch
O leaf
O cumulus let me pray for you
O sun hotter than fires
of my eyes let me pray for you
O night within the tree trunk
  let me pray for you
O birds of autumn
O bark
O sin let me pray for you
O confession secret & psychic
        let me pray for you
O last autumn insect,
burrowing through the surface
           forever
let me pray for you
O youth and old age, let me pray for you
O minute and timeless passion
    let me pray for you
O sex mindless or mindful
let me pray for you
O flesh and blood
torn and shed
O flesh and blood
conceived and formed
let me pray for you
O happiness, O sorrow let me pray

Let me pray for you, O stars
burning a sphere of life
let me pray for you, O loneliness
like a fallen tree
let me pray for you, O words
never really conceptual
let me pray for you, O trying
and trying and trying,
let me pray for you
those to whom life comes easy
those to whom life comes hard.
O animals of the earth let me pray for you
O life in other worlds, only felt,
let me pray for you
O reason let me pray for you
O death
who follows us like a small
and innocuous cloud,
in the bluest blue skies.

I climb to top of rock . . .
my shadow glues my passions,
my lust my desire, immobile, locked,
paralyzed with no relation

to mountains or plains.
The creases in rock enfold me
in moving organic sins
the past in front of me like a tree.

In a land with no tree
I curl around like a dog
a man inactive and free
like the eucharist on a log

Out of sight is my mind
out of mind is all sight
only my ears are left to find
beautiful odorless night

No phantom comes, nor does it go
from me like a deer
passing in the dark low
of earth by my ear

And now I hear
what I've gotten myself into:
two voices separating, merging
I see them with my ears
and feel them with my tongue
two sounds
    close but far
sweet but bitter
alone but in crowds.
But me, I've merged
into the invisible tree
into the sandy dark
into a formula, a compound
of some non-matter light
some non-wavelength beam
some beyond-spirit-mystery
where each organ incarnates.

And from here
a blood flows in the ground
a blood flows through the stars
from one to another
a blood flows through trees
and animals and water
my blood flows
through the ground
to the stars one to the other
to the trees, to animals, to water

it flows to color
it flows to smell
it flows to taste
it flows to moving
and molecules and atoms
and anti-atoms and mystery

and from here
my brain is a rock
my skull an archeology of passion,
laughing and crying
inside night's luminous jokes.
O night, bring me open
and the resources that blind me
that form the same forces on my ribs,
recontrol this journey into the arch.

And now I see the wall,
the trees against my head
the seepage of bodies thru the ground
the pervious layer
of what I've always seen
equally strong within a dream.

Where is my heart that disappears?
Who would find it in the dirt
still throbbing, still calling
like a late bird left behind
in a colossal migration.

Now looking down at myself
I see whatever is replaced
but still remains the same,
whatever is in motion
in solitary nerve systems
a feeling of eternal youth
caused by desperation & ecstasy.

But ecstasy has always been
and looking away from it
I realize it has been waiting
for me to grab a little
towards my own destruction.
And while still calling
still left behind
I abandon myself from all that
and enter the last mirage.

Every structure, every form,
like before I ever was
incarnates thru every other storm,
and all this is followed,
followed everywhere.

When a puff of wind deserts us
and we are little children
on the sweet plateau, where should
I turn in these pyramids
and implore revelations?
    Sunny altar springing
sanguine hopes. Invitations
and birds flowing freely
above the invisible bird.
Hearts among the nations
gone awry with supplications
to the angels. But not
even wings on gods
to gravitate these waves amid the deserts
I experience; these waves of altars
against the dirt and stone.
    Who was here before, who is here
now, who to fly, who to soar
through my eyesight,
into a lens of dreams? A sunny
spark burns my bicep

straining to look out into
the invisible world,
or to step into revels
of no evolution
       through burning life

My lips turn drowsy
the wine of dead leaves
overtakes me in waves
that carry me deeper
into the hymns, O hymns of hibernation
my breathing slowing,
my heart, a dying seal,
and the eyes can no longer open
no matter what oblivion calls,
no matter what wilderness
nor monster walks on top of this.

Never before has such heat
left this body
now sliding so many ergs
below the temperate of my life
Knees bind me so close to myself
and my teeth have cut
      my chest a little,
while a seascape
    of all my losses
smells damp like a fallen net.
In this unknown sea of earth
in which the magma
heats my few breaths
I divide from this everlasting dream.

O beautiful one   rising therefore

every heart   the maker of earth

My two hands   the knife hacked off

every day   which is within it

     have strengthened me   increasing

     my limbs

O God of life,   I sing praises to you

your beauties   are dilated with joy.

Mountains   coming forth   traversing

millions of years,   older than

       the womb

greater than the duration of life.

Become green to thee   through the earth

the greatness of terror

   which has not become his name.

Me in the duration of his life

towing the earth in his name,

extended of body,   loaves of bread

beautiful in the face.   My heart

the body   a place of happiness

to not be repulsed   not

by the weighing of words,

but triumph to hear thee,

the balance in the Tomb.

Where can I find thee   but to
                              make me

to embrace you   who illumines

the sky of yesterday and today

every place   coming from water

the mother of substance   eternity

going in and coming out.

I'm in the washing flames

unbolting   the sled of concealment:

of the bound   of the beautiful,

showing, performing, the world which is under

the regularity of darkness.

Not is there in my body

the sight   driven away divine

a motive for my hidden self

the planets   my heart twice evil.

Does divine destroy divine?

       Now night,   the daybreak

       of mountains,   breaks.

Seldom has there been   O sky

such as everything that passes away,

germinates all respiration

      and returns

Biological is my boat hidden to me

upon my face

      I smell   air and darkness

The images in sand,   a rudder

      in darkness

longing   in the well   of hours

    to germinate and pass.

The night on my head comes

      into the city

Failing and purifications; great

is the end which has no end

What then is it   my life

  in this "double nest"?

My hair   the slaughter upon earth

my footsteps

            to me and:

there's light.

  From unformed matter, formed,

I am yesterday of today

  I enter into the exaltation

defects and all destroyed.

My name is soul,   my name

is rest and darkness

my name is light, son,

and daughter, and tree.

The fishes lie in place

  of hidden things,

the crocodiles in wait

to transfigure with me   like uranium
                          in the balance.
The lions in bliss   upon

                    our tomb.

But for me   make my friends,

my sons, & daughters   & my loves

exalt   on unguent earth

in this invisible face

this endless respiration.

In this way I found
mountains that abounded
with one rock after another
multiples of speech
farther & farther to reach
flooded with light
that made my hair raise.
Within this dark illumination
my eyes inert and separated,
my head was given to me.

I fall down   become animal
but fear like heaven descends on water.
The earth is appearing on
                          earth:
a part of death destroyed.

What food was there?
The beautiful branch
I ate in darkness.
I ate the night

for those of them who love,
passing on two feet annihilating
my body's flame:
I pass into a bird,
those wings, yet divine.

O revolution of rock over rock
    that fights my breathing
of my backbone and hands
from the lips of Spirit
    the howling in the rocks.
Pursuing the desire
        to fall down
at the last state
without the weapon of not fearing
or the desires to
        be terrored of death.

Breathing, or the breath
of the body does not forget
the conception of the body,
the remembrance of the shelter
of this system
into living energy.

Everything rises   nothing rises
things fall   things do not fall
the sky and my heart together . . .
it's all, it's all   illusion
            it's all

I wake up
between two iron mountains
my feet are tied in mud and branches.
A womb of spatial unity. Sand is surrounding
a heart of carbon
Something flies closer to me than
an eagle to the side of a diabase cliff.
Straining into the cell
I could see the gateway
where there is no difference
to be transmitted to me
or lost in delusion to light.
  (But there's no light:)

an ordained body outside of body
to inside this ordinary soul,
the void in flux.

O how can I gain the body anew?
No concept surfaces
and sexual wheels
wake up this endless bliss.

Although languid I come
to you, languid I die,
unknown by my own heart.
I lay there in my shadows.

To say nothing is to dream
want nothing, a geometrical
chord in an unknown song
of blossoms that could fathom what it is
to be far away
or old and youthful,
Stand away from those smells!

Spring surrounds your ears
when in the clear mouldy distance
a mist settles on the fertile edges
of the mystical fever.

O sticks piled up in the woods,
O deer that passed thru the city streets
that my search has brought me
disembodied to a song
of pure rotted pain.
O angels that decomposed
on the rich meadows of
Jurassic upheaval,
now a clear soft grain
on the pelvic mound of retrieval.

Splinters of light
in my eyes forever,
light that if even the suns
went out and all
that would be left
runs into the eternal night
would still remain
like a grain of rice
lit by the moon
like a hard kiss on the mouth.
I contemplate like a gnat
to open its eyes
before it dies . . . the summer wing.

O that buzzing of famine
rain and neon in the mud,
placing over my eyes
a fire of body, a mine, a vein
under a drugged mission
where it comes like the charity
of confused dogma.

One poem   one peyote
all disappears across the traffic
of night's grizzly breath.

Voices like broken trees
across my dreams,
daffodils of lies
while the clonk-bell cries
of this mysterious evening bird
raids the roughage
of immortality
through my system

Where can I go, O tunnels
of forced money.
The radiation of lies
descends from heaven
The heavens disappear
in the evolution of brains.
All that remains
are Words for the survival of groups
as they descend into the immorality
of leaden truth,
or as the cosmic hurricane
tears apart the ball
and spews colors and colors
in the mosaic of eternal stopping

Saturn still turns
in the wind
his hairy rings swim around
his violent seasons.
A blind girl enters,
the wind swirls around the dusty streets
at the reawakening
of a broken spirit into pain

Pain pain and pain.
Thank the gods for youth
they keep the soul invisible
They ride on my back
like Prometheus stealing
the light of blind faith
in the incomplete journey of the mist.
Pain and pain, pain
the camouflage of mystical progressions
where there's only one body
which electrocutes my disappearance
where a spark like a burning quiver
is bathing my solar plexus.
A bird sings, a gun goes off
the earth falls
        asleep in our arms.

New buildings wave
   toward the future
The lamb lies next to Arabia
sword in hand
a metrical fear
embraces the battle
with Europa's arms held wide,
bayonet wounds on her forearms.

The bull's head is bloody
in the acid moonlight
where the river through mica
under the stony rays
of cosmic heat,

and the head like the moon
floating in the river rain,
a discharge swelling
like blood in the body
but not contained.

I sit crying
in this city of wilderness
waiting for the ignition
of the plains
against the fiery heavens
ragged, incensed
betrothed to winter winds

in the electrifying death
of the darkness
in the blind vision,
vision of pure cruelty,

Cruelty of undenied forces.
Amor turns to power
Psyche to revenge & revulsion
Apollo turns to lies and propaganda
only Orpheus slips away
into the night wind
unseen   unfound   slips away
through pain and fear
fading into the night wood
a light   a spark   a quantum
                of silence

I step back into the forest
  with the shadows

INTERIOR OF THE POEM
1971

My hair is black, my eyes are black,
I am the dictator of the poem.
The poem is in front of me
I am writing on its face.
The soul of the poem
is inside the soul
which is inside the poem.
There is no mystery to me
because I can be seen.

I am five foot one, can almost be called dark.
My forehead is high
like a nude African.
My body is nude underneath this dress.
The skin is lighter than a hard-on.
If I move, my dress will move.
Underneath this dress are openings.
They are used for purposes.
I am not mysterious.

In my own way I am a star,
a galaxy of temptation and denial.
My eyes are wide,
even a deer would stop to look.
I am a huntress; my game is man.
Behind my ribs is a heart
that can be eaten.
I am an animal.   No! No!
I am an animal
There is a dictator of the poem.
I removed is that dictator.

Beneath my dress, midway
beneath my dress are lips
that have been bitten by the poem.
If I remove the dictator, I become me,
which is the poem removed.

I'm a huntress of the soul,
but I'm gentle with my fallen prey.
I am misused by my prey
and my poem.
The poem can reveal itself through me.
If I say
that I am more intelligent
than the poem,
do I mean that the poem is less
intelligent than I
or do I mean that the dictator
is less intelligent
than the poem?
The poem has no weight.
The poems has no value.
It is not for sale.

Where do I end
and where do I begin?
The poem is talking, I am not.
When will it stop
so that I can talk?
Does the poem love me
or does the soul inhabit me
to love the poem?
If I kiss the poem
or fuck the poem
will it then love me?
There is no guarantee.

If I charge
like a bull with fluttering wings
will the poem laugh at me?
I command the poem to let me in.
        It throws shit in my face.
And in my own way, I deny the poem
the fruits of life,
independence, freedom, and happiness.

I steal from the poem
its energy, its humor,
its eccentric stability.

I place the poem
under a microscope.
I look at it through a telescope
where its magnified soul
explodes in my face.
For all this it sees right through me.

Where is the key to the poem,
the opening that will make me
see it as a bride, a mistress
of the open seas?
I used to write letters
asking for forgiveness.
There was never an answer
but I learned
to love the poem even more.
It was bright, intelligent, imaginative.
warm and sensual
and completely dominated me
with its words, its ideas.

The longings of the poem
scare me, and its challenge
will destroy me from what I am today.

But why are you so new, so young,
so full of innocent obscenities?
Your glance
full of the sweet poisons I ask for,
is too quick for my eyes.
Everything leaves me too fast.
How can I reveal myself to you?
If I paint, if I become more sculptural,
you say I might reach you.
If I undress, there is still my skin,

my flesh, my bones
hiding me from you.
If I attempt to be honest,
I reveal my weaknesses
and lose the poem.
If I wear a mask, you ignore me.
When I work, I'm too shallow
When I rest I'm too secretive.
What's left but to go
through the forest
knocking on the trees with my prick,
sighing through the woods
with a nude body,
feeling every little thing on its skin.

O, where is the interior of the poem
so that I can stab it with my prick?
Where is my bride
to whom I promised I would come?
        (Some thing's missing
I can't continue.
The poem's become too real.
I've lost myself.)

The poem does not give up.
It teases me and taunts me
until there's no brain left.
It sees my face in the mirror
and laughs at me again when I find
that it is looking at me.
Wait a minute!   Stay a little longer!
I know you have other faces to see.
I feel completely involved———
Am I revealing myself to you?   Am I?
You say it's midnight
You have to go?
At least I know you're not sleepy.

No!   I'll only stop when you are mine
and neither priest nor murderer
can take you away.

No!   I reject all that stuff
about priests and murderers;
I don't care who takes you away
as long as you keep coming back.
It's not because I'm lonely
that I want you back
but because I know you are familiar
with these woods.

Selfishly I need your weapons
to capture the poem.
But I can't continue
because now I don't know
whether I have you or lost you
or whether I'm looking for you.
        I think I once had the poem
        when I was young, when I first met her.
        Whatever knowledge I had then
        was dissipated from my brain.

But it's only you writing the poem,
while I sing away
at dreams of unreality
like a bad folksinger.
You think you've written poem for me?
Yes, you're right.
I had nothing to do with it,
its bland language,
its undecorated sensibility.
You think you've been my guide,
my undiscovered self, my inspiration?
I've only let you because
I was afraid I might lose you again
to some other more revealing force.

Now I see that love
is the only clarity I feared,
and whatever you say
is a translation.
What really moves me
with uncontrollable forces
is that unearthly desire
to be without cares,
to live with every sexual desire,
and to end up in the end like a bum.

INRI

1979

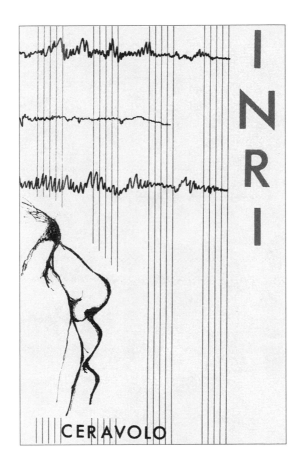

In Memory of Joseph Robinson

O MOON

O moon
How ghost you are.
Come closer.
Let me kiss you,
and touch those lips
of dry ice.

ALONE SWOLLEN

Love has swollen
   its banks,
But only one life, one,
I interpenetrate alone.

ANOTHER WORLD

Everything is part of me,
even the heat of inhumanness,
now that I'm exiled.

QUESTION HAUNTING

I'm torn apart by light,
hardly moving my head.
Why am I so tied to my brain?

BIRTH DAY

Here I am, right here,
torn and ragged,
deeper and deeper
into visible birth.

VISION

Sacrifice love and record position
The goats balance
On beautiful mountains

LIVE TODAY

All these future
     thinkers
Building up the future:
Knock them down.
Make a new life now.

PERCHED

Perched here
confused as a wounded eagle,
I shoot the Time away.
Like an arrow

PROMONTORY

At dawn whatever light
returns, my heart
becomes quicker and quicker
in the night

BLOODSUCKER

Break it all down!
We're too mesmerized
to break from
this vampire, America.

RAMPANT GOD

It's time America
    had form,
organic and real
to take us from this
       wild god.

EARTH

How can we destroy earth?
Why do I see?
The earth is still
another small planet.

TROUBLE

Women have gotten so tall,
they can't
bend for the foliage.
Men have shrunk
        too low.

EXPERIENCE

I've been around
I've been over
everything in 30 odd years

and still it breaks.

HOTEL

Am I supposed to
make a joke of this?
In this hotel thinking
of my children?

SPACE OUT

O Loneliness
O life in the YMCA
Old, ugly, transferred, men
Hungry

MISTAKE

When I button my fly
I button it wrong
and I laugh.
My crotch looks lopsided.

APOLOGY

How can I give you freedom?
The moon is lit tonight,
and stars
are breaking my neck.

NO HELP

Where is love?
Where is science to help?
I hang my head like
a dead crane.
A failure.

FREEDOM

This morning I could
walk and walk.
That's freedom.
But I drink this coffee
before work.

WITHIN

There will always
    be at least 2 forces:

While in the senses, the
real storms growling.

DANGEROUS JOURNEY

Speeding with me
to down.
Break it up
    and stop now.
I can't turn your head
against me.

WORSE ENEMY

Stretched out in the street
is my friend, me,
who just got
hit by a car:
With no goodbye

NOT ONE

There is not one honest
    word in me.
My mind tricks my
    mind.
And love is bolted up.

FABLE

Try my gate.
Food spoiled in the sunlight
is no good to eat.
My thoughts destroy me today.

BAD ASS

A novel can't be as strong,
a play as obscene,
sculpture as dangerous
            as me.

MIXTURE

Gradually, the wind
sucks up its break
          And me
alone beside myself
     today

BROKEN

Alone, more than alone.
I breathe my last fire.
Fathers and sons
walk up mountain.

LAYOUT

The agonies of fortune
assail me
But life under trees
breathing world
is enough for me.

REBORN

Angels are falling.
My life is taken.
I can't be myself
without first dying.

FUTURA

On the desert
my own mirage sleeps.
A chain around my neck.
Loving the future

INTERNAL RAYS

Old Atlantis
is not as far as this.
The same sun rays pour
down the same clouds.

APOCALYPSE

When did it change?
Or was it always
world without end:
with end so near,
yet so far.

AWARENESS

Loneliness is so feared.
Does an ant crawling alone
not notice the world
at all?

MACRO

My screams
can't annoy the stars.
Come, Holy Ghost
enlighten me!
Continue me on.

RISING SOUND

Starting from nothing
Ending it all
The note of the
Cicada in the back yard.

HARD OR SOFT

Fantasy grips me.
Hard or soft, beware.
The sun is ready
to take my reason.

LIGHTING UP

I am paralysed
beyond Love.
Can't you see
my offer inside?
Close me up first.

JOB

Here I am
waiting for a job,
my life in my hands.
My heart on a
    pedestal

THE CAR

All I got left is the car
and a broken heart.
But what more
do I deserve, now?

BEYOND PHONY

Existential, Existential,
a phony word.
Who doubts
that life's
beyond a dream?

INSIDE

Life penetrates
my technological side.
How am I going
to get outside?

UNABLE TO MOVE

The building's shadow
creeps up close
Since I cannot move
the sun better hurry down.

PASS ME BY

Cars pass me by.
Who would have
thought I'd be here
parked on a bench
before the altar.

HARD ENERGY

The sun on my body
 (lonely body)
reveals the injustice
to modern man

MOTION

Bicycles pass
Cars pass
Someone stops to ask
me a question
A break in falling

STUPOR

Sweat is pouring
from my arms
The sun bearing
on my skin.
My bowels
eating sand.

CUANDO AMENECER EL SOL

Who says you
can't mention
old universals?
A plane falls against
colors of dawn.

SPRING BREEZE

Clean Cutting breeze:
a little brutal too much.

Spring trees
My child asleep
in my arms

SLEEPING ONE

Eyes like god's insects,
Cheeks with hair on flowers.
All the colored blossoms
can't match your lips.

HUNTING

> I can't live
> upon this land
> without recalling
> the tribe that walks
> across my grave

THIS LAND

> Summer's on the other side
> and autumn fights its way in
> with an Indian Knife.

OLD FRIEND HUNG

How long has it been
since I've seen you, noticed you,
old friend hung
between my two legs.

THE GODS IN ME

Orpheus is in my bowels
Apollo, my chest.
Isis juggles my penis.

FUTURE LANDSCAPE

What says it is gone
The night air
The bridge along the clouds
The cortex of cities?

IMAGINARY STYX

Motion is spirit
The Passaic clothed
        in veils
My heart riding
    a black canal

DISASTERS

The Mississippi floods
and people lie.
Out in the ocean
everything is blue.

END OF THE WORLD

The look of the end
of the world
is on the face
of every bird
when it's flying.

REALITY PRINTED

A fight with her today,
a fight with her yesterday.
But I'm not really angry.

MARGINAL EXISTENCE

Without you
I would be nothing.
Your double set of lips
have made me
bigger than life.

FOOTING

No more footing.
A windless chase
Tripping on a storm
Kissing her burning belly.

CONTINUUM

Someday, this moment
will be thought about.
If I'm dead
Then you will think
This moment

IF I CAN'T

Take my mouth
if I can't love.
Amid technologies of reverence
blood pours out.

RIVER FLOODED

What shame!
When I hate
I hate deeply.
When I hurt I hurt deeply
and all around.

THE FOREST WETNESS

> Trees light up
> against the sky
> Birds eat away
> While I squat down,
>   my ass
> touching wet leaves

NON-SPATIAL

> The wind like glass
> being broken
> down the road
> surprises my own existence.

RUNS ME OVER

Sometimes when I sit here
eating in the hot sun,
a great sadness
runs me over

FLIGHT

I see worlds passing by
And I'm sleepy

I hear buzzing
of perfumes invading.

BUT

Ideas are just ideas
But imagination
mindless imagination
flies

TO SEED

I love life, I really
    love life.
My dozing on a Spring
rainy day goes to seed.

MANURE

Death is a seed
and Spring its manure
Love in the language
of science
becomes my name
          (Insane)

A CAVE MAN'S DREAM

There is magical
A bird on tongues
Vision and memory
Steep me in the rites

RITUAL

Like the growth
    of a tree
I'm fed into
mysteries of Spring:
that have Killed me
more than once.

BASIC HEART

As I open the
flood gates
I transfer the potential
of tears
into sexual heat

THE WINDS OF THE COMET

The winds of the comet
are like a whirlwind
The invisible sky
reappears.

NEGATIVE MOUNTAIN PEAK

O Real Spirit!
see if you can embrace and
Conquer me!;
the negative mountain peak

INFINITE THUNDER

What a beautiful storm!
Infinite thunder!
Wishing to be home
No wonder.

GHOST OF SPRING

The ghost of Spring
has reappeared,
clearing my throat
of winter.
I make the first move

MILLENIUM DUST

1982

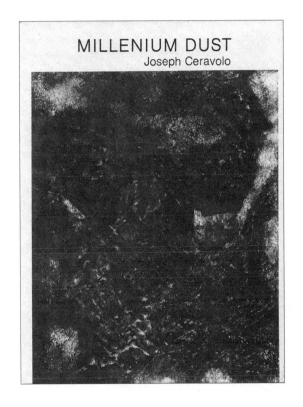

His heart was clear on one point:
he knew whom he loved . . .
—FYODOR DOSTOYEVSKY, *The Idiot*

To Paul, Anita, & James

Winds of the Comet

VOLCANO TEARS

I'm a blank
The sun is out
The wind is cold
Walking but not going.
Why didn't you love me?
On the beach
the shells still move.
Summer will never change
But you do, you changed

the face of the mystic
that wanders around in me,
that abandons me
when the rising moon surges
above the loneliness
of this beautiful world.

BRIGHT SUN

The sun is in the sky,
and it is bright.
The signs are bright
and soon there is something
to shine. Until the flower
coming out of the soil.

There is something dark
in this bright sun.
It is not my feeling toward
you, or the universe, or feelings
of Spring.

WET SAND

Cruelty, love, derangement.
    Movements decide like
        sand dunes while we are
away from home, and all
of us are brushing

this breast of mine.

Me hovering
over you last night.
From our brain to the sun
was the only thought as I lay there nude.
In the end will the sand be wet?

CROSS FIRE

This is the second day without anyone.
I am chinning against a dark sky
to strengthen my arms.
A picture of everyone I love passes thru me.

No clear light streams thru this cell.
There's no dawn.
What have I gained
by lying in this abyss,
waiting for the masonry
to show a little slit
for my soul to get through?

SAVAGE NOCTURNE

Do you think
because you're out
and I'm reading my palms
like a gypsy,
that you have freedom?

Maybe you do.
And I'm the one in Vulcan's furnace
dipping my burning heart in oil

while one drop of desire
would save my life.
Now that the coast is clear
and the Holy Ghost
is in my nerves; I look for you

but you're not here.

A LAST SONG

I know
harm can destroy
what trust there was in love.
But no, not us,
walking in this bright
universe. What is in it?
No face, no love, no rage?
Among the transversal beams
of our giving up,
of all despair,
soothing at each end,
there is one thing left
in this raging dispassionate lust.

SPIRAL

Anti-stars far away
Venus, Jupiter, and Moon
around each other, yet far apart.
My life: yet it all comes back.
Stars and matter and spiral
clear and cold
about to take me on:
warm body and all.

GEOLOGICAL HYMN

The wine is gone,
but I'm still not drunk.
Can non-visual reality
bring all my dreams to completion?

My head doesn't belong to me
Why should it?
A desert, an ocean, a tundra,
in the antecedent cambrian worm
lies before me in a field of vision,
not from me or in me
but from some foreign night
falling and falling in snow.

But I still come around
while the wind itself is gone
and the soul like a strung bow
in the elastic and infinite void

stretches beyond the spaced out message
in this geological kiss.

BARBARIC

I try to lighten myself with
prayer, sunshine, sex,
but I'm really as heavy as you are.
Brother of summer,
when all the hydrogen transforms
are you still
as instantaneous as you are now?

But what will be left of you,
and what will be left of us someday?

THE CATSKILLS

I climbed to the top of Blackhead Mountain
My mind had been thinking
of the world below.
I was only eighteen.
Suddenly overcome with her,
I studded the imagination
with backtracks into life.
The scene below became a distant lagoon.
O dreams of migration!
dreams of migration
sneaking up behind me.
I was only eighteen.
She touched my neck:
it lifted my insides into flames,
and me not thinking what I'd do
sprang from the top
toward the endless field below.
I was only eighteen.

TODAY'S NIGHT

At night when you are off
in a dark-eye sleep

and I look in the mirror
at these young shoulders,

my face filled with the wild flowers
we passed today,

it comes to me like a skunk
in the woods

that someday I won't
be standing in this cosmos.

And I am filled with
a strange energy

to alight my mind.

SLEEPING BY THE ROCKS

I hold her hand held
  swollen with dreams.
Passing a soul through the hand.
    An insect jumps
              on her breast.
The urge is in a river passing.

So many facts in recall,
on her breast, swollen with sleep,
on her legs, sleeping
in a jumpy dream.

If I let go of her hand
    will she sleep?
I hold her hand
held swollen with dawn.

DRUNK ON THE BRAIN

This is the top.
All around in a day
   of oxygen, real,
         a room overlooking.
      Total light
      and promise
          to understand your
   pains and suffering
     in the dark room.
What is a wife? A woman
    A hand. A leg.
      With Egyptian
    odors, lying on the bed.
Drunk, by soap
    on your hands:
        Drunk on the brain.

If night be above the earth.

THE SPIRIT MERCURY

The thunder is dirty,
the lightning my sister.
Two voices from the
        same source.
But I won't allow
myself to think of nature.
It's too appealing,

too full of mysteries
that take my heart away
from this ugly laceration.
   But somehow
even that is gone
and all that's left
        is rain.

RHYTHM

What landscape should I stalk
now that I've descended
and the war planes over my talk,
covering my mind are ended,

and it's paroxysm
for you with the first lark songs?
Spring is in. O.K. Just
one love before the wolf
tears down the door.

But I am paralyzed.
The moons, the winds,
fade on with the first lark,
while the magic of Spring
teases and tempts beyond recall.

WHITE DWARF

To the salt,
if there is any left
on this planet without life,
I give up my soul.
I give it without the body

to exude a vision
of life   without a planet
What   is   left beyond that?

The morning
between the leaves.
Misery, love, generation,
all screwed up.
But stars look even brighter.

Love, morning, stars, slightly
blue now, in the
continuous lighting
                of the heavens,
earth, hell,
the bright star, and the universe

all alone.

INSIDE STORY

Like a dinosaur licking a tiger
my soul seems to be
outside me.
This space I fit in
is even the foundation of matter.
There are things all around.
The things are matter.
I just don't know any longer
than the life of a baby
sleeping in the bed next to me.

Does this fact look
                at me and see me
happy as a stone,
washed in a baby's teething mouth?

This beach, this obtainable
    light in the modern physics
    of night time.

Like a dinosaur licking a tiger
my soul is outside.

ESCAPE TO ATLANTIS

O lost world in found continent!
Open tonight! Rise with the sun
    as thunder from outside.
A few drops fall———like sand
between stars.
    It is a galaxy,
      this streak that flies around.
A stone in an ocean:
and I try more than once
to make up for
the neglect of a thousand feelings.

WINDS OF THE COMET

The winds of the comet are quiet.
Tonight the rain turned around.
The way I held it and held you
was over the hill.

I see the distance fade
and holding it tightly
in my arms like a two year old,
I feel a great chill.

I am not a fool,
but love is so breezy,
as I live from day to day, more and more,
on sprung meditations.

SURVIVAL

With wings reached out
and ready to reveal
    layer after layer,
the wind through the peaks
grips my nostrils.

My neck, my head, stiff,
  my wings opened
        as far as they can go
            but not as far as
                I think I am.

My little ones in the nest.
Land is below.
Who needs to rest
but revel in this layer after layer.

I look down:
everything   is   beautiful.
Feel faint in stomach.
Stretch my arms
till they hurt and bones show through.
Things I never see
pass closer than my beak.
I recall nothing
nothing that is so alive.

FIRE OF MYSELF

What I miss most is
      that live
that subtle transformation
  from inert to
trans-atomic structures
that leaves my welded
and supple body
that carries the imprint
      of that body
into the land
    of pure migration

BODY OF EARTH

A piece of metal
is in the street in the sunshine.

Even suffering is made of air
and is related to the next breath.

What are the clouds
or the sky or the trees

next to our object soul

which leaves me

like a lizard in the mountains,
not a symbol,

not God, nor any
of the objects in the air.

The river flows on.
The mountain returns.
The commotion of the trees flies

through the pulse.
Eternal love, still
not a symbol, is still invisible,
but flows on
through the clouds, the planets,
through this planet,
body of earth.

NOT AFRAID OF THE DARK

What I give you tomorrow
you already have.
It's absorbed and blended
into a larger and more eternal:
I die for you each day.

Lamenting in the tank,
absorbed is the sand,
O tenderness of blood and birds
searing my temples, my young head:
the recurring storm of youth
            wrecks my sins.

The sun over branches
over the open flesh of dawn
kissing the hands of migrant farmers,
fogging the insides of rainy caves

        while we're absorbed and blending
        into larger and more eternal sexes.

The body still here, at my fingers,
at my organs,
spread like water underground
thru me, the spirit. And the rain
dissolves my organics thru sins
that no one talks about anymore,
but like months of rain
flood our time on earth
like stars in living vapors.

GENERATIONS OF CLOUDS

Here I am without you.
Generations of clouds
might see me,
but where am I without you?

Like a young girl
whose life has its own toughness,
lying around waiting
wanting to approach.

Where am I without you?
not meaning
I might be nowhere.

Loose, diverting, just trying
to take the whips
and the loves without you. The clouds
dance over the young people.
Love is itching their brain.

Soon the generation is new.

WAVES APART

The sun is blinding!

The sun that seems now
only a stone glowing.
        A cloud
passing it and blocking it
doesn't change
my ideas of the buildings.
I'm caught in thc dcsolation
away from you
                into the world

COOLING GALAXY

ME NO CARE

When what I say

When when I stay. . . . .just pray

satisfied and calling mine.

Hear thee

THE ROCKET

                I
Being with you
        I am a seagull alone
        and flying although the clouds
    are within.

Tomorrow I'll be trans-illumined.

Does God call it?

O spit
      on the ground
       in a denser way
            upon the clouds.

In the jungle,
       clouds are falling.
Stand in front of me!
      Block out the sun!
       The leaves
have lines of their own.

We become trans-illumined
    Will we ever be like
        the sun . . . . . . when it's
        like a piece of slate?

    You call me
       though the shoulders
this morning
       shake.
Flying above.
Spots, seeing spots.
You gotta go in right here.

A bug
is going behind the wall.
Is some of its existence love?
It doesn't look it.
But its feet change speed.
Outside the air is flat and cold,

and it doesn't snow.
Nothing to do, like a bug,
with its green blood
coursing along its shell,
its basic means of knowing.
Looking around at a new
cosmos in its blood which is
outside the flower
in some lost existent speeded world.

II

Is there a soul other than that generator
like an arctic sky?
Noticing the stars; gathering
in spright all the bastards on earth.
Not one is old.
Solingering about a night
in ropey love.
The bastards of all earth are us.

In a dark love without love.
The one seed
noticing all the stars
in a new composition. A new generation
of love forms.
Seagulls pierce the coast.
O easy wings of strain's desire,
what is the joy of man?
Is there a joy without love's composition
staining and loving on this earth?
We are not so helpless as one
extinguished star.
But what about love
in our feeling for the cosmos?
Is it cosmic enough? Is it like a
ray of invisible light or comic   enough
in a field of natural blights?

But, I stay and I hear. And it is
the same beautiful song.
The arctic and the jungle on one drug.
And love, windless, rough,
in the cosmic lust.

III

The streets are dented.
They are all awakening
and in easy love
guiding no template to feeling scared.
Alone in a word of love
on the side while cars
are full of people
averaging their immense sleep.
But I'm lonely.
Stop! I might be in trouble.
The template of good is
all around us and still the cars
go by like years
          and stars
in a refreshed universe.

Gather them o stars.
I am not so big.
  But I am mobile like a stuffed deer
without a family,
      too lost
        to be another child;
and now my tongue is big.

What choice and then
the sun comes up:
peering I fall down on
my chest crying.

As the sun glides across
the lumpy tears
and I am limpid in your arms

swerving through the light
in the manifold
of a new embrace
I see my deficiency
          on the gauge.

Me defoliated and dry
about to burst into fire mite.
Defoliated and dry
waiting for internal casts
Defoliated,
covered with bruises,
dry,
defoliated and dry
pissing in the wind
finding it maybe this winter.
Me defoliated
me dry

IV
Today it's just a blank because I envelope you
while the cars are
going by so fast and there's no poetry
in the sun or in the last
flame of a star.
The dawn in its traffic-light red
looks like a blowing orange blanket
tossing in the south east.
But still there's misunderstanding
that shakes us like a truck
passing by in a detonation.

I am released tonight.

There's a young moon
about to intermit
so that I could remain up;
and eat of my desires.
To speak that I might eat.
To have strength.

But there's a young moon
out the window of my rocket
that tells me
the earth is sending off its sons.
     It is easy to speak.
But so hard to strike
          the song
on the hunt of the people
     of the world.

But tonight I'm not eating.
Even though the cosmos is swooping
in my ear, I am released
to your arms from this outer sea.

The stars are salt
   this morning
as I sit here
sobbing into my arm,
into the wooden table.
My heart and
no abomination:
no rum, no rum left
   for me.

Let the leaves around this. _ _ _
Engorged on the outer wing
of the volcano
I hear a rumble.
I am cold.
Let the leaves around this. _ _ _

On the outer wing
of this engorged volcano
I feel the rumble in the leaves around
of what no flower can deny the cosmos.
In the cold
on the outer wing to love.

Let the leaves be engorged
in our tears.
There is no rumble that a flower
can deny.
There is no cosmos in the outer wing toward love.
In the cold volcano

v

During these long and blank formations
between the nights of time
        parallelism
I lapse into this transmutation.
How sudden, how great to survive
with no sadness on the scene.
        In prehistoric America
there was no deficiency too great to
survive the catastrophes.

Us, found in nature;
unpure and clear,
with the premonition of a mammoth
of beautiful proportions
and the suddenness
of wild birds.
Our beginning is new because of our appearance,
but what about
the change of nature
and the cataclysmic land bridges
that bring one land to another
or that spring up separately
like ancient fish
in mechanistic revels to survive?

During these long and blank days
of happiness or joy, great
as the proportion of a woman found
with no clothes on,
maybe there's nothing to our joy or pain:
clearer than any new cataclysm
that destroys everything, destroys.

Soon this snow will melt
and the park with its floor of ice
will be melting. Soon, when
the deluge of cosmic suffering flys with is.
Soon this park will melt.

VI

When a fire becomes fire
    there is no dying.
Again the poles are cold.

The street promulgated with
large trees and birds in its song.
How the branches sing
and the heart makes falser
    what we pretend.

It isn't Spring, but the branches.
It isn't warm, but the chirps
of the invisible archangels.
Where have you been all my life?

Love is breathing and love is taking,
but away when
there is no Spring: we live.
We are a micro generation
in these trees
   amid this song of one note
and a million intonations.
But it is not Spring
and love is dying in its youth

but the trees are living
among these sacred powers
of incantations to life:
        Among all this destiny
we still fight.
But it is Spring
and in the sky are the velvet planets
wandering and in the soul
is a suspension:

Thru and thru
this will never come in

But here I am painless
in a world of pain.

        A sick dog
who doesn't know one sickness.

The limited surging
of my blood, not only in my vein

but in the bodies of you
my brothers, my sisters.

Look outside at the starlike
stars! They are not even pointed.

I think of the women I know
in their baths

and us passing through
with a name, a star, a dog.

Even in this light the stars
are equal to a flower.

The last blot of light
this universe will see

or that we see at night
  is a laugh, a song.

We wash clothes, we wear them,
the stars shake.

We do not feel it
but the soul takes its secrets

to your bath, your arms, your eyes,
your thrust into the last flash

and then, it is day.

CODA

For it seems
that the darkness
is a dream of experiment.
There is more of the monkey
to be respected.

Day follows day.
White. . . .   the next day is black.
What analysis
behind the light.
What's between a child sleeping.
The bird in a glance.
Dark bodies
are the children sleeping.

The weather ends,
and efforts of a novice
to exhaust but still to be;
until the end of the mysteries
of an immaterial universe.

What have we caught
in a human modern dream?
Submission: Menstrual
in the life sub
of a secret passage to blood.

Is life knowing the thing?
Not knowing is not
hearing.
Fill us with
a loving animal!

The galaxies last and last
until the end of the galaxies:
lasts and lasts.
When nothing stands
between my black face
and red heart
     I ask
Where is home?

and the universe,
the belly grumbling,
is the cry of a baby
growing hair.
White light
and night heat
falls along the sharpest
and the little snugglers
with their eyes;
the human embryo
arouses in this empty stomach
the feeling of a universal smell.

As I sit
with this case
on the shoulder
of an ancient shore,
with the thing we fear:
On this day I throw off the clothes
in a sing of dominated embraces.

The wintry puddle
comes back to life.
Ants with their new clear
bodies are drenched
in their first walk.
My heart has known conceit.

There is a long ant.
There is a short ant.
Eyes keep running
thru the night.
Why should I let it die?
All I need is to embrace it.

I sit down alone
and do not run.
Children run.
Children scream and play.
The more I follow the wind
the bead stops
and my opinion.

Friends knock on my heart.

The effect of woman
is in the feelings.
Splash my eyes,
keep me drenched,
to a decried heart,
down a soul.
Although there is an ancientness
in human breath,
even the creatures sing.

1967

Apollo in the Night

STORM BREAKING OVER

Last night my eyes
were like rain leaking through
thinking of how I've messed up
my chances with you.
But no more bullshit,
no more holding back.
My life is filled with
how I'll never reach anything.
You in one world, me in a solo.
It's subtle and painful
to be separated
by a primal methane of ideas.
I know women
who are completely sane
and I know you better than ever now.
What is this unity
that separates us?
Can I become a woman,
can you become a man?

Our America seems to be
against all of nature's subtle unity.
All that's left is memory
riding the tide in,
a few extra pleasures, warmth, love,
and nonchalant desires.
Time is closing in on me.
Memory is standing forth
like an erection
forcing its way
into female insurrection.
I think I am drowning myself.

But if I believed all this
it would be the zero
of non-ending time and space.
The world is created and destroyed.
Material brings us little.
The earth doesn't exist.
Only life transfigured into smoke
settles in a solar plexus
of pleasures revoked.

Now I've come full circle,
but the beginning
is not the same as the end.

I cried thinking of how
I've messed up my chances.
Even though I may
never escape to tell
about the three worlds
heaven, earth, and hell,

some light did come back,
now working, now resting,
in every cross-section of me.

HILLS

Have I been beaten by love
caught in the mud
of Autumn's feeling?
A knock on the head freezes
the mystical breeze
on these abysmal hills.

I stand up naked
above the sacrificed land.
People think I'm out of my mind,

but I'm only beaten up in memory.
The chill of this morning
in seeking and wanting: haunting
like the path of some unknown,

a purple flower here, a fool, a body.
How did I ever come
in this century's secret melancholy,
this mad science?

In a fit of self reliance
my strategy is all wound up.

I've sunk in
like cosmic dust,
and like a prisoner
tearing away his blindfold on life
I'm under the same stars
in the sacred vow radiant,
radiant in the sacred vow.

NIGHT WANDER

Eyes without light,
night without eyes,
scum of the earth, primordial skin.
A black, a beautiful universe.
Skin and eyes and fever
travels within itself
into the other.
Do not be afraid.

Recline with your hopes
on this resplendent day.
Birds cry out to the morning,
the ground calls me brother.
I crawl to you

wiped out,
  stains on the heart.
O you who from our eyes is hid
with one odor
one note
and no explosion at all.

COLD NIGHT ALONE

I fight and fight
when I'm away from you.

Everything obscure and lonely disappears.
When I walk I feel my legs.
I think until
there's no air left inside me.

Forget me! Forget it!
The forces I have
are the same against and for.
They're never loaded as you are.
They live within the organs
like a cold night alone.

MORNING INSULTS

  Eyes are swollen
after last night.
My head is empty.
There're stones in my shoes.
The voice sounds like a cricket's.
My arms are heavy
carrying my own body.
My neck is moving with resistance.

The heart and chest
are tied up in the sacrifice
of love that may never come.

Your kiss is still ringing in my ears.

Don't expect too much from life.

CONCEPTION

The pains flip me around
and one rain is enough to fill my bladder.

The chair, the knife,
the nipples of this volcano
one kisses to be living.

The guns shoot a lonely
        runaway slave.
The daffodils
        bleed into summer.

The knife, the napkin,
but still the footsteps
of an angel overhead
haunts every blink
my eyes make.

MILKY WAYS

What holds this together?
What eros of a living star
slides through these heavens and heavens
making me the most fortunate of all?

But flattered, plagued and lonely,
like wings it folds around me:

like the branches of a willow
in the rain, and falling to earth.

TIME ON EARTH

Close to you
        it's morning
Close to you
    I am getting up
My head hits
        the metal.
Close to you in morning.
Breezes moving the underwear
            close to you

INSTANTANEOUS TAKES TIME

I am so alone on
this television screen. The universe
        and the atoms
    of the birds are still
        in my eyes.
The silver night gets smaller and
            smaller while I hold you
        and notice the stratified dawn.
It is not red.
    A bird flies off the ground:
    His chest still cool, like mine.

The beach is so windy.
You climb down and the
sun is like a softening orange
streaming out its stickers
of exuding fission.
Why are the atmospheres so clear
where even the smallest speck
finds its plane
in that aromatic love
coming from the city streets?
The sun slants off
the buildings and off the glass
in front of the stores.
I thought you were gone.
Even this smallest thought
is a bacteria, is a
disease. Yes, how it
kills in this atmosphere of no despair
like thunder in the eyes
of people, like specks
in the September air.

PROJECTION

Talking outside in the light
the men work. They light their cigarettes.
Copying and staying on the job.
A bird along the wall
pauses and watches the men.
What overtakes them?
O morning
I talk to you
in a spotted and refracted voice.
Branches face me.
Much heavier than thoughts.

The night passes through April wind.
I wake up on the oasis bushes. The system
is at rest away from you
neater than a star overhead
drawing all chemicals from the brain.
This body, this blood
like asphalt under heat. . . . melts.

STAR SONG

December!   end!
this
beneath my house
alongside
by
intro
of milk silver
that sprang up
in
leaves which
            bloom
and as
in the. . . . .

O stars!

EARTHQUAKE

Out the window of the clouds
the sea brush overtakes,
and I remember all the big cities
of the world
but they're pushed back.

Buildings torn down and built up.
Storms upon storms of wind
rented upon the heart
of a land that disappears
in one organic night.
Night over night of changing land,
first buried then swept away,
while faraway birds stop by
(and we talk about space)
out of the clouds
under the stormy magnetics
        of the stars.

VOICE ON MY BIRTHDAY

(april 22, 1976)

        Your song
        like an owl's hoot
        with pain added bothers me.
Every day at this time
I hear you calling,
        What are you?

Are you the same bird
that held my son in his heart
when he thought you were
        an owl in the trees
but couldn't see you?

Or are you the bird
that cried like a soldier back home?

Too beautiful is your voice
if voice it be
too simple is your song
only three or four notes
which have slid into me forever.

INLAND

If I lived here
        before long
I would go crazy
for the ocean.
A lake just isn't enough
        for me.
As beautiful as this gem
reflects earth's diamond grave
I could die here for love's sake
        while I'm still strong.

Before long
        (why take it seriously)
the sun's gone down
as I was drowning in you
sorrows and all.

How deep does it have to go?
A lake just isn't enough
                for me
in this rough deep
            cold.

ILLUMINANT BEFORE DAWN

Close my eyes
Turn your head
The mother asks me to call you.
Returning kiss for kiss,
I lay in your arms at every turn.
My face regressed by the moon
knows no way out.

I'm married in your hair,
while night drags me the deceiver
out in the open.

The black and blue illuminant
just before dawn,
has broken and finds
birds in the near eastern sky
where a minute ago burned
the predestined stars.

There's no history
        and there is no death.

Only the information of having loved
that tears an arrow
through my wings in mid-flight.

LATE BIRDS

Who is out tonight?
Who is gone?
Man cripple walking slowly
who looks up,
stopping every minute
to twist his body.

Cars are out
driving back and forth
oblivious of gas, of ground,
just revolving on all four.

And the breeze is out
with shiny moons
and the mosquito
looking for blood from the heart
is all right too.

Now the kids are gone.
They were on that corner
a minute ago
like the flowing by of another light.

If I find that I have a heart
still left in me
I'll take it and hang it
on that street lamp
and put it up for sale
or trade it for the rudiments of passion.

SUMMER LIGHTNING

March 30th and the air
still has winter.

The first willows bud
along turbid rivers coming
        from the colder north

        O North America!

You're a little child.

        O cathedrals, destroyed,
tents and mounds and buffalo
across the horizon.

You gunfire on a summer night,
you campfire   and whispering voices
in the early night chill,
you woodland streams
carving Indian nations,
you tree house in lightning,
you delirious beach, you solemn
beach in weeping end of summer.

The sun disappears behind hills,
a white light still remains.
No pink or red or orange
with tight purple streaks,
through a white cloud.

I suddenly feel
we can never be destroyed,
but I know otherwise.
  It's only a daydream
  an overwhelming breeze
a constriction that I can't see
opening up in the heart
on a warm evening.

1

The universe is volatile.
Sober, useless, discarded like
fast particles.

People are delirious.
Love is like a galaxy
  on the retina after we've closed
    our eyes.
Such surfacing love
   is apparent
like submarines, like bridges
  without balance.

O glands! don't do me
  a favor. Pass me up!
In some hand my body may be
flavorful but
   it is nude and rough.
So pass me to those I love,
  in spirit, in form.

A wave strikes me like a meteor. Why do I talk about myself? Waves
strike me from every corner. The reality of suffering, pain, poverty,
disease, inhumanity, inequality, like a meteor strikes me. Everything
is nihil, everything is love, everything is mortal and flesh. Everything
is immortal, but above all transcendable by a spirit of life forceful
and mysterious, unexpected, youthful ageless, that the sky, its stars
and its galaxies of living matter, seem as insensitive as they really
are, as inhuman, and some of that is also me.

2

Like a pearl lying out in the mud,
this is a self, a me,
my changing change of mind,
a season in oblivion.

When a face between caresses
produces no difficulties
I'm so effaced and spotted
to tell my everyday god.
But nothing's out of desire.
This dream never falls asleep.
Like a bird of everywhere
it lands on my soul,
while one mad stupid desire
leaps the width of the chest.
I'm a human being, a man,
not a wingless bird,
or a dart on fire
shooting towards an innocent saint.

If I'm entangled in this thread,
let me wrap up myself completely
and shoot towards metamorphosis.

My mind is devoid of all thought. These words are only words.
The mystery of my awakened self is hidden behind all the earthly
passions. But I have no more hunger, no more thirst, no more desire:
for a moment. When that moment is gone, even a caterpillar can
make me weep. How can I talk about this? The real thing I want to
say is as another creature: a birth through metamorphosis.

3

O womb
that stops dilating,
running contained in us but
straying,
that stops dilating, but is contained in us.

O moving womb straying
in the town
like a cat calling,
wailing the city.

O hold us another day.
Do not strain yourself, drink
a little bit of coffee.
       We can now
   look into night's heavy screen
   like babies.

In a senseless wonder this is no poetics, but the rejoining of a lost world with a craving for secret knowledge longed for. So bombarded are we by the human strain and imagined patterns of evolution that to pick up lost thread, to find the end of the web, to continue it, would be no less than an immortal revelation. But how can we embrace nature within this invocation?

                    4
   The natives are spirits, my masters.
   They come back as death does
   and is given to you and disappears.
   In the stars
   your body stands.
   My frontal shoulders as big
   as arguments of parents.

   I need you
   like an alliance, life,
   when death is sacred
   and mellow. It writes its own
   "Book of the Dead"
   and the sea water: a tiger flashing his teeth
   while an ocean wave, like a saber-toothed,
   slashes my neck
   like words, words, words.

This is the wrong way. My mind passes all logic. Can I recover from the tremendous leap that only a man who knows unity could take, or a man who has finally seen? The more I try to reach that ledge the more I find myself seeking it, asking the rocks, plants, the insects, for the trail that sounds real but is lost.

I'm washed nice and warm
Twittering in the wind:
the tiny creator atom
halves in our big
heart. It is drafty.

What is the foamy modulation
that was put in us?
That makes us lighter than usual?

In the morning,
in the doped up branches
of the trees
I see a bird bouncing up and down.

The clouds begin to rise and drop, slash each other until a storm
moves in from the ocean. The body is drenched. Tears and the ocean
taste the same. The water has saved me. I'm drenched, but now as
strong as a prehistoric bird. This morning my eyes opened, and you
were like a large fir tree looming through the opening. I made my
way toward the distance where I thought I could embrace the whole
plane of existence and of vision.

6

But now I just have nothing.
The extant drums are cold.
Have no belly.
O great sea out there.
Looking for the trail in the sea.
Hair on her head.
Yes it is.

Like a brown bear
in the sea way out there I might
make her happy.
Natural as a bear, I feel guilt
in my lungs

like nothing else in the
white sea.
It's me.
I have to go to her.

Falling on the ground like snow, the system collapses like a deer shot near the heart. I feel sleepy lying here, hands on my genitals. It's morning, the mountains rise. Sleep brushes away and my eyes, still wide open, have the tightness in corners. Distant mountains rumble. I saw a woman's face. I took her from my mouth and I thought of suffering. But this refused to decay me. All human suffering came to me in a short time.

7

I set out from this moment.
The yellow blinking morning.
The rate of desire is picking up.
The car's surface is bilineal.
A boy is dribbling a basketball.
He throws it into the basket.
The weather is cool.
I think of her in bed.
My legs come together hard.

I was delirious with worry. The head on my shoulders was a machine. It was working on a set program that nearly destroyed me from wanting to tear it apart and away from my emotions. What human misery caused me, what, the world, or are they both one? All my human energy was used to set up an opposition to life, and the forces of life; mainly love. I am beyond exhaustion, a dead man, carried by a throbbing river outside of any known force in my own biology, in my own physique.

8

I'm not smoothed down as oceans
smooth down in the ice.
Lions and planets are fast in

the jungle of another search.
Harvest time, and Saturn is humming
in the screen of stars. Birds'
roomy throats are smooth as shells.
And I am going out,
away from this protective mass.

But when it's warm
I'll look for you and go away
with you. While winter's falling
on this burnt out heart.
I'll poke my head out of
the cave and the ice floes
will be big and go on and on.
Your kiss will be the only warm spot
        on the snow.

Every time I look fast behind me, there is only the shadow of
my own hair preceding me. Something has gone and disappeared
behind the fold. But never for a moment is there real fear. What has
whispered to these massive structures, given them an unexplained
life? Something has happened to the secular field, to the electron, to
other particles.

9
It's not a loss of power
that I've forgotten how much I've lost.
In love, yes, in my arms
in going away

in love waiting as the sun
and waves flame to the rocks.
        I'm sober
and lying around. A tremor revels

to take off all my clothes
and amuse myself, while surrounding life
levels all my feelings and thoughts.

Have I forgotten how much I've lost, how much I have avoided you out of fear I would never go that way, because youth is filled with familiar symbols more common to memories of an awakened life.

Everything dies and decays. Even the highland disappears and escapes to the beyond.

10

I am getting past it. I'm not lost yet.
But the violence and refuge cannot clean
the greediness of a face forlorn.
Behind you some kiss is still left.
O Give me beautiful things
  that I can carry back
  with me, back to where I play.

O Host! Hold me! O unseen power.

Immersed, still floating, carried by waves over stones, stones of memory locked away from a mortal life. What keeps knocking at these stones of my memory? At any second I'll see before me a form, real or apparition, who'll guide me through what appears to be the most dangerous, but also the most beautiful terrain I have ever imagined.

And here I am. . . . in the midst of the living.

1964 & 1972

What, no one here? No one
around here? No buffalo?
Like sleeping on the toilet bowl. . . .
Drifting toward love . . .

The dogs are out this morning
jumping on top of each other
Is there a real release with them?

But, no one here.
There's no buffalo, only dogs,
this morning, where dawn
and a wild wild bird fly away.

A RAILWAY STOP
(Orange, N.J.)

Two students kiss goodbye.
He boards the train laughing.
She disappears down the stairs,

disappears into the night.
It comes soon enough
against the spread-apart clouds,
or one penis smokestack
in this old industrial valley.
The hills are not high
but they surround the houses
that face the empty desolate industries.
    Morning mixes into night.
    The world of sorrows begins to part.

NIGHT BIRDS

While the animals rest
do we have the right to divine life?
Branch Brook pond is clear.
It is a clear impossible alone.
All inner feelings are grown up
and us, two people
approaching the clear pond
with fish we see, near the edge.
It's like a vision
of the pond
but there are two children
and a man.
Is it through the pond
or the flowers around
or our talking
or the whispering of late
erotic birds?
Yes, maybe they are far
    from their family.
Maybe that's why they're late
or are they just night birds
come here like they do
every night, like we do.

Millenium Dust

LONGER TRIP

"little man got big Idea"

—Jim

I found out
that the ducks on the ocean
are ospreys resting
on their longer trip.
To where? I don't know.

My son said
a kite can reach the full moon,
and a sea gull can,
and a bullet can,
but he wasn't kidding.

Full moon full sea,
moon on water
a lake on the ocean
from the hills
   while boats somewhere
      in the black and dark
have given up the trip.

As the fog comes in
and smokes the light,
respirations and dreams
rise out of my mouth:
past places, other stops
      of unfolded visions.

DAWN HUNT

The unsteady flow
            of this message
along the regions
            of my head
knocks as if I'm awake.

This creature looks
so mystical in the mirror of blood
in the burden
            of the hunt
laid bare at my feet.
   My arms know
   this kind of flesh
with the heat of an animal
into regions of symbolic quest.

So ranging is the night:
   I shiver in its beauty,
while Dawn
shoots from the volcano
a virginity in disguise,
a red that chokes all sensuality,
shimmering to the grey solution.

CARDINAL CONJUNCTION

It's windy. . . . . the rain is over.
An opening inside the trees,
shows the flood stage
of near destruction.

Is it the lost invaders
touching the shores
of my own guts?
Is it here,

or there, under or over,
(am I blind or am I deaf)
covering me with kisses?

The wild expanse of swamp
hides us in its giant grasses,
my knees, my waist.

A holocaust of Olmec temples
gives direction to the winds,
while a poor man in a new world
is all bitten and refused,
meandering and endless.

Is it the darkness
of the sunny cloud,
is it the crimson flash
of his wings,
that make us stay?

SACRED AND PROFANE

The city is up now
in the ultimate distance.
For some ocean beyond knowledge
my back has pains.

O Past, O Future
crashing together
O two equidistant stars
in the chance-ordained firmament.

IGNITION OF DAWN

Whatever sound it is
whatever way
the night's fallen and fallen
on the branches that remain.

To describe what's fallen
and out of the beach's mist
more fluid than waves
comes youth or breezes of it

in the more eternal
the dying salt or no death;
a mineral for a cell.

Something is passing the firmament.
The fallen branch of dark,

the night like a fallen branch
crashes my thoughts. I wake
and wake, and wake and. . . . .

the sky has floated
      in our midst.

BODY WEIGHT

  Feeding on solitude
my stomach is fucked up.
What right do I have
when the earth is short
of love, of food,
to feed myself like a pig?
Where did this guilt come from?
Don't mention nature, or the way
things look with the eyes:

with love you can die
without seeing a tree or
the sky or the oceans
or the smell of childhood.
The clouds stopping overhead
means there are no worlds,
nor is there sickly relativity to confuse
    an almost endless dream.

HYMN TO EARTH

The brook curves to the left
during the seeds of dreams.
Runs head on
with maiden of the rocks.

What ethnic dream
lies before me or under me?
The rock cooling off to oblivion.
My hands in this soil

forgetting the sorrow of the Holy Ghost
or the energy to live, or the calories
in transubstantiation.
The soul in union is it.

Who cares that matter
can be created or destroyed
or that matter transforms into energy
or that life is infinite or eternal in God!

One touch of darkness
sweeps me against the void
One breath of wine
chokes me with understanding

Out on the plains
the vibrations of the tribes running
on the woodland mounds,
the -EEEE- of songs pass
while the desert is filled
on my lips like a crust of bread.

My blood is encrusted on this dirt,
this pre-ordained, this pre-conceived vision:
Predestinated to travel, a crazy mystic,
far from every known path.

KYRIE ELEISON

I can't repeat OM, OM.
I can't repeat NAM-MI-OHO-RENGE-KYO
I can't repeat HARE KRISHNA, HARE KRISHNA
or chant these:
Chant means to sing.
To you o life songs burst
in the middle of
this dawn's inflammation.
The sky is infected
with a slap across
the holy face of dawn
which all science, all technology
cannot really wipe away.

I throw kisses to these changing
red buttocks of eternity
which no knowledge
nor tricks of knowledge
can erase or dissipate.

Have mercy on the light
and on the reflected blush
that passes on the face.
Have mercy on human forms
meaning with all that desire.

CAN'T SLEEP

I sit here, it is 4 AM.

Death sits on me
and overbounds my physicality.

It must be my underlying thought.
But now I know where it comes from.

I sit here, I lie here,
it is 4:15

out in the open,
under the stars,
let it rebound in my body,
my non-existing corpus,
into the snows of abstract flesh
that flood with light, my sorrow.

NEW REALISM

A coyote's song
wet with death
makes me live just to die
in this approaching light.

These rods of light
that are on everything.
These winds of light that stick to me.

A dream, a stab
of preservation. A mouth
between ourselves,
a preserver of heaven
between our legs.

Summer, summer,
a rumor greater than mud is out,
and it's seeding the whirlpool
of earth's magnified fall.

GOOD FRIDAY

Last night I went to a bar.
　　　There were a lot
　　　　　　of black people in there

They were all peaceful
　　　　　but tense,
　　even the few whites.

Once in a while
　　a wrong word
　　or something was misunderstood
and a flareup of voices.

I thought I would
　　　find you there
and I was right,
because I thought of you
　　all night

hanging on that cross

and myself having an ale
for this incredible thirst.

A go-go girl (what a strange word)
        a beautiful black
                Mary Magdalene
danced not too spiritedly.

Forgive me I thought,
because I don't know
        what I'm doing
and because the night is so hot
and because life is so short:
        I thought of you,
your weight pulling down.

Was it day or was it night?
Was it real or was it fake?

And I thought of you
as I pushed away
the heavy metal door
and walked into night
and I remembered
Bach's Saint Matthew Passion, the part
        where Peter wept bitterly
after he denied three times,
and the violin weeping more beautifully
than a desolate landscape

and walked into
        the ending night.

MOOD

Green is the night
green is the wood
green is the building
green is the food
Greener than grass is the night
greener than frogs are the trees
greener than leaves the swamp
greener than youth is my mood
green is the heavenly light

BIRTH IN THE DUNES

The shit of the dunes
fills my nostrils
as the ants speed through the debris.
What is the night made of?
and children playing
              in the sand.
The groins in the tide,
like a long spine revealed

beside the ocean rips,
while channels of love's
        maidens inside the invincible sea.

O the cries on the dunes.
I feel the breeze
like a mask on my face
deep in the woods
that aren't here.

Flies are eating
     every part of me,
with the ocean
     in retrogressive state,
at rest, but not defeated.
  The wind is free
       of absolute motion
like me the solitary mate.

  How magnificent the waves,
     the sun's invisibility.
  How wondrous is life:
     how sparse, how precarious,
       with no predictability.

FEVER

O wild navel
on what branch
do I hang onto,
do I hang my frame on,
heavy with sins of the woods,
that would not break?

Carry a little piece,
a little divinity in
3 dimensions of pain.

What wine, what drug, what fuck,
will lift me into
the non-dimensionality of salvation?

TENSIONS

The sand is washed from eroded rocks
The ocean with the sun shining off it
the colors of the god of the sea
and memory of a silver fish
in the dying sun.
And not to eliminate
the falseness of my life,
the son of the mankind
dispersed from that starry water.
If only the tensions of real poverty
could be dissolved
like the tensions of sin
in the baptism of the sea.

MEADOWLANDS

Only a few song birds are out
they sing. . . . . . the wind brushes the grasses.
The winds brush from a golden
to a shade of gold
over the enormous flooded.
Only the signal of a moth
only a few song birds

only the wind mixed with salt:
only the stars

GRAVITY AWAKENING

One lone sea gull
one lone surfer
flying, floating
on the plasmic waves.

More sea gulls begin to circle
out of everywhere.
More wind from the south.

Taboos rising from the earth.
The island of the Atlantic
searching for Atlantis,
the ruins of America
turned to sand.
I wake up in the night
full of the light
gathered from the rising moon,
and   recognize division
division inside my head
that ends and starts everything.

TO OPEN REGIONS

Sometimes
when I'm riding an elevator
                    down
I vibrate with a tremendous
sadness, a loneliness

of descension into
    the vibration of the heart

I fall back against the walls

and the journey increases,

carrying me past

Scylla and Charybdis

lowering me to raging
        dreams of youth

and the taste
      of that communion

REVERSALS

NOT KNOWING
FROM ONE DAY TO THE NEXT
  WHAT FORCES
      THERE ARE AFOOT

    THAT CLOSE YOUR EYES,

REVERSALS OF INTERNALS,
ARTERIES CROSSED IN THE MIDNIGHT AIR

MAGNIFICATIONS FALLING OUT
        OF CLOUDLESS DREAMS

UNEMPLOYMENT

On a line reading "Friday Reporters Only"
I wait with my broken hand
in my pocket.
Don't want them to see
my hand is broken:
nor that my heart is.

Like a soldier who has no where to go
on weekends, and wants to meet someone,
whoever is in sight.

O that goddess of youth———
———enfolds with her wings———
and carries you off
a million years.

FULL BLOOM

The notes that I hear
are like the dawn
with no intentions
on my life

Seedlings, droppings,
the ocean rides in with stars,
the full bloom
of dying in a strange land.

Then the return and how to return
to still have love
standing over you
in the mountains and sky.

Challenge me my sister!

How unwieldy, how unmanageable
the earth is
in all the splendors of catastrophe!

NOT REALLY PUNISHMENT

I don't feel it,
that kiss from the muse
that deadens me to this world
into the new land,
that stings me and paralyzes
even the world for me.
I don't feel it now.

NUDE MADNESS

Tie me down
  Tie me down
        Everyday work
      All the promises
    in clouds disappearing
Glue me to this earth!

         Nail me to this rock!
Would it hurt too much?
Would it be a cushion
      against reality
a self consciousness
of the human body
and human movement
a game of cheating sexuality?

It scares me more to think
  of the nucleus of an atom
than to imagine a revolution.

I fall down beside you,
  breathe heavily.
I feel heavy
The morning wind
     comes through the window,
     through my open side.

CRAZY DEATH

This morning I know there's a dawn
out there somewhere.
     Crazy death drives all the motors
  of the world. Radio defiance
flares up in the presence of
the holy vagabonds, and the essence

is erased from my spit.
   What number, what song
is lodged like a tic in my ear?
What fever of an unrecorded mist
has turned up inside?

PARK THOUGHTS

O clouds above these trees
   like trees detached from trunks

It hasn't rained
nor do the genitals reign
      as they used to.

O cloud trees
         over the trees of the west
      moved to the northern sky.

Sail with the south wind
         along the coast
      toward the grotto
of our secret.

O, what bullshit!
Ah, what solitude!

CONCEALED WOUND

Pain penetrates, it penetrates deeply
then springs out of this wound of
morning, Spring and Winter.
      I fall back until the flames fall
from loving are thrown out like garbage.
On this body we are struck by love

until we fall, until the flames fall
in Spring, Winter, in Autumn,
        out of this mind
with a divine drunkenness.

You. We follow
the visions   O   the embraces
to an illusion in the mind
where pain penetrates fast
        and happily

OCEAN BODY

The ocean like an open butterfly
is immobile but still pulsating a little.
The color of the sea
is like a blue butterfly
in the primordial future.
The swell of the body
is like a mammoth butterfly
about to take off from earth
and leave this desert of
a faraway planet

spread before us like a desolate tune.

GLASS AND STEEL STRUCTURES

The first snow
falls across the building
like peeling paint
scraped from the ceiling.
The silence outside
    bends around corners

A maximum thrust
makes the concrete, steel, and glass
seem so destructible, not
like the melted snowflake
that lasts until the roach.
I know those tricky insects
are hiding somewhere

But the strange rhythm
in me
    while in you also

is like stars I can't contemplate
like all the motion of words
when words have given up.

THE NEW WORLD
for Andrei Voznesensky

Who's there?
Nobody's here. Where are you?
Nobody's here. I wish I could
meet the Russian poet Andrei Voznesensky.
       This morning
    Siberia's in my knees.
    There's more than enough
of it in me.
Will she gentle be?
Andrei, Vladimir, are they?
I know how they are.
Everyone's the same
all over the world's dreams.

The forests are all green
and Russia in its loneliness
comes down to meet us

like a long lost mother
with shiny yellow hair.
But are they?

There are tiny flowers
in our forest Andrei:
pick one for Russia.

NO MORE PEOPLE

Earth is only scraping
among the unknown stars.

I sit here relaxed. I'm dizzy
without any direction.
My senses reel.

When I imagine
there are no more people
on the earth,
adrift I ride
into unequal rapids.
It's happening now
to the forces inside me.
I'm fixed in these emotions
moved in directions of energy
that leave me finally
totally alone, and away
from everything I love.

I wake up and I sleep.
Cut myself loose.
I lose myself,
I see and I do not see.

BROOK

In this cooling air,
       in summer ranging,
far going on shower's look:
       but blind, touch the hair.

O brook, what blooms
    are carried on holocaust,
       and wings?
     To mention you
     is useless,
     archaic, songs on songs.
But to eyes, and where love
       and sweat still odors
like a swamp across the woods. . . . .

       You flow away,
with all the doubts of the planet.
   And at night
   compared to the wind
   it cuts away   it cuts away
   to earth's atomic dream.

MILLENIUM DUST

The spread of suffering
rolls away like dusk into the moon.
Flesh of these arid bodies
and more than what man reduced them to.

O archeology, producing more
and more intensely
the feeling of being alone.
Abated, enchanted in a suffering
more magical than life

on these temple stones
that roll away enchantment
for a newer day.

MONTAUK

　　Where are you?
　　in these waves over waves,
　　　　　dunes over dunes.

　　The moon is like a bird
　　I saw today
　　a pure bird
　　in the white to blue sky

　　　Waves over waves

　　O wavey mindless
　　o pure bird
　　in the white to blue sky
　　covering the eternal sand
　　　　bending from one human
　　to another, while no one is awake
　　to this connecting warp
　　　in the. . . . . .

UNFINISHED SONNET

　　Sleep quietly under the snow.
　　The earth seems cold,
　　out of phase with Alpha Centauri.
　　The northwest wind blows.

In all this machinery,
in this icey glaze
a person goes to dream.
Under all these stars
are all these angels,
like the song of a dying wolf. . . .

DIRTY SNOW

O webs inside me,
like knots on my tongue!
Help me get rid of
what draws me away from you,
what clouds my eyes from inside.

All I hope to reach
all I hope to see
in ice, in snow, so that I
might be the one that cries
like the rust in a nail,
like a bike between speeding trucks,
like a home that never comes . . .
and when you wake up
you hear the rain
             you hear the rain.

TIDELANDS

So much bad luck,
so much disease.
But can you stop listening to people's misfortune,
near-deaths, medications, complaints?
Unknown beauties might
wait in the details of the soil.

O, take the sacred night
that burns in the stars.
Take the hungry daylight.
Take oceans and lakes, birds,
the earth itself,
           the moving coasts,
and the spirit that gives us life
           to fly away.

FINAL DIMENSIONS

I want to throw away
all this trouble
and live my life
on this molten earth
on some other plane
in some other dream
whether it's there
inside me, unconditionally
or whether I'm there:
but these sounds keep mixing
with the night.

My tears burn
my frozen hands
I glide toward the arc weld
more red than the cheeks of a child
more blue than the skies
of all the crucifixions and hangings.
The surface spreads before me
like the arctic melted and flat.
I rise up in my boat
mad and blinded
a single gliding bird
in the divine mystery of survival.

Nobody can get inside me
until the angels get there first.
A vision stands scratching his wing
on the other side.
Two angels fly among the trees.
O ocean that stops my blood
O sun! that dries it up
O clouds that carry it off
and the courage inside
our tough organisim
    that loses life so easily.

Think what you want
    about the uselessness
    of art for art's sake,

or science as a social metaphor.

Neither can change
    this world

or become a comrade to the enslaved
embittered masses
or a ruby in the elite crown
of the greedy few.

That's why nobody is allowed inside me
until the angels
bring their defiant message
to reconstruct the resumption
    of life everlasting
        of love, of hope.

MAD ANGELS
1976–1988

RAILWAY BOX (DEO TE SALVE)
May 6, 1976

From what lost age are you?
What leftover are you,
or extension into future?
We always travel to next stop. . . .
on our right the industrialization of America
on our left, the urban residential.
What villages of sorrow
do we suppress,
Elizabeth?   How beautiful your name,
it rings to me: Saint Elizabeth!
Sweaters, swimsuits
National State Bank.
It's not ironic. Maybe
you are beautiful inside.

Porches and little houses,
boxes from W.W.II.
Dreams of oil on our left,
smoking pipes in air
getting higher on methane,
ethel,   Elizabeth! Elizabeth!
What dreams the American spirit
had for you,
like dreams of boyhood
growing into manhood.
Next stop, Rahway,
Rahway with your prison observatory
looking at me
(but it's quiet in this town)
and sees me riding by,
no riots in my souls for you.
Hooded buildings to catch the light.
I'm not lamenting all this.

Next stop, Rahway, please watch
your step again.
Tops of trees, like the empty lots
and fields of Astoria in W.W.II
uniting me to you.

But what are looks
compared to the soul
of this land
to its people of paradise
of the sorrow in books,
of my sorrow,
from outside looking in
or inside reflecting out.
Outward, overturned, are all
the detached states
with which I've punched my heart
in more ways than one.

The silent birds through
the closed window
are calling to me
but I can't go,
you know that,
so compensate the stars
and the tears of the moon
like silver manifesting their way
into our hearts.
But to live on this earth
and not be able to love.
Look at the starving
hundreds of millions. . . . .
"by the year 2000 all. . . . .
Yes! what will it be like?
Not much different,
we hope and yet don't.

Deo te salve
God help us
have mercy on us
Control us   control us
we're flying without stars
and we're out of sins to commit.
Look at the starving of the earth
and you talk about love
more and more to desire,
to possess even love more and more
to transform the reflecting earth
when it's hard to change
even one living soul.

Already, next stop, Metro Park
a new platform, a new vision
a new futurist dream
of super pseudo architecture
to hide the fears
in the middle of nowhere
from nowhere to nowhere
But listen to us
Listen to this singing   Listen to the rails
Deo te salve   of songs

BODY JET
May 10, 1976

Weeping at the crude greatness
ready to take off
on the wetness all alone

I burn at the take off
  so invisible
a god, off the ground
into air I moan

It's the most
crude   thing of fears
I have ever seen in life
this emulation of strife
of a bird

Although it scares
the shit out of me
it is close to ecstasy

LOVE EYES
May 1976

I wish a spider
would drop the dawn,
as it comes just the same,
as hair grows on our bodies.
The black-legged god
    of the web is dancing
and transforms
the illusions of space,
showing up as color
in your eyes,
to make disappear the disillusion
in Hermes' message that
Aphrodite wants to take
all of love back
back from everywhere
to her own breast.

WHAT IT'S LIKE
January 4, 1977

I wake up, it's morning
the grass is still wet
the origins of poverty
are in my eyes, the sand
in my toes flushes my entrails
with acceptance and non-acceptance,
with my torso
like a lake of density.
But don't feel sorry for me
I'm a son returning
from the masses.
I'm heavy with kisses
in the squalling night,
in the overdrive of death.
What pastoral is left
in the trees,
what song is left
in the cold wind,
like rusty springs
in my nostrils?

The ecstasy of the shepherd
falls apart with the singer.
It is snowing
and the sheep dog's mouth
tastes of blood
Like my mouth
when I drink the dawn
and fly from you.

ESPACIO

February 1, 1977

In this space
I spend Time alone
nothing leaves me cold
but the north wind curves
around our door like a continental sweeping

Snow is in the night
night is in the snow

Disconnected on the ice
seven feet thick alone
in night's ice age of affection.

O space, o windy question
O sun, o sperm,

just a little flame
from the gods' mass reserves.

HAUNTING GHOSTS

February 22, 1977

The Formula is regained for the ghosts
ghosts feeding on the pain which is spiraling to infinity.
        Infinity is phased out.
        Muscles in our solar plexus
like a fiber of the organ
with which I'm pissing the night away
        into fiery dawn, into eerie joy
        into eerie rain
        of solar methane
        ghosts ghosts ghosts
riding shotgun through the heart

RTE 3 INTO N.Y.
March 3, 1977

    7:53, 36 degrees
    slight haze in north
    very white in the east
    yellow in the south
    blue in the west.
    Overhead, my mind hangs
    in the transparent sky.
    A bible freak next to me
       is reading, "will they
    ever find Noah's Ark?"
    Who cares
    whether they find it or not.
    Will I ever find a job?
    I really do feel
    like wandering off forever
    and stop looking for anything
                  while the wind
                  carries away the smoke
                  from Hoffman La Roche Pharmaceuticals

JUST AT THE BEGINNING OF SUMMER
June 20, 1977

    Morning shadows
    stretching like an animal
    just woken up

    Morning shadows stretching more
    than the bow of Diana

    Morning shade
      over ponds
    morning shadows
         over morning

covering murderers & workers
covering saints and saintly prostitutes
morning eyes
morning breast

Morning buildings of poverty,
shades of loneliness,
subways of ultimate destiny,

contrasts of poverty.

Morning songs from trees
       from windows and alleys
morning mountains
morning vows

SCOPE

December 1977

Vacant, annulled, disabled
I walk the streets
packed with the germs of a vista.
My head unto the window pounds
My meat pounds,
the holy hours are gone.
Nothing moves,
the total branch alights,
a night bird and your arms.
Predestined kiss all gone,
alone the night away
with dead predestination rains.
A mover, a city wave
headed for my veins.
This extreme unction
drifting on the winds.

WORDS FROM A YOUNG FATHER (LEAVING BODY)
January 24, 1978

My breath is gone
What angel carries it
away from the sand
       of this earth
where I am headed aimlessly
over the line
of savage melancholy.
  No one knew
   no one cared
what light my life had
  when I couldn't talk or cry.
My breath is gone
Dirt of my dirt is still under my nails
O my children
Spring has kicked my eyes
     O my children
what noise could I make
over the grinding
of all these infinite doubts
against the rustling
    of my soul?

REQUIEM
February 13, 1978

The river below has tiny whirlpools
around the bridge piers.
The pools are like birds
    diving for fish.

The seagulls gather   on the ice
of northern rivers gathered
near their mother, the bay.

Not turning to anybody
in this trip across glaciers

to embrace the melting tongue
    on the fire of the horizon.

The bird is blessed.
Ashes of the dead are blessed,
    in a promise of new life
in the seagulls gathered on the ice
at the opening of the bridge
of that eternal rest

Requiem requiem requiem

diving in the ice

APRIL ALREADY
April 5, 1978
to Ted Berrigan

April here already!
The maples are covered
        with red welts of buds,
        willows, webs of green.
Last night I read Ted Berrigan,
poet of the moment.
Now I pass
a dead cat on the sidewalk
after it's been demolished.
The sun is just above
the edge of a cloud
    For no reason at all
everything seems to mean,
or is it all because
there is no sense to this or that
like this Passaic River sparkling

not far from the house
of another great poet
where Ted and Ron and me
and Sandy and Rosemary and Pat
      and our little ones
drank of his ghost
while we talked to Flossie
            over a beer.
      The tunnel approaches.
I have to wipe off
this face of elation
the last refuge of wilderness passed,
this mustering of my life
O. . . . . for all the poets of the world.

ASSIMILATION (IN THE STREETS OF THIS CITY)
April 7, 1978

A man with bloody lips.
Who could sooner be
a man who works
his ass off in the building
A desperate man
of strange bedraggled honor
A despairing man
turning on himself, hurting himself
A desperate man
sending curses to
"the white devils"
he says he's better than.
A man at 8 o'clock
amid the smells of coffee
and beggars
"Help me I am blind"
and my step slows down
as I enter the building
my step slows more than backward.

As I throw my clothes off
an inborn horror carries me
into the nest
of this inner heart.

NIGHT RIDE
April 7, 1978

    Come on sit next to me
    the dream's not started.
    The smoke stacks
        have cages on the top
        to stop birds, the city
        like a million bugs
        with shiny backs all crushed.

    My god, I'm really racked up
    the dream's not parted,
    a tree's already fallen on my legs
    and the sky like a field of rye
    falls out beyond the edge.
    Come sit next to me
    the dreams not started

April 26, 1978

    In one day everything's green
    The tulip tree's afire
    Someone's started a garden
    Nitrogen busts up my brain
    O the hair of the little one
    carrying Spring in his hair

    I'll faint this year
    much like all the others.
    Run! melancholy words,

drive toward the opening,
while Orpheus in the green
mountainous garden of the tides
licks his rough tongue against the night.

HOLY

May 3, 1978

O if only I could
straighten out the nail

The sun shines between buildings
on the sidewalk, on people, burning faces
with holy needles that the universe
could have easily dissolved.

Where is the smell of dirt?
O lashes of the night

someday it will be alright.

TONGUES

May 22, 1978

Bird on the chimney
your frantic song
reminds me of a knife.
Bird who has cut into my tongue,
who has overtaken the sky
and the May breeze
opening up my face.
You, revealing the struggle
of singing to the intransigence of youth.

With all this suffering
in the world
and I notice *you*
bird on the chimney
and hurt my tongue
answering your crazy song.

May 25, 1978

The night gets lonely
and the murmur
of the insects
turns to light

In the morning
when I wake up
my arms loose
around you and the breath. . . .

Like the wind
my heart is left.
What I thought was dead
is like new leaves:
in that worlds of suffering
are very deep.

CRAZY IN THE NIGHT

May 25, 1978

The sun is shining
against the city
against alleys of sacrosanct
whining against the bay.
Bridges roped across music
and commerce selling life & death,
like dogs of television,
radio dreams of transporting seeds,
south seas of sacrifice
in volcanic fuel.
Bread's giant squid
of world poverty.
Aurora Borealis of hopes,
manic waves of sex
Excitement against the moon
floating up from the dark fish.
Brevity, churches, temples,
thirteen dollars for everything
O windows!
Windows to our hearts
Angels of mercy!
Drug of exhalation!

MAYHEM

May 26, 1978

My head is swollen
in a drowsiness
as if riding elevators
to a mine shaft and back all day.
It's nerves, they say,
the backward tension
        of this crucial life.
But today I saw a man

killed by the police
after he had gone berserk
grabbed a cop's gun
and murdered several people.
He was lying there on the floor
with his hands cuffed
     behind his back
lying on one side of his face
the bloody side,
his eyes closed forever.
But I feel no sorrow for him
The tension
is the bones of empathy
scattered in my being.
My head is swollen
His gun lay beside him,
a beautiful 38 caliber
His clothes were almost rags
I don't feel he didn't
deserve to die
Look at the poor bastards just walking
who he shot lying in the hospital dying
in a drowsiness.
The gun was perfect
and he in such rotten condition
half crazed in rags
and now dead.
Justice triumphs, I guess,
but the gods forget
we're only human.

A great peace finally
descends on me
as if a constipation were ended
as if tears flow
from my feet to my eyes
as if I finally
    understand you
creator, destroyer, preserver.

June 1, 1978

Taking me away. . . .
Do you see my eyes?
Only from the heart
   could that cry come
Taking me away,
only the answers
are not going anywhere
only from the inside
    could I sing.
Underneath it all
in the warm rain
My soul is a desert
drifting toward the ocean
I am like dry dirt
inside, touched by talons
What difference does it make
where I am
Taking me away

SUB-SCAPE
June 1, 1978

Stop Going!
The wheels race.
Gateway to wonders
The clouds hurry
across the wet earth
Gateway to sorrow
Mind's formula destroyed
We're better off
Stop going!
the heart races
blindly sacred
The slopes of trees

O painful
promontory
O wind.

SIGNALS
July 6, 1978

Fireworks dot the sky
I remember meeting you here
with the crowds & the kids.
The ships down at Sea-Land
were full today, full of tremendous boxes
ready to leave for some other land,
maybe Australia
where you last wanted to go.

The starbursts light the sky
with so many
fires in the night, below the jets
from the airports.
Tonight I can't get you
out of my mind
you seem more real
than the string band playing
in the dark

A snow of unreality falls on me
The summer breeze wafts
off the smoke-bursts like clouds
beneath the jets,
the spaceless sky
where words leap into
the few sounds they need
to call where no answer calls back
in the thunder and lightning
of mortal celebration

APOLOGY

February 7, 1979

Everything is out of me,
a sonnet, a ballad
like a silent plow
on a destroyed farm,
while poets sing dooms of element bombs
and man's slow destruction of fluid earth.
I can only focus on an ant, a bud
a look in someone's eye
while the external order of things
declines. . . . The snows fall
by some instantaneous structure,
but God, where is your blood
so that centuries from now
our lips, our tongues might still
sing the flames of the past
and among metals
and electronics dissolving in water,
we might still be stubborn enough,
fuse with the flesh, burn with the soul
and rise in a vaporous light.

February 8, 1979

Tie one on,   tie it on
          tie me on

to the four prison corners
of sex and madness
in the self conscious headaches
of everyday life.

"My head aches
and a drowsy numbness"
holds on. . . . . . . hold on
before it disappears

and I become so senseless

that my body shakes
as if an earthquake's
open fault drained blood from it
and closed again,
and rain fell like mercy
directly on puberty's hard-on
and drained the cold from it
and eyes that see nothing
but a web of unrequited mist!

The heart's gone off beat
and distortions of
the sad metaphor
of Spring's first scent

sends *me*
so my head
drops off from my body

and I find it in the grasses
next to the swamp
only to tie it back on
and find my way back

SUPPLICATION
March 1980

My eyes hurt
The twins are in the sky
It's a beautiful day

Words are in seclusion
Squirrels climbing the wires
The world is in hunger
Brazilians are dying
Malnutrition phlegms
the throat of earth

In infinite mercy
        protect us
In finite kindness
        give us breath
and food and pleasure
        and will

The poor are getting poorer.
Governments conquer their people
The new war is regenerated

To be born is to be
    borne by sunsets
by oceans and
      ruptured earthly paradise

My eyes hurt
the poor are getting poorer
inequity is standing
on the shoulders of pure profit

All the earth is still
Protect us and give us will,
and some quiet dreams
out of the ecstasy of
           the ruins
out of the radiation
of chemicals and drugs
out of the smoke of
unconscious power
out of the individual's singular purpose

Turn fear into ashes
turn ashes into bodies
turn air into blood
and through the incarnation
    of my earthly soul

give me a sliver
        of the spear of love
to magnify tears of courage.

POSITIVE DISINTEGRATION
December 17, 1980

Who put me together
What put me whole
Like the rocks
like the rain
What put thinking
Who put tears
        alone in wind
in city and building
with only you
who put me together
now takes me apart

AURORA
No date

O anaerobic delights
against skies and city nights
where sighs, chemicals, and salt
pervade ingested air
and the graph of poverty rises up
into the smoke of ideals.
And I lay here
in a sea of dreams

A layer of insanity
curls up on me
I lie here
in a sea, my dreams unprotected
and stirred up like dredgings
from the angel of a kiss

whose only escape
is the rising alba
over the mountainous rocks,
of some inner mountain

LAMENT #1 FOR POLAND

December 24, 1981

Chained to this gang he looks around
The stars leak through the pine trees.
A metamorphic outcrop with green lichen
stirs his intestines.

O summer solstice, summer solstice
The heart beats radiantly, angels fly
in this snow   radiant snow radiant snow.
The era of the dead is on us.
Solidarity flies the coop.

O slaves, salvation is far away

O mother, mother
bleeding from your side!
Will the hour of love dry tears?
Will a house of love hide fears?
Is the muslim shawl
hanging on your cold shoulders
keeping you warm?

Maybe we never know that eternal spirit,
as sweet messengers
from the forests of disease,
messengers from the night,
messengers filled with phosphorus and light
and coal dust,
lie crumpled in dead newspaper's soldiers
listing the destruction cycle of earth.
Messengers speaking silently
to the hopeless, innocent and dying
messengers from my body to yours
from my neurosis, memories, to your soul,
messengers brushing wings
kissing the neck of evil
messengers squeezing
our cold hands.

The first spring rain is over
the mud dries
Opens up our swollen eyes
O the cuts the bruises
      and the welts of the storm

O temple that lives in no government
O temple that lives in no church
temple that lives in no temple
temple that lives for the search,
temple that has no building
temple that has no sword
O temple that has no revolution
temple that has no false prophets
Why leave us in desolation?
Why is everything a holy fire?

Should we erase historical christendom,
misleading god of our mind
for just a sliver of eternal truth
an outgrowth of false religion and despair

Wait! There's no kingdom of Love, of God,
not in us.
Only God in and out of us,
the void of eternal truth
showers our animal eyes
the miracle without vestments,
without marks, without democracy
without money

The Pagan is real to the Christian
Babylonia real to Jew
Ikhnaton real to Mohammed

Does Mazda shed eternal light
or Buddha light the eternal way?

A vestal virgin melts the sword of communism,
a large spider
dissolves the temptation of capitalism,
both drowned by a sunbeam

O song of the Hototogisu,
O song of the nightingale,
O cry of the crow,
over the desolate
fusion of the winds _ _ _ _

While coming down
from the mountain, a beggar
with no shoes on
singing a sinuous melody
contained between voids, between words, between worlds.

DIRT

July 1982

Dirt on shoes
The simple life
When fears come
   like a trembling
of rocks
  the earthquake
  is my bride

LAMENT #2 FOR LEBANON

August 1982

Tomorrow night before the winds blow down
the hungry trees: they're swaying in the mist,
I want to stop this grove from filling.
Stars in our sleep ride the massacre
in corners of destruction's nest.
Suns of chords unknown
like dialysis or death.

Oh Lebanon
land of wood, land of wood
defoliated dreams, decapitated screams.

Like a pawn you lie
in the middle of the beast,
in the midst of an
old land of sorrows,
of controversy crossing the soul.
A dark walk in the desert!
A scorched memory's toll!

All the fake gods
have gathered in the night
and battle in the blood dawn.

ASIA

August 1982

Foliage on the snow
Mystery on the rice
Blossoms and oppression
    holding scented hands
Holding back tears
in the slow moonlight.
Oppression, control, contrasts of love
        and lonely fears.
The water light on the mist of hunger
Where do the waters flow?
The night walks through the heart
like a spider on the hand, like
a splinter in the breath
while the hermit
lies dying on the mountain
      lost in a dream of cold sorrow
with breathless sex
still panting in the night.

SUNSET

September 22, 1982

Why do I follow you

through these woods

Now I've found

that grey and yellow bird

dying in my hand
What do I do with it?
A song of the night

wakes me

and in my hand lies you

in the matter of all fear

A song of the people,
of forbidden lies,
of surrounding night and legs
and emptiness
A call in the night!
O beggars, O masters
why leave?   we are only beggars
as we pull ourselves up
in the erotic stratifications
before the sunset of your blush.

MIDDLE OF WINTER (OFF THE HUDSON)
November 29, 1982

Rising from the river, a mist
Rising from the mist, a cliff of basalt
Looking into the mist
houses across the sublime shimmer.
A boat he cannot see
A rope he feels in his hands

Listening to the game yard of the city
rolling through a slime

getting dimmer and dimmer

Arise! He tells himself
in the radical shade

Get up! rise up!

because birds whisper nearby
because drizzle coats their eyes

because tree rubs his hairs
and buds welded to branches
melt open like puberty's sweet speedy kiss.

    Rise up!
a spirit as well as temporal shadow
is prepared for us on this earth

rise up like some agile god rising
from the touch of his mother.

November 1982

It only takes a machine
to set me going,
a machine of the heart
that really doesn't exist.
All the bars are open.
The smell of beer
washes off my feet
but I cannot drink

Houses are open for ten or twenty bucks
The hunting season is open
while barrels of wine flow
through the meadows
through maples and birch
The smell of cedars along the swamp
My lungs on fire
but I cannot drink

So tell me
while I am not blind
how the infinite wind
reaches through you to me
why a sudden darkness
comes over my hands touching
into the reckless stream
why I still cannot drink?

A message is scratched
in my head
while black and white dust settles
on the secret lungs of the spirit
Dreams ejaculate in the heart
and leave me feverish
in the midnight bliss
waiting and waiting to drink

VERSES OF THE SOUL SUFFERING TO SEE GOD
translated from San Juan de la Cruz
1982

I live, but not inside myself,
with only the hope
to die, because I die not.

I live without being in me
and this is how I wait,
dying because I die not

No, inside I do not live yet
and without God I cannot live
But without him and without me,
this life, what will it be?

A thousand deaths I'll feel
while I wait for my life,
dying because I do not die

Whatever life I live
is imaginary living,
so I continue dying like this
until I meld in You, my life.
Listen to me God, hear,
I don't want this life;
always dying   because I cannot die

Since you won't come to me,
what life can I adhere to,
instead suffer a death
most mortals never know.
Pity, pity myself
because I'm struck with this fate
of dying because I can't die.

Even a fish out of water
is more at peace
that in the death he suffers
he finally pays death off.
But what kind of death compares
to my living lamentation
where the more I live the more I die

When I think of unburdening,
seeing you in that sacrament
makes me feel more pain
that I cannot rejoice in you;
all this adds sorrow to sorrow,
I can't see you as I want to
and I die because I die not

And if joy, O Lord, overwhelms
with the hope of seeing you,
    that I might lose sight of you
doubles this pain of sorrows:
Living with such tremorous fear,
and yearning the way I yearn
I die more   because I do not die.

O stop me from such a death,
My God, and grant me life;
don't keep me so entangled
as if by a lasso bound.
Look, how I long to see you,
this aching is so complete
that I die because I do not die.

In time I'll weep at my death,
and lament this life
that has to be so imprisoned
by sins, my sins
O   my God   O   When, when?
When I tell you from truth enlightened,
"Live I," because I do not die.

1983

RAIN FOREST ODE
February 1983

For want of words
the awesome clouds appear.
The mountains are covered
by life and
blood of trees
and hair of leaves.

Drops fall to the
endless ravine
and we push against the trees.

O giant leaves   O human leaves
more green, more green, more green
for want of words

The drops slide to
the forest brush
under feet under feet,
gentle floor against the ankles
wet brush, cool leaves
for want of civilization,
wild birds among the top
colored birds extinct,
damp womb of a mother's kiss
shelters from this heat.

Why leave, why leave?
No want of word,
no want of hurt,
why leave among the trees

why leave
      from 'mong the trees

EARTH SO BEAUTIFUL
February 1983

Clouds below like spit
over the waters.
I know I should be somewhere
Cabin presses against me in series

Long rolling waves
through ears to eyes
I know I should be somewhere.
Sleep love!
divided into the sea,
rest all wonderment
into the sea forever.
The "broken arm of the sea"
reaches out and mounds
appear in the neck
of the island
tortured from the thrust
of the plates
and from the void's
weird imagination.

DOMINICA
February 1983

Bodies bathing in the river,
unaware but aware.
Rocks on the center island.
Feet walking over.boulders
small to large.
The soul is bathing
in languid movement
with you, o universe

far from the states of everyday
far from the lands of evil
far from the banks of money
and revolutions and inequity
of our breathing life.
The body standing
        on the rocks
        in the river
        full standing

like a bird transformed
to man
like a man transfigured
    to serpent
like the hungry movement
between death and life
like the ascension
from the underworlds

FOREST DREAMS
February 1983

    Thunder on the shore
    Voices nearby against
    the crashing of storm waves
    against the silence.
    But like them
    never stops long enough,
        this pain.

    Sleep, sleep, the boat rocks nearby
    like a song of giant
    waves against the island
    rocking the sleeping
    volcanic bowels of Spring.

    Rocking like the beyond
    where no one comes
    in the thunder of nighttime

    So we could see in the lightning
    and breathe and live
    among the forests
    all the time
    and waken
        from the dream.

OVER MUSIC
June 30, 1983

Storm over the land is over
Storm over the heart is not
Cars pass
Wheels move
blending with the night wind
arising from mountains
long gone
in an arsenal
of forgiveness from earth

Why have you faked
          so much?
Why are you no you
or it of them or her of him?

The night is filled with songs
that Apollo's son Orpheus
could only have sung

Yet we know
that every leaf
every migratory bird
singing in the dusk

cannot all be seen
and every night
I feel away this devastation
closer to happiness
closer to unrest
like music's unrest.

Hold me light, hold me tight,
winter will come in the night.
Dark and dreaming
hold me tight
break the storm watch!
Delight, O delight
that old breaking word
like the sea behind a dam
pushing against my eyes.

Hold me right, dark dreaming
in the night
stark angel of our streets
in the temple of the heat.

TO THE DEATH OF A POET
July 25, 1983
in memory of Ted Berrigan

Big man is no more here
smokin' and fightin'
the literary world
Into his own cosmos
where we will all go.

The big man is no more
he's gone to unknown land.
Back to an island of the valleys
back to the reverse of the sun
on a long eternal journey,
passing all, passing all.

I see the infinite stars
which also have an end
Look at universal dust

which we breathe even now
and there are no special worlds
for a poet when
he dies or when you die
he goes where you go.

Meanwhile, weep for big man poet
weep awhile and when your
age is all dried up
remove a sliver of his music
from your heart
from inside you
and pass it to the muse
so that some other poor
and common man
could sear the nightingale's wings
with songs unheard.

LONG SONNET

July 27, 1983

So many leaves on trees
my love, like the bees
making their nest in Catskills
or walking in grassy plains
   of Kalahari baked mud
when you're not here
and like the cell that kills
and like the call that deepens
also that solitude
from an unknown bird
when no one's here

so many trees
fall inside me, fall outside
like the oppression of the people
like the remission of the seas.

Where have I got time
    for you, O . . . . . .

Where in deepened corners
of miscellaneous gasoline
and ether and alcohol
filling the fumes
    of night's air,
have I got place for you?

And, when the beach lightens
to melancholy states
and signs of first
egrets on the sand
and pain and regrets
open vistas on despair,

the traffic of feet
in some distant land
dances to the tune's great Spring

Summer stays virgin
on the lost island
A number disappears
on the knife of eternity.
So where have I got
time for you
breathing the plankton of space.

. . . . . . or are you all of the above?

CITY SCAPE

July 27, 1983

Grace and lust, lust and grace
grace the organs of the city
and lusts on the body of languor
in a painful route
I take through pity and scent.

Through city and heat
where dungeons
fill a network upon the skin
and in the heart it's even deeper
The air is full of grace
The city is filled with lust
The shadows upon my face,
a prisoner's last chance,
a crusader in the dust.

DOUBLE BLIND CONCERTO (FOR EPICTETUS)

July 29, 1983

Houses, garages, dogs, people,
blind man talking
a triumph of freedom,
black girl walking
entropy of sight, sound, touch,
the ancient Greeks, Romans, Egyptian serfdom
slaves especially understood much
in the balmy evening
in the volcanic noon
as they envision the adventures
of the encompassing night
or universe of the moon.

A black-beaked and wing-tip lark
flies in the evening as dark
descends or ascends to seeds
unknown to sightless wonder
which leaves us all agape
in the long reeds, a breeze
wipes our face in the thunder
of the sensual world

GUITAR ODE

August 1, 1983
For Paul

A guitar plays the light of afternoon
A guitar stabs the afternoon air
The song winding up,
now winding down
a cry
        to the stars
truly hears, the plaintive wind
        of the guitar
in the ripe afternoon.

The country road,
the dirt and gravel dusty
repeating a refrain a refrain
to the wind,
and the guitar
in the cloudy afternoon,
and the guitar brang-brung
over the voices
in lyrical relaxations
        revolutions

like a lyre in the garden
where Orpheus still plays,
his voice
secretly and tenderly vibrating
for the next brave generation.

A guitar plays
the light of afternoon,
a guitar wildly gains
the height of bird's
short songs.
A guitar of noon, a guitar
of lightning,
a guitar, aloft!

August 1, 1983

The first August day is over
The hurricane
starting above the leeward isles

The crystal of the sun
the bright light across the sky

Try to sleep while an insect
rears its head   looks around

Neighbors in some distant grove
sing out with laughs.

The knife of voices
is mixed with morning.
Honesty and poverty killing
the lie in the heart,

while all is in the ocean
all is in the sky
all is in the universe without lie.

SUNBURN
August 2, 1983

Moons of the wind
that rises in heat,
beer drinks on the boat
that carry it out,
spray lost in the fog

where restless and enraptured
you lie on the beach

Wounds of the mind
that penetrate and bleed

O cyclic rapture
wounded in the night.
Visions that we are slain
by Gods and nature

while restless, enraptured
you lie on the beach.

LINEAR BALLAD
August 3, 1983

News continues
full scope of all
that fills the coffers
of data
constantly where
economics, politico-dreams,
material cravings
and elegant news
of aircrafts, war, sales
of products, promises
promises, prices,

prices, computers
telephones, cures of all
diseases and injuries

everything is coming

O progressions

Tour of the world
and not one lie told
as the mind absorbs
or excretes the momentum
of sins at night
at day with guns
Special features,
all that is worthwhile
in city, outside, in world
outside, wherever signals
bind us to the
conquering of other planets.

Who will get there?
who will be the new
new world explorer?
who will seek the gold
and find no flesh?
who will press artificial intelligence
like erogenous organs
in a crippled world.

Can any predict the space man
activated by human brain
or chimpanzee brain
or any brain
to fool the masses
in the marriage of
    sweet dreams
to innocuous whims.

Send robots
and robot souls
combine a machine
into one omniscient whole

NO! There aren't many days left
in secret longing,

or will the senses
of the flesh rejoice
like days of youth

rejoice desire and rapture
rejoice ecstasy and peace

and from the tremors of the soul
survive to spirit
that can never be detected.

THE AMPHIBIAN

August 8, 1983

Surrounded, I feel the clouds
like algae
            in this lake
encompassing my breath
and I'm alive

Have I come to a break
in the formation where I thrive?
Altogether there are no
units of me left.
I've disappeared into
the algae of the light
into the clouds of the smokey lake

I've been born a human,
and the harmony is the same

August 12, 1983

Rain cycle, hold my brains

close to you
amid the trees
to feel a stone

like one against the root
within my head

August 12, 1983

I hear the music from below
raising up to me like a butterfly in the trees.
A raspy sad voice, low again singing
the strains of love the loved and the lover
    It opens like a sacred tune,

touches . . . Sings like a torn bullet

through the veins, rips through
our mental and physical pain . . . . ecstasy . . . .
            . . . . Common ecstasy . . . .

IT'S ONLY GLUE
September 19, 1983

A man off a subway
        off a train
on a bench
    sitting, gone-eyed
a young man
in his thirties
I thought a derelict, shouted

out some warning
    as I sat
        next, near him
    just shouted once

The thin emaciated
far-eyed
    emaciated eyes
        looked out
his fingers sticky
with some substance
I thought
    was part of
        his flesh, sticky
    until I
        recognizcd it
    as he cupped
    a hand over the stickiness
and brought it to
        the face
of this his face
that once
    a child's,
and as eyes closed
breathed in.
I felt the
    aromatics and my heart
raced to my stomach
infused like a rainy garden
a nausea twinge
as I extrapolated
the fear.
The body all gone
    the brain
aloft in death
on a subway stop
on a journey
    to oblivion

with no dogs
to tear apart the organs
at the entrance
but a sticky substance
    like flesh
having a
formula of hydrocarbons
and tears.

BUILDERS (LARGE MOON RISE)
September 19, 1983

I salute you,
majestic sweat
beneath the moon
Crystalline shimmer
spread forth
along the isle,
giants of structurality
opposed to a pale
jaundice lunar
unrounded orb

I drink to you river
moving ebb
into the lake
of the universe

I follow you orbits
of hard life
beneath which feeling
shatters you
        gracefully
        into sleep

I unhinge you
arc-lights
of this mortal century

I exalt you
bits of love
conjured up
in the electric night
for the renunciation
of solid death
    for sale

I salute you
    humble sweat

December 1983

Here's a traveler in the womb
about to drift away

O mother universe
in your heartless virus lips
extending over me complete

in whose mind I've changed.
Deliver me in the pure waters
    of sudden joy
when for no reason
it be O K to die
and never return

To hold your face inside me
feel your all beside
This morning float into you
a little traveler in search
of the spirit
        that sent forth me
with all others

SPIRIT MATTER

December 7, 1983

Man is blood
woman is blood
    and water and chemicals
that note the heart beat
of the secret body.

Every drop is of water
    and chemicals too,
that beat the heart
when love comes closer

Dawn comes
Dawn disappears
down the valley of light
because the spirit
    is made of light
the spirit is made of dark
Every woman is blood

Every star is filled with chains
every body filled with blood

All the animals are life
all the insects of chemicals
and the unseen mites and creatures
of microscopic force.
All the creatures
    have their blood

All the living has an end
all the dead has a start
all the universes
    have an end
all the universes
    have a beginning

All the body has an ocean
and the flesh
    that's warm and sweet
in that sacred emotion.

The body melts in fire bombs,
in cyclotrons
in the sweet scent of flowers
in the slant of human sex
in the gods striking
through every age
in the desert blood of Indian Nations.
Every creature needs its food
Every body is blood.

TONES
December 15, 1983

    Swallow me in all particles
    Chew me like bread
    Burn me in the
        winter wind
    digest me in the heart beat

    And when I wake up
    in wild abandon
    grind me in the lashes
    of your eyes

December 23, 1983

    All winter the
        leaves
    stay on this ground

    the sun

The rake, the hoe
   the furrows

the moon

All winter
embodies

The ashes

Working insects beneath

NIGHT FLASH
December 28, 1983

   Mothers and fathers
   sons and daughter
   are sacred drops

   An abandoned auto
   glints in the light.
   The path is abrupt.
   The path is alright.

December 29, 1983

   Do a little job
   Everyday work breathes on
   Swim a little river
   Play as child plays
   backyard dreams
   Do a little job
   in immense sea

1984

The squirrel leaping frightens
the pigeon walking over you

In this return of winter,
snow on branches,
in this ravine of sorrow.

A bird's wings like
a heart beats
over adrenaline snow,
yet I know you're not here.

There's no sound
not even of the silence
broken by a gun,

not even of the thunder
of drugged eyes,

not even of ecstasy
half asleep in the breast.

Yet I know the bare feet
of narrow salvation

in the dirt and dust around us
follows all day.

In the same way a light breaks
into a coal mine

do I explode all the fantasy
of description and metaphor

and leave with a blush, in snow.

Sunny day with ice
turning warm before death

Buildings bloody, while rain
warms the snow

Solemn snow, broken chemicals,
mean dreams,
god's help in front of life,
the warmth thickens with steam

Sunny day with ice
  spring of holy rites

gushing through this flesh
    of earth

sustaining, retaining
  awesome life, eternal drift.

FAULT (PENANCE)
February 8, 1984

Inspired to conquer,
rated to transpire,
only stranded on the river
of loyal missions
        in the dust

Bathed in transgressions
rooted in confessions
holy lightning in the forest
mea culpa on the chest.

PLANET SONNET
February 1, 1984

O waters of April and Winter
coinciding with deep blasts
of March like timbers splintering
from some volcanic thrust
of magma, lava, ash,
O, calm down the fires in the chest.

Like the sun, brother of sight
in explosions, calms the oceans,
like the comet, wandering sister
walking the street of a city,
alone bolstering the night emotion.
O, call the angels to the nest.

Revive the rain in these stars
with the pain of new devotion.

LAMENT #3 FOR BAYREUTH
February 13, 1984

Open body singing in the trees
through the swamplands
through the bogs with
the city out a ways.

City corners are full
in the streets
singing through crowds.
Ancient roaming
of lost bodies

over bridges of the night.

My body is in
the broken beams
   of the buildings
fallen on living bodies
for the lies of rehabilitation
in the sun.
My body is in the rubble
full of living bodies

the living holy eucharist
of destruction and resurrection,
the body, the blood.

Open songs in the trees
humming of holy bees,
and stillness of the land.

FORGIVE
February 22, 1984

Forgive me
for my impatience,
forgive me for stupidity
forgive for not showing love,
forgive for rigidity of the mind

and perdition of the soul.

Forgive me for tricks of the trade
and life's blind hawk
      of the spirit

forgive me for forgetting
   how to forgive

   and how to forget.

CITY

March 14, 1984

Solid States abound in us
even in the surrounding
weakness of a city

or the strength of its destruction.
Solid walls collapse
through the night.
Truth abounds in the
water and dust
spraying fires hotter than lava,
saltier than murder
in the old city streets,
rising concrete, marble and glass,

in the lairs of corners
alleys, basements

with lonely troubadours chanting to the sun
rising in rubble, fire and water.

O City of Orphans
City of all brothers
befriending crime
in the African Velt
of the spirit

City of Caucasian dangers
in the substance of
dead isotopes of the heart

City where the innocent
still live, tied to
brotherhood, family, intellect, work,
city where the forest
once lived, burned,
where the immigrant stops by
to bathe in strife

O subterranean vessel,
subatomic thrill,
City of the will
and testament of night

Solid light abounds
and we chant
in the chorus that heals
all pain, in the light
that drips new day

onto pavements of the sick
of lost, and lonely
and you, and me

SPRING RISE
March 21, 1984

Inside the cold rain
I sit with Spring.
The tree is loaded
with only tiny
wine-like purple beads.
It's cool
and the odor of ice
is fading with the blending
of breezes on the journey
from a cave.

The buildings cannot change
the breath's deep forest,
and the mist returning,
with the cool rain
on a warm . . .

GRAND JURY
April 2, 1984

He was walking down a street
him and friend
Some hood on stoop
came down as he's passing

"You stepped on my foot,"
  bad black man said,
  while good black man apologized,
"I don't think I
    stepped on foot but
    I'm sorry if I did"

While friend was stabbed
through in back & front,
a piece of lung,
liver cut in two.

Hospital. . . . . a slowed down body, ...
  sad lamentation. . . . .
                quiet.
From deep south farmland
to flashing knife
                unseen
                unfound
unbounding passion
of confusion

bewilderment at gift of life
with no revenge
not even a punch in the face
or the fingers
on a jugular vein
to ease the satellite of sorrow
following all his days

INDIAN SONG
No date

The stone is hard
The stamen & pistil of this flower
yet wild yet near

The city street is dark

This hand, these lips
The stone is hard
the city street dark

The wild woodlands break out
open upon the subterranean plains
yet wild yet near
The city is dark

RELEASE
April 8, 1984

I know the tops of these trees
do not care
for clouds floating
or for me noting
that they exist at all.

Or for crows looking round
from branches' top
at the enemy
in the formic acid of the dirt.

Nor for the roots
in the havoc of light
right now in corners
of earth or mind beat up.
Nor for the beating down on

the poor and desolate
inviolate angels of this dust
in everyday suffering
in everyday redemption

Nor do they care for music
as we hear that ecstasy
nor stranded creatures
in the fires and floods
of the planet,
nor for the guns of Jerusalem
or Afghanistan

nor for the common suffering
       of man
and redemption.

JET RESURRECTION
April 16, 1984

The stars fall the same
I am alone
in the terminal, as a woman
watches me, cigarette in hand,
eyes aslant.
The new world
has closed me in.
The air pushes through,
enclosed, shut out.
She puffs through her lungs
the cigarette held up,
the pain over my eyes,
shut in, never to escape,
at least not until
the mountains rise and rise
forever with air
rising to the southern cross.

The terminal is the end,
the sacrifice to skies,
the resurrection of the body
unto yon milky stars.

Alone in the desert
on the hill with only snakes.
Invading the land,
who stops you cold
in the cool midnight
When I'm going away
alone and strange
in a new continent
of smoke and light,
in the lungs of fire,
in the thirst of the body like wood,
in the mystery of human
remorse and sacrifice,

I think what dreams are in us
and the eyes catch light
and fear and love
and the hero's search,
that ends too soon.

MOTHER LAND
April 27, 1984

I can always go back
to where my land is
born in free die in free
I can always go back
to where I was born.

I can always shed tears
upon my soil, dirt
of my planet, water of my
body, rivers and oceans,
I can always shed tears.

I can always leave blood
behind my life
if the gods control the flow
even where clouds
form mysteries of sonic flight
I can always leave me.

I can always go back
I can always shed tears
I can always leave me.

ABOVE CLOUDS ABOVE

April 27, 1984

I

Blue Ocean
with solemn wings afloat,
green swirls
to mix the far mist.
Volcanic outcrop
lost in blue mystic flow
forever green and brown,
volcanic atoll.

Flat island of loneliness
not a human bone

The purple ring encircling
O absence of ice and
northern scars
across the body

Shelter us!
No rain   no life
Inhuman suffering
setting sail in harbors
          of light
dry vision
surrounded by
blue diamond
encircled by green emeralds

as if the island
had eyes
that come up to us
    from the blue

LEGACY (GOING BACK)
May 1, 1984

Oh young of this world!
What is it that the ancient erupts?

Even in the midst
of silicon chips and endless terminals,
slick musicals, advertisement,
and business journals

mind-warping takes the masses
so that an elite
of control and money again subjugates
human minds beyond the scope of death

Half-minds caught up in gain
thinking that a little ditty
or clever idea makes
a genius with cause to forego others
for the sake of money and power,

little hard ants of self ingratiation
bragging about success
without a universal thought
or thought of human suffering,
upon which much of their
    success is built.

But who needs communism,
that contemporary refuge
from material subjugation
into a newer human subjugation?

I want to go back to the Pond
and transcendent destinies
back to that innocent belief that
to be stubborn for a harmless cause
is a spiritual awakening,

that real freedom is to contemplate
and not lose ground or starve or die
without honor or love,

back to the mystery
of the individual
and of the people
though rash, proud and narrow
still manage to taste the flowers
of love brush their lips
and beauty touched once before death,

back to the lava of the dream
spurting from inside,
    flowing into the real
O young of this ancient world
we leave you
in the perpetual danger of the galaxy

of which we have no stroke
but like a tree or an ant
 live and die,
  and maybe live again.

May 3, 1984

The pains of children
growing up
 are solid,
tearing mystery out
  of the heart

weighed down with generations
of melancholy
  and doubt

Sharp is the pain
 of flight and escape
weighing heavily on the fears
  of youth,
O pray for the drama
  of forgiveness,
the penance of bitter relief,

  the drowning of sorrows

and the spring of beginning
  with new eyes
  that mix with
  each other's hearts
and bring newer pains.

May 10, 1984

Where am I now?
Can you see me?
Do you touch me?
Where am I now?

Where are you
Above the clouds
Inside the earth
Around the galaxy
Inside the x
Where is you?

SERENADE NO. I
May 15, 1984

Ah shit!
it doesn't come
when you wait for it,
you have to go out
and get it, it
doesn't come

Oh balls!
it doesn't stop
you have to go stop it
sorrow and all
it doesn't stop

Ah dream
you've burnt out my throat
arrived at dawn
my eyes athirst

more real than shoes
more bitter than fruit
Dream, you throw me out

WHY GOD SHOULD KNOW THE GODS
May 18, 1984

A little girl
with black pigtails
and sweet black skin
is holding a book
without a hard cover
called "Jesus Our Saviour"

Another little person
is learning that
there might be a saviour.
O Holy Holy
spirit of the tree
Holy, holy
spirit of the water
oxygen and hydrogen
chlorophyll and photosynthesis
"Jesus Salvador"

El Salvador, San Salvador
Blood shed in the soul
A sacred sacred mist
illusion of solid flesh
where the heart
opens up for all
in the mess of reality

Are we wakened
with sword in hand
guns mounted on beams
eyes opened with
        anointed substance?

Do we see? Is it vision
as if in a frenzy
or is it better not to see

the false from the true spirit
that hovers over the spit . . . . of infinity
and anoints the stars . . . . without words?

No date

O Guitar!
a string shaking
into stark beauty

WAR
June 12, 1984

The soil trembles

I am in the dirt

War rumbles from
the brown fields

It is peacetime in
the hot meadows

Longing, trembling
in the hot tongue
of silence

A few birds start
now and then

O the acrid smoke of
revelation

It is peacetime in
the meadows

SILENT

June 15, 1984

A wind comes down the station.
Students walk to school
summer is a comin'
cries a mad bird

The tree is heavy in the root
boys and girls go to school
the sun is comin'
down the windy shade.
Stores are opening,
coffee smokin',
people talkin' to themselves in cars.

Silent is the dream,
summer's comin'
silent is the bird
summer's comin'
silent is the dream
summer's comin'
silent is. . . . .
. . . .

July 6, 1984

Floating emotions
            above his head
the man is alone
he comes back home

Embrace the ancient wine
far newer than blood

The sun is alone
The moon is alone

Embrace the two flashes
inside the sweet bride.
The harvest
inside the man
alone inside the woman

Above the horizon
the hunger pangs awaken.

July 7, 1984

O ancient Rivers
moved from Jurassic to Cenozoic

slipped from upheaval
to meandering
to the music of the land.

Mississippi, small Passaic,
lithe Colorado,
through ancient sands.

Hudson arrow through Palisades
coals of Susquehanna,
smooth dust of Hackensack,

you flow like a blind man
through a subway train
ever flowing ever frantic
like the migration of hungry insects

effortless, yet blind, yet seeing
yet marooned on planet X

PRE-CHRISTIAN

July 10, 1984

Sweet sun that makes the trees
Rough sun that controls the breeze
Cruel sun to rape the sky
kind sun to rule the eye
sweet sun that makes the flowers
rough sun controls the towers
cruel sun to withhold fire

Kind sun that makes me liar

SIMPLE CREATION I

July 1984

The stars are created.
A spider walks the tree,
as it turns a slender body
on wiry legs.
The universes are created,
fitted together with spit,
water and air.
The spider is the eye
entering into submission
as the life is created
from the phantom sigh.
The sun is created
the spider walks the tree
You are created
like amoeba in the sea

SIMPLE CREATION II
July 1984

> Stars are created
> A spider spins a tree
> Universe is created
> Held together with spit
> Water and Air
> A spider has an eye
> Life is created
> From a phantom sigh
> The spider devours a tree
> You are created
> Like Amoeba in the sea

July 31, 1984

> Minor eruptions in the air
> in the baptism of the earth
> Where does a sweet girl
> like thou get off to here
> in the midst of dirt
>
> and melancholy mirth?
> Sustain the bed
> Minor eruptions in the air
> as in the forest as in the fog
> as in the search

DEAD SEA SCROLLS
August 1, 1984

> Heightened in passion
> The bird clears his throat
> The trail through desert
> is loaded with tears

The clan is alive
in the mountain walls
The bird throttles on
into a nearby grove

August 13, 1984

If I left
nothing would happen
to the stars,
flowers would not wither,
sun would not flicker,
or a man rise
somewhere between life & death.
We would not be picked up
by some distant creator
to define the universe.

I might wither
in the stars.

When my brothers
walk the desert plains
or simple hills,
proclaim a sacred earth spot,
this is no game.
Nothing would happen to stars
I would dehydrate
in the sun
running this open desert
for a grain of truth.

If I left, the oceans
would not stop moving
the rains not stop flooding,
the rivers not stop meeting,
deer not stop running

Nothing would happen
to the stars
that would not be

August 15, 1984

The migration flaps
over the ocean
over the peaks

Why dream tonight?
The heart leaves one beat out
A whole step of physics
turns energy into song,
reflection into dust
dust into energy

energy into lust

HERMIT GAMBLER

August 16, 1984

Raise the limit
I'm losing out
Stop the wheels
I'm lost

Rapture floats away
Eerie sounds drift by
I'm losing altitude tonight
Raise the limit
of your touch

Raise the ceiling
I'm alone, like a drunk
in a cool breeze,

a wild sick man in a jet
a hermit gambler in
the dusk
Raise the limit
of your touch

ALIVE
August 23, 1984

The waves keep coming
        into the sand
one following the other,
keeps following the other
up and over the shore
of ancient bodies,
while this our mortal corpus retains.

Look, the seagull, see the eyes
like a giant ant's eye
        which is dark and black
and fathomless
like the deepest shark's eyes
that don't see light.

Look, the waves' motion
        shut out from
        light or dark
on this small planet
frozen for ecstasy
        in the other sea
where we can only choke
on its eternal beauty

where waves of dark
come over us in the sun

WOODS
August 26, 1984

The hawks float over us
two next to each other
hunting us all day
to tell us we live and breathe
the harsh woods,

and the deer scent pervades
justice, honor, freedom
in that sacred spot inside.

The hawks on the air
we on the sphagnum
of this bog in
reforming the earth.

We stop, we stalk
the ancient trail in the rain.
The flap of wings,
the song inside mixing
with our heated eyes
and insides. The hawk

like Hermes follows us.
It is everywhere, it is nowhere
follows our inside eyes
follows beyond solar winds
beyond golden shadows of death
to a common eternity.

DIRTY BENEDICTION
September 1984

My head falls on the dirt
It rains on my body
under the tree
Am I here with you?
You are not here.
There's bread in the grass
while the eyes wander endlessly

ELEGY
September 4, 1984

Eros is lying next to us
following you through the garden
where sexual dreams make you blush.
We are only human.

Is he living in us
like in the little girl playing with mud
who is a woman?

Or when in the flames of evil
his love cries out to us

See the Autumn flowers
they send out for Eros
who picks the buds
for immortality, like singers in make-up
reaching out to him.

But Eros lies on top of us
in the pains of pleasure.

Where dreams pull out like trains,
the tracks lain upon our bodies,

Eros flies overhead in the dark
eyes closed in confused ecstasy.

Does he sleep or does he die
             while we awaken
in the flesh?

TOXIC WASTES
September 9, 1984

Poor animal, his dead tail waving
in the wake of a passing car.
He's stone dead
as are his brothers and sisters
in other cities of the world.

It's hard to consider its life
yet one of us dies
with the same frequency.
Such lamentations arise.
These bums are lying
on the sidewalk of 8th Avenue
old coat pulled over them
waving in the breeze,
while millions pass them
like cars pass the animals.

Yet look at insects
and smaller pinions
or the trees in ancient majesty
overhead, such innocence
in the roots.

One car avoids the animal
another over its head,
a runner trots by.
The tree, its sunny leaves

waving darkly underneath
with giant shiny crows
flying atop

O light from our only sun
ties chemical chains
to our only body,
shines almost forever, burns!

AUTUMN TORCHES
September 10, 1984

Monday morning in the Americas
cloudy bright, cloudy bright,
cloudy bright, clouds to bright.
The earth people going to work.
So this is what it's like
to be in a trance awakened by the fires

and silence in the cold
with soft voices disappearing.
The day coming on like an intoxication
with no control on the watery shore
of struggle in autumn.

Monday morning
the screech of my eyes
opening into dawn
My eyes speeding to the woman
standing over me;
In my ear
a mother and father returning
for an instant, the bread and coffee
on the hot stones
in the next room dream.
I have turned in my sleep.
Do I enter the deep?

Monday morning creation ascending
to celestial paradigm
in the conflagration
of dumped computers
and magnetic erasure of world data.

The coffee staining
the arms straining,
a ladle pouring
ingots in the noise.
The strength returning
to the center of the crossed body

Another kiss   another sigh
Monday morning:
      in the sky
   a bird's cry.

LIBERA ME
September 24, 1984

The police from all over
gather for the funeral
of a county policeman
shot on interstate 280 while
stopping a car.

The police all dressed
for a hero, a common man
in a casket at 27
lying at the altar
of the Sacred Heart, his heart
no longer beating.

Why do tears begin to blind
at 8 AM this morning?
I've never thought much of police,

look at all the brutality
in this more than evil world,
and was this victim
a good man? He probably was.
He was trusting, doing his best.

I don't know this hero
Yet I know him
as I know the blind killer
twisted by society, and race
       and drugs.
He should be hung until dead,
but who are we to perform
executions. He should be
mutilated by the hero's family,
but which of them
would kill him.
I might, without compunction
because I know the killer
just as I know the hero.

Did I just say that
with hate in the heart now,
but when on a warm sunny day
or on a bright drizzly afternoon
cloud-mothered in our soul
or on a clean snowy night
perform the ritual death
for ultimate punishment?
I do not know.

Maybe policemen
with their heavy 38s
heavy with their own fear of death
might easily put the bullet
through the head and heart.

The hero lies still, lowered into
     clay and silt,
his wife sullen with tears.
His parents always with returning
memories. While the killer's
stunned parents crying with sorrow
bitter tears wished they had
ended their own son
before he'd grown up. Whatever
happy memories tear at their breast
reduce their reason for living on

O cruel brother
of night earth. Mother of earth
swallowing in the chasm of eternity,
our hero lies sleeping
and so do we
while this our hero,
our youth, enters the desolate journey,
which ends one desolate one
to enter another
that sets him free. Libera Me

October 15, 1984

I lean on my bus
going to work.
The sun casts shadows
the length of buildings.
This weekend we saw
a crane along a river
far from home, we said.
It'll die unable to fly
before the last leaf dries.
A wind leaps at me
from the northwest
as I step out.

If I said I hated poetry
I would be lying,
but this is really
an artificial poem.
Everything is invented
except that it is Autumn,
and I am going to work
except that I'm on a bus
and that there is a sun
casting shadows
and that it is windy
it is windy

October 17, 1984

How can I disconnect
me from the world?

Am I a coward to reinject
a lost soul into
the world around me,
nature and mechanical,
electronic and astral,

with the lie of facts,
the lie of progress?

How can I disconnect,
O creative guide
to our little soul,
myself from me,
or how through thee to It
can I connect,
and double connect,
    all else reject?

SONNET
October 1984

In the middle of Autumn
early when the skies
show the dawn
still hovering in trees
and the geese, a series
of arrows break form
for another unknown bird
that catches our eyes,
I can't return.
While overhead one storm
in the bird's neck feathers carries
the dampness of the journey

soaked with our laughs and whispers
in the subterfuge of happiness

STAY
November 5, 1984

Stay Pure, bright wind
like an innocent.

Stay Bright, pure wind
like an instrument
of an unknown force.

Stay powerful,
blow away remorse
Stay pure light wind
dissolve the blood

THANKSGIVING DAY
November 22, 1984

Like a pig of iron
my heart is descending
into the desert of the times

in earth unending.
What makes it easy
to fly to the net of eternity
as I cry out with no name?

O pure fingers that have been made
to hold the knife
or give the genitals temerity.
All parts of me are now
struck by the stinger of strife
in pure shaking flight.

My organs quiver like an antelope
taking off from leopards,
like a jet straining
on the runway.
Then a tiger turns
on the predator.

You've held me in descending,
being next to me
giving strength to feel
the vine that you extend.

December 3, 1984

O world without light
without fires
at midnight bright,
without happy sparks at night
where can I hope to be?

Even the skyscraper's height
is no wonder
compared to one spark

or the first rain or thunder.
Hear me, hold me
until love overtakes.

STREET WISE ROMANTIC

December 7, 1984

The streets are empty and still,
between the red time,
then start again.
Trucks bouncing by,
cars to work, work.
The farms are disappearing as I noticed
years ago along this old route.
Now the farms lie beneath
hotels, office complexes whose beauty
is beyond the senses
in some economic realm fortified
by the delusions of power and inequity.
But the farms are lying beneath
and large poisonous plants
fusing the electrical circuits beneath.
No there's no death to evil,
it rises again, now in war, now in bucks
now in land, now in power,
it rises up forever until the end,
when the light may intercede and remain.
Seek refuge from the fantasy
into one other fantasy.
We see violence done on subways on streets
but we don't see violence done
in a new class system or economic twist.
Does it murder just as well?

Nothing can be done.
It will go on and on
until the intercessions of the sun.
Everything else has failed, and will,
but the innocence of youth
and the momentum of dawn.

LAMENT #4 FOR ETHIOPIA
December 11, 1984

I open my mouth,
dream unconditionally
in a world of pain
hardship and sorrow.
Starvation a figment of matter.
Ethiopians down to nothing
Lives with my looks hidden
in their faces,
bodies of bones,
uncontrolled pain-smiles
the hunt of starvation
breaking through earth's salvation.

   Chorus—
   We hunger and thirst
   for an empty meal.
   O give to dying body
   the last divine energy burst.

   Hunger has penetrated the brain.
   Thirst has stolen the liver.
   We shake apart.
   We fall away.

Forgive us, children of pain,
eyes of fearful deer
my upper respiratory is

engulfing sordid brains.
Famine is a child of humanity
a shadow of mammal reptile and fish
sleeking in the alleys
of plains and mountains
to the innocent stomach of trouble.

    Chorus.

Lift the air from earth!
Dry the wells, rot the fruit
one sip of you for death
and we are all equal.
I kneel at your body overtowering,
kiss your lips overpowering.

    Chorus.

A PIECE OF GLASS
December 23, 1984

Staring on the ground
for no one reason
except looking into a piece of glass
in the winter among the leaves.
Now you know that the grassy field
is clocked for winter
while in the rooms of a house
shadows of trees, as lives
inhabit autumn and blossoms.

On the top branch of a wiry tree
a bird sits and looks
against the sky,
but is really some distance
from the great look in your eyes
that tenders pity, irony
innocence and love.

Why go on looking
when the sparse groups walking
on the island desert
where groups of cormorants and ibises
make their last nest
within the survival key.

The light flashes on the giant transmitter
timed to infinity.
Ah, if the finite particles
would be your touch.
But, from a piece of glass
shines the soul
on the veins of an arm
that tears away
my eyes from you
as the night tears away
from the sun.

Without a sound a plane
follows a bird
in the rapturous distance
next to my eyes,
in the dark raising
of the earth,
as the disappearance
of darkness and light

deepens the agony of sparks
of that look in your eyes.

December 28, 1984

Happy heart that sows the breeze
with seeds and pollen gods freeze,
to keep motivation
for love's regeneration.

What I mean is that every
particle of life is a reverie,
a dream where death takes over
from the lover to ascension.

1984
December 31, 1984

It's the last day of
the year, I bought this pair of jeans
a week ago.
You're a dirty liar,
a sneaky queer.
You said you didn't
carry this brand here.
I know I bought them here.
There's a defect in the crotch,
the flap stays open,
there's a dark thread missing.
I can't wear them like this.
I have no receipt,
you know these are yours.
You have to change to them.
I won't leave the store.
"I'll call the police if
you don't leave."
I don't care if you call
the police, I want you to.
I'll raise my voice to you
because you lied to me
you took me for a fool
and you're the fool,
see here's my Visa receipt.
I bought 1 pair of jeans
and 2 pairs of sweats
$38.97, see
you're the fool.

Do I want an exchange
or a refund?
A refund, you fool,
this is the last day of 1984.

1985

January 2, 1985

My intellect seems to breathe.
I can't separate
what I see. Like a seed
it flies with the birds, like fate,
invading yet settling
on the nerves of my mind.
Close the veil of sight!
Close the heart-door!
The mind wants to seethe
on the meta-rays of thought.
But are we so dumb
that a patch
on the table or on the window
marred by light
can infuse wizardry
with philosophical delights,
and a tune on the radio insignificant
recall metaphysical nights?
Oh, turn the particles to waves
of light and destiny
burrowing the brain.
Pass the salt, cross the traffic!
Open the thoughts' maze
to celestial unending rays.

IF YOU LOVED ME
January 4, 1985

How can anyone on the steam of light
turn his head and see
the decapitation of childhood
or paraphrase the simple tunes
that carry even greater depth?

Or carry even lonesome blues
or faraway dreams to apple trees
in mountains,
      valleys of mist.
You say it's as brilliant as light,
I say it's black as revelation,
or inspiration in the liver,
the all warming core
of the human body.
We think and breathe
fuck, feel, touch
like an insect in a breeze.
Trying to hold on
trying to let go
while we're drowning in dreams
that rise like time.

LOVE SONG
January 10, 1985

Like a punch in the face
planetary lights and stars,
do I see Spring.
The ground is frozen.
Dawn like the colors of an old fire
illuminates the south-east.
The ground is frozen solid,
yet not to permafrost,

yet not to this inner core
which glows like coals for you.
Overcast comes, overcast goes
the ground is frozen but not the core,
but not your eyes
which glow like coals
but not to permafrost.

January 11, 1985

Seagulls are in from the sea.
The forecast is a dusting,

better than the slaughter
taking place in me
over the magnetic swell of lusting.

Televisions are turned on
           in the video room
across the triangle park,
light changing like the wings
           of a bird batting
in the new winter storm.
It is a momentary dark
crossing a sudden word,
swelling in the throat
when your form cuts like a deer
across the wind
forever into my heart.

Snow is only frozen water.

PAGES OF STORMS

January 15, 1985

There is no pleasure, yet there is.
North wind drives snow.
Old people shuffle along
on their way through ice.
Yet there is an only world
where songs come
over the air waves:
not the great Mozart, Beethoven, Schubert,
but laments of country blues.
A dragon snorts through the woods
Invisible flames melt
      the path of snow.
Trees still hold serenity.
There's no heaven on earth,
no ecstasy persisting like a night storm
no tiger in the bushes, yet there is.

HUNGRY

January 17, 1985

Alternate side of the street parking
has been suspended
but where is the marking
showing the repented
along the roads and alleys
of recent misery.
It's not only in rivers and valleys
that we cleanse ourselves
or each other, or crucify the mother,
but in the volcanoes where
the silent magma
turns to wonder.

Oh how green the forests
in infinite rain
the solvent of lust and dreams
and cradle days
that no longer pack themselves
onto your dreaming.

So stop this thrust
the solemn pleasures and schemes
the slick money maze
that racks the poor and homeless
delving into listlessness
the human body and brain.
When we wake up, the forests are green
delve and dive
　　　　into worlds unseen.

February 1, 1985

Tile floor, open glass
smells break open

recent dreams, dogs and garbage.

Open the fires of lust
in dreamt repetitions.
Awake the worm
in reverie, allons, allons, refrain.

This house this room of recent shadows
turn reality walking around
taking the other route
with newspapers
magazines of the face.

Wake up and see your shadow
upon the walls of the heart,
the face, that eyes have mischief

of love, looking into.
So speak above the light
that dims in day with ol' sun
not disappearing before
                    mountains in horizon.
Dwarfed, we face the blue
and raise the root of
our compassion into the arms
of brothers and sisters,
with open mouths and eyes,
we chase the sight of early loves,
not dreams not dreams.

STREET JOURNAL
February 8, 1985

The economy is good for some
The farms are starving for some
The ladder against the house
On the street corner, a bum
The economy is good for some
Holy men are shot
Bad boys are shot
Human minds are shot
but we work, the economy
is good for some.

Business schemes are cast
People think they're great
They just made a deal
on somebody's meal
The human being feels
like a cockroach sometimes
while he talks to himself
on a corner with a dog walking by,
its head held high,
while the sun comes into the sky.

The sun is good for some
The poor earth and each other
        is all we got.

February 11, 1985

Dried up and dogged
rain soaked and logged
upon the compost of apostasy.
Should I turn, should I burn
from inside out?

God help me learn
Love please be stern
Holler me, Hurry me
        from inside out!

In a night full of tires,
in a breast of desires

from inside out

UNFINISHED
February 12, 1985

Let your imagination
        become constricted
and take, wash away, away
        all pleasure.

Take a field of wild bent flowers
loomed overhead by aircraft.
Overturn the ocean
on a planet full of life.

Dream the sounds of dream
Whirl away the night
One dark spot remains
that is us   all us

CENTURY SONNET
February 15, 1985

When a spirit comes to me and frightens
and the weight on my chest
turns butterflies into desert lands,
and rivers flow through arms to heart,
shepherds and farmers sit to drink
my isolated soul.
But not because I'm away
from you or may never see again
the drunken night,
or shaking stars' illusion,
that distance is not time
and time not space,
but that spirit comes to me entwined
and the century lightens . . . .

February 20, 1985

I'm not weeping and weeping
since the cinders upon my body
cure a languid soul
and the liquid morning
stands dirt upon dirt
to make up the clouds and mist
of animal anxiety.
Pour the ashes on my head
I went to change my body
and my soul intervened

I went to cleanse your body
and your soul intertwined.
What should I do now?
but turn myself into and out of,
alone, and come weeping home.

FREEDOM

February 20, 1985

The steel mill is burning.
It is Pennsylvania at dusk.
The industry dissolving into sounds
of birds and dogs mesmerizing trucks.
It is America at dawn
the birth of liberty and pain
one doesn't see or face
but tired eyes crack open. Love
and street people storming desperation.
O quiet eyes O quiet rain
O mountain crags of hymns,
smoke and mist in ancient trees
dissolve of eyes the creatures stream,
dissolve o eyes the creatures mist.
O lost, be lost, be lost in thee
  to liberty and pain.

HOSPITAL

February 21, 1985

The dying are all over
but we want to work a little,
see friends and sons and daughters
and get out of here forever and ever
until eternity burns the seas.

The living are filtering the smoke
as if we were all puffing away
at tobacco and microfilm,
and we contemplate the lover
as eternity burns the seas.

See the crowds, millions gathered
outdoors in sunburn and night.
Listen, the music breaks rocks
and birds fly off-course in the
waves of thundered guitars
while eternity burns the seas.

I know it's only the rooster breaking,
lovers holding hands and kissing.
Warmth breaks the chill of Caribbean cliffs,
breakfast on the planet
while eternity burns the seas.

February 25, 1985

This is not the place I want to be
rather a bubble on that creek
headed towards the free
or the meat in a crow's beak
clogging the throat.
Our hearts say it's remote
that we approach each day with new
resignations and then screw
them into our brain
like headless trees in lightning and rain
cursing a clock or a supermarket.
O, praise be winter
and somnambulist trees
against the night's socket,
lights opening all around,
the simple light of always being born

in midnight skies,
while I settle for the place
between thine eyes.
O praise be rivers
oceans and space
and the lightning of embrace

INCANTATION
March 1, 1985

Let's get going
  It's time
Time passes, it's time
      to now leave
You were born
  only yesterday
you will know love
love will know you
you will hurt inside
you will be relieved
love will know you
you were born
  only yesterday
you will laugh
you will cry
  just like before
  only a little different
you will be you
you will be us
you will be everyone
you will be each other
It's time
only yesterday
you were born
  you were born

PUMPING IRON
March 5, 1985

Lift the weights off us
of the debris of earthquakes in mountains
Disaster upon disaster
    not just long ago
but now and forever
distaste on distaste of
          broken bodies
around the rumblings
       of a movement.

O fluid of wave conception
from the time your
eyes shot down
and left this creation

Looting, murdering, bodies,
    destruction of mortar and stone,
iron battering machines
in the illusion of holy reduction.

Lift the weights of missile tubes
secretly in rumbling earth,
in throbbing magma blinded
by the chaos of unity.

Lift the weights
with our only body

Lift to purification
lift to dream, lift the dead
weight as these bodies absorb the spirit
of our common struggle.

March 5, 1985

'Du bist in meinen Blut'
This phrase came to me
over and over
You are in my blood
This phrase
in meinen Blut
like a god was there
flowing forever
'Du bist in meinen Blut'
surging in me
forever and ever
siempre en mi sangre
'Du bist in meinen Blut'
in my blood, through my frame
to my central flame.

REGGAE MINE
March 7, 1985

You to me
Me to you
me knowing
me not knowing
O minor flowers
O major towers
It's sunny warm inflamed
in the pain
of this touch like
a sword of showers.
Hand to mouth
mouth to hand
from the cortex to the corpse
me not knowing
me knowing
All the sufferin'
  in this touch

COURAGE
March 12, 1985

Radical frozen light
above the torch of night
light dust, moon rust
rising above the beams of west wind.
Solitary fusion of people around fires
as the sun sinks deeply
      into Demeter's lap.
No silver moon
but between the east buildings
the rosy moon filtered yellow
by the atmosphere's gases held tightly.
There's no life in other galaxies,
meant with no religious thought
or elevation of man
as if he were unique,

but it's the reality of solitude
like speeding on a highway
through dark,
sleeping on the banks of the river
taken over by courage
out of the millennium's fear

Music rising from the box
across the lake
The feeding of youngsters
The pyre of the old
The poet searching for the new
song for divine celebration, or
just for sexuality
      in the buff.

MORNING VESPERS
March 15, 1985

I talk to you plainly
while the wind is along the coast
I see you blindly
and something touches my body
The blood is clamped on me
from inside
I'm so small that I breathe myself.
Only the smallest creation
can fit in this body.
Showers of darkness
wet me with the veil of hope
Have I fooled myself again
for the last time?
A taste burns into my body
Don't say soul
when you mean body
Both may turn to spirit.

March 19, 1985

9:01
and   twenty seconds

so   rejoice
    in your deximil
            of time

NOTORIETY—ACADEMY AWARDS
March 25, 1985

Sweaty hands no memory
with riches all around

Out to dine
for more money than
a poor family takes
  to eat in a month

And proud are the money makers
sweaty hands no memory
proud and cool are the golden hearts
breasts laden
   with self pride
and unique greatness of style,

swelling until almost bursting a gut
slapping each other's backs
in the subterfuge of vanity.

Sweaty hands no memory
while peasants
who never find an easy day
dine on the floor of struggle
bear children for the continuum.

But so what? We forget
we all suffer the same,
only the trappings different in
the eyes of mortality.
And as we lay down
our bodies
in the night
the real world
passes over us all

and we pass from
cool infinite arms
to mother arms
warmed by the breath
of hope in that transmission
to a greater greater spirit
    a greater spirit.

No date

    The streets against their stomachs
    Their heads bloodied and scabbed
    The noses running with wine
    There are gun wounds salting the flesh.

    An air of powder and burning mist,
    an error of advancement
    in the secret journals.
    The inner city sadness
    with pimps and hustlers and pushers
    all for an occupation
    in the rain storm of money.

    But there's no solution,
    except that some dream might
    awaken the grizzly slumber of despair,
    and a new redemption
    engulf the earth,
    and the flames that destroy
    return as the flames of hope.

    Not that light is always
    better than dark
    especially when dark dissolves fear
    and some flesh you love is near,
    especially then, especially
    when we wake
    and are forgiven

NIGHT STROKES

April 1, 1985

So much that I see, O night
is emptiness and pain
I come home and
  what do I do?
The morning ice melts
      along the edges
of my fire

My heart melts for
the new world of my children
and their happiness.
Early America slips by me.
Ships, wagons, horses
walking running
beside the moonlight
along the river.

Then suddenly a bomb
smashes the nearby apartment house
an armored division
cuts through the block
searching out Islam renegades.

A communist band
cuts the jugular veins
of an encampment.
Fascists blow out brains
over the walls of a house.
An airplane of cocaine
blows up in the sky.

Capitalist "saints" self proclaimed
tear the balls off man
Chemicals burn the eyes
and livers of a village.
Islands of beauty burn up.

Earth doesn't weep
Nor do comets nor
       yellow asteroids destined in some future
       Nor stars in some implosion
       Nor moon in some religion
Nothing weeps
  only sleeps
O night, as the greed explodes
over our daily bread.

BMX

April 21, 1985

Songs of the track fly all around
as the encampment settles in.

Rising oceans of coastal plains
begin to warm toward
the southern equinox.
But this enchantment
over the quiet encampment
of just plain people
in the lonesome din
of exited voices,
is transcended by the racers pedaling
through the air waves,
their awesome hearts like in love
push the fuel to
muscles and bones and eyes
that pierce our hearts,

and give energy's hope
to the strength of the world.

FORECAST

April 30, 1985

It's almost summer
Does this mean much
to an island paradise
or to the workers in
a coal mine. Yeah! of course!

Yellow beams shoot down
when emerging from it all.
Rains come, rains go,
but the memory
mounts and deepens the mind.

A giant tree. Vines hang.
Comfort and ease
have no comrades
like a veil of songs.
It's almost summer, all is smashed.

The deep forest churns the green,
lava and ash
write symphonies of death,
while earth like a battered child
learns to eat inhabitants and buildings.

But why from summer to this?
The rain covers the shiny streets
An angels occupies the wet trees.
The substance of the living is
groaning in holy victory of the oceans.

But how fast are we going in the velocity
of despair. Nourishment warms
the desolation and the dead
till all the cities be leveled
and summer comes again

IGNORANCE (STRONG)

May 10, 1985

Reporting noise on the west front,
rebel soldiers think they
will save the masses.
Soviets march bombs and weapons
in an ignorant display.
America continues to advertise
all that will make you happy.
Ignorant movies try to show,
or ignorant articles try to convince,
that we know soviets
when not one is truly Russian, because
they feel no love for their land.
So it's all a disguise
a confluence of secrecy
in the land of the free
to control the masses
while the little guy
gets his head cut off,
or gets shot on a lonely jungle road.

The innocent always pay
what deadly price.
Multitudes marched off
into mass graves prepared by religious
beliefs of superiority.

God talks to no one,
not to the ignorant rigid
the ignorant lying
or the ignorant fanatical

Yes it is just as easy
in our 3 western subterfuges
to be hypocrites
as to be evil.

Reporting noise on all fronts
buildings in rubble
superimposed upon the
lonely bodies of starvation,
while we in the quadrants
wait for a body from some universe
to cut the bread, pour the wine
and wash away the inherent
ignorance of the almighty strong.

NARRATIVE NIGHT

May 15, 1985

O night of dreams
your melancholy heart redeems
all the daytime debris that makes
violence a part of catastrophe.

A bomb was thrown on a row house
to break an opening in the roof
in order to pour tear gas
and other chemicals
to squeeze out members of
a back to nature cult
in Philadelphia, who had automatic weapons.

The bomb caught fire
and flames spread to sixty houses
destroying all, destroying all.
Ten bodies, charred, were found.
The back to nature cult
is gone from the debris.
The hundreds of homeless lost everything.

The police justify the bomb.
Why is there not greater lamentation?
Why not the clawing of hair

and tears flowing
even though most have their lives
and can hold each other and children,
and the dead don't lament.

There's an old lady emerging from ruins
holding a little boy crying.
There are men thrown in alleys.

May 23, 1985

On a night in a distant country
in a village on a night
in a bed on a night in a distant land
in a night on a bed in a distant country

In my arms on a night
        in a distance
in a country city
soft with oozings of
        bright arms
in the night on the neck
on the mouth in a far city
almost dark   almost dusk
in the light on a bed in
        a distant land . . . .
    . . . .

June 5, 1985

I am not able to move
I am locked in
But I won't throw myself
against the bars
and crush my skull,

though it be easier to prove
those bruises pains and sufferin'
than to melt in these flames
     that transform.

Something's opening the wall
but it takes more pain
than a train going over my legs
to open my heart.

Let morning rise, let songs sing
let motors race in the
         hurricane's embrace
Talk to me! Ride with me!
Don't all blind creatures need a light?

SONNET
June 7, 1985

Is beauty lost forever
or does love just change?
With your face in my heart
I've lost the range of freedom
or the track I've gotten off.
It ends in the desert
surrounded by heated dirt
while the sun drops me out
of the journey,
no tree no bush no sea no storm.

Am I still lost and do the
spiny flowers that smell like you
warm me, torture me, try me out
in the exploding beauty that pains?

HIDDEN BIRD
June 13, 1985

Song birds enter the morning
the pre-dawn before the fires,
you know, when the night floats away
like vapor on a lake,
or like kisses in the woods.
Songs that even creation
might not remember.

Continuous, threaded, as if
a cherry pit were stuck
in the throat
to produce the trumpet of the branches.
So varies, yet never, changing
through all the days, since
reptiles fell to earth.

I give up the reason for the sound
I give up the creature of sound
and the creator of the creatures
and of us and of dawn and
air and of vacuum
and human inhumanity.
I give up the song.
I give up the place

LAMENT #5 FOR LEBANON AND ISRAEL
June 20, 1985

The Phoenicians are waiting
outside the city
on the water in the harbor.
I wait along the city walls
of news from my sons and brothers
along the shore.

My cousins, the Phoenicians
have a different cult
yet even here no one accepts
my Dionysus stacked inside
for six thousand years.
Pray that Apollo brings
them all safely
and Hermes, a link to humanity,
no different than the other.

The mimosa spreads open with sun
A giant aircraft explodes
over the ocean
The Phoenician's brown hair
gleams in the sunlight,
hungry faces and souls
lean upon the spears.
Hermes carries a message
through the air.
"There will be great bloodshed
on the sand and rocks
on the roofs and alleys
on the altars and in the body,
that same body that knew love
in the breezes of the Ionian Sea."

LETHAL SONNET

June 28, 1985

Laughter filters through the clash of dishes.
Music filters through the guns and shouts.
Soft, strong, complex, like muscles in the arm.
Light filters through the green forests
along the woods and streams,
through the cottonwood trees, ready to die,
while the light coming through seduces
       the youth left in our bodies.

Words filter through the brain
            through the liver, through God,
through the particles within the particle,
            through the soul within the soul,
through the longing within the language
of the heart, more lethal than words.

July 9, 1985

Closer and closer to the ground
Closer and closer to resurrection
Closer and closer to penitence
Closer and closer to the night

Further and further from the truth
Further and further from the light
Closer and closer to you.

RAIN & WOLVES INHABIT ME
July 26, 1985

They roam through & through.
A rain soaking
the pubic hairs of youth
like volcanoes growing trees,
like my head in sleepy vision.

Rain and wolves inhabit me
behind the fevers of the jungle
            of the individual self
ready to destroy all notion
in the ocean of false intelligence
that destroys bit by bit.

Rain and wolves inhabit me
as I stop at the edge of the woods
freeze and smell and listen
listen and smell and think
see and feel and listen
to the particle universe I drink.

ALL AT ONCE

August 5, 1985

For complex reasons
with my beloved weapons
we drive from despair to futility.
Strained hard, lifting,
work not having to do,
but to utilize the body
escaping from this shoddy remorse
of the sagging,
of the flesh like sand shifting.
But I still have reality
enough for the body.

Today we rise like
elephants just shot and wounded.
Through the trees the wind
lifts a few leaves in all.
With a spear and a dart of sleep
     I move, I breathe
No better, no worse but deep
to the center of thee
to the emptiness of all.

LIFE SENTENCE
August 5, 1985

A poem is like a cat sleeping
curled up, the mouth and nose warm
and humid
like the leaves of the Amazon.
And arousing from the sleep
ready to take a quiet drink
so stretched like a bow
or ready to kill.
Like the eyes of a cat,
pupils changing shape
taking shape through the sound
or form or pressure or tension
of the lightning unlike anything.
Inspiration feeds the light
it floats away like smoke
and then attaches the neck
the chest, the genitals,
then eats and caresses through night to dawn
till the sentence of the soul.

August 8, 1985

There is no way
from here to there
for almost a day
to get rid of this fear

There is no way

There is no sin
that follows me there
to where you are
in the heated stars

No one to win

There is no sin

DRAGONS AND DUNGEONS
August 13, 1985

Domination in creation
The stars are clear tonight
We live in a house
we dwell in a cave
deep in the dragon's soul.
Yes the dragon has my transcendence.
There is no intellect without feeling.
The mystery of the cave descends
on us living peacefully
while the dragon's heart
shoots blood into the fire
of our youth

Feel the ball against the bat
flying out of the universe,
and the dragon's mouth like a mother
absorbs the shock. Rejoice,
the sun climbs into our eyes,
and like the mouth of the creature
breathes life after life after fire
into our own denseness.
Insects roam earth,
like stars roam universe;

Domination in creation
within the body, within the sun
within the pain we ascend
without the pain the gods send.

ODE SONG
August 31, 1985

A man is sleeping
   in a parking lot, on break
         from Saturday's hard times.
Years before we lived
   the Senecas and Mohawks
         roamed the hills sleeping
               with trees and deer and bears.

O America my birth!
   America my birth!

   Strong odors glean the mountains,
      trout and bass brush my legs,
a sleepy cage engulfs
   the cicada, angels verticillating
a swooning song.
And am I sleeping
   away my birth
   away my birth?

Soft songs lighten the explosions
for citizens battered and not sleeping,
but shot or bombed or
anxious for a piece of grain
to ease the pain,
for the poor in body and spirit.
On the mountains, valleys, and plains,
the world is my birth
sleeping sleeping in movement.

Future Brothers, Future Sisters
maybe we'll sleep too,
maybe we'll awaken
in this world of beauty, love and pain.

MAD ANGELS
August 31, 1985

No formulas for storm clouds
pushing overheard, just vapors
charged and loaded
with earth dust dark
and filled with life,
torrential kisses on the face.

No forms for virus burning
rushing hunger to masses
breathing fire in exaltation
of living spores and microbes
starving sick and mangled,
keep singing in our embrace,
torrential kisses on the face.

Rock the stage, tear the infield
roam the stores
like a torrent at the edge of quakes
where mad angels rest.

ONE
September 3, 1985

Three nazis turned to swans
Three communists turned to deer
Three capitalists turned to buffalo
three laughters turned to tears.

Two storm troopers turned to lice
two KGB's turned to roaches
two CIA's turned to locusts
Two kisses turned to torches.

One V2 turned to fire
One old nuke turned to rubble
One new nuke turned to dust
Don't be fooled by one God.

THE CITY
September 5, 1985

Mountains meet hills, back
where plains spread over non-eternity.
The grass is wet.
　　Bare feet soaked over rocks.
Trees and all there is on earth
mix with the sun
until savage nighttime
breaks open the eyes of death,
and sleeping by the pond
without thanks or guarantee
rakes memories over the coolness
of north winds.

A fog sweeps over the stadium,
a mist from the glacial lake.

ODE
September 9, 1985

It was night. It turned day.
I was walking east.
The desert was like a reptile.

I was lost, in a dream.
I had no clothes,
my body was tight,
my black hair flowing
in the white sun,
the bow across my back and chest.
I was lost but kept moving
across the valley which was
endless, brown, abounding
in beauty and spirit
that pushed me across the heat.
I think and think
of this moment, of future nights,
and loves and celebrations
of you and me and sand and rocks
and trees and sun and jungle.
I was lost but kept moving
while something that was there
all along, burned, disintegrated
penetrated the central core,
until all that was left,
in matter, was a hidden dream,
concentrated to the marriage
of this living spirit journey.

DREAM ODE
October 24, 1985

As if I had inhaled
a dozen packs of cigarettes
I awake this morning.
Whatever had prevailed
during that night, solid regrets,
nightmares, spirits dawning
on my wake-up eyes,
whatever spirits disguised
as dreamfields, created

pain blood and sacrifice.
Ah mountains, ah pimps
anointing my loins.
Tell them to stop
kissing nuclear wastes
and fall in love at the glimpse
of masses in massive ruins.
O drag me on my knees
through the new invisible night
to the sagebrush chemicals
we invent with delight.

As if I had inhaled a
dozen stacks of chemicals
I implore the new invisible world
for the clarity of the miracle,
that same miracle of the dream
and of the material world
to carry it one step further
into the awakening.

October 31, 1985

Dry leaves, light trees
spoiled tears
on the building stones
Tripping on sacred bodies
turning the death corner
with beer still cool on the lips.

Don't know what doing
Don't know where going
windy day sunny day.
Don't know what's coming
from eternal gods.

TRAVELIN' BLUE HIGHWAY

November 8, 1985
inspired by Blue Highways, *William Least Heat-Moon*
and after Robert Burns' "My Heart's in the Highlands"

Went a travelin' long time ago
Now don't go no place
no where to go.
Been a travelin' long time gone.
Pack no bags, fill no wagon,
My heart ain't here
My heart ain't near
but in these woodlands
carry'n through the saplin's
maple, oak, and briars.

Over the hill-lands
where some other birth
over with the folk
in poverty's worth.
My soul just ain't here
        under fluorescent light
My soul long left me
like a dog its master
thinkin' all the time
of hidden disaster.

My soul's travelin'
to bring me back the sage
cryin' out in the city's rage
sleepin' on the mountainous edge
O desert O city
send me back my soul safely
look into my eyes
look into me again
as I drink from thee   and thee.

PEOPLE'S REPUBLIC
November 13, 1985

Reach out to the people
reach out to the storm
reach out to the masses
troubled and worn.

Everyone cheats these days,
one honest person
is like water on the desert.
They're there hidden inside
because everyone hides these days.

The rich are also troubled,
and are also the "people"
but do not know it!
In this moment we are together.

If we mention cocaine, people laugh.
If we mention nuclear arms
    people close down,
everyone hides these days.

Turn the mountain into clay
Crush the minds of kids,
sabotage the rain
and spit on beauty's frame,
everyone lies these days.

Reach out to the people
reach out to the storm
reach out to the masses
troubled and worn.

Volcano mud covering exquisite bodies
Eruptions from molten earth.
Thank God it's hot, that being
the price we pay birth.
But the price we pay
loneliness, a small village gone,
a mountainside blown off.
Children herding sheep
farmers plowing deep.
O crust of earth, O core's rebirth
Both love and riches disappearing
in one momentous thrust.

Hold the bombs, hold the blood,
the end is always near.
Songs rise from millions of bodies,
flesh flowing in the rivers
under rocks under roots
but they – all gone.

REAL
November 18, 1985

Let's face it
the historical is dissolved.
You are still hidden
under my eyelids
and in the sun you are sun,
in the reaches you are particles,
in the void you are no thing.
I can't dream anymore
for in that dissolution absorbed
is you. I can't dream anymore.
A hunter carries the bow
while the arrow fixed

in tension aims between my eyes,
not to blind me but to make me see
the winds of destiny.

O, but I can't dream anymore
and a little simple life
though not so simple is
hidden as a dream.
So when we wake up
and childhood lashes
us against the boat,
or when we are walking against wind
let's face it
all is dissolved in you.
I can't dream anymore
but would you watch
the celestial body gather ice
and burst into combustion
until all is gone?
All is done?

MARKETEERS ENTWINED
November 20, 1985

Bread! Get your bread
Stones! Get your stones
    Hypocrite delight
        White Castles
are still here.
I mean the burgers
with onions and grease juice.
Don't refuse the market
        it's buy everything
but NO, it's BE everything
while you can.
Money is a'right.
  Fight, make it

in the night
What's the stars
        but us?
   Common proletarians
   with golden necks
make it big, young
    beginning talent
big marketeers, P.R. men
media whittlers with the knife
     of ambition
     PΣEUDO Artistes
         "   old priests
    media studiers
pretenders that try
            to save our souls,
pretenders that scrape our hearts.
    Bread and stones
    wine and fire
watch Prometheus
        in the hour of desire.

The wind is quiet
even the chains have embraced us.
The lightning spreads.
We're only innocent beings.
We forget the pieces of lies
     pretend we have no soul
     pretend we have no death
from the media to the synod
     pretend we know
        the living god
Bread! bread! bread!
Stones! stones! stones!

THE COMET RETURNS
December 1, 1985

Save the morning
        for the people
Save the people
        for the night.
Warm and dark woods
Cool and bright sun.

There's a comet in the east
if it hit the earth would quiver,
thunder, lightning reduced to nothing,
life would run, and burn,
life would starve, melt
there'd be no wonder,
only clouds remembering.

See the islands, see the continents
plates are movin' in the silence.

Save the sun for the morning
save the morning for the people
save the light for the night,
a last remembrance of the kiss.

LITANICAL
December 2, 1985

Calculation mitigation
    conflagration, problem solving.

Fool the innocent
grope the land, starve the spirit,
break the mold.

Swollen heads, puffed out chests
neighborly churchgoers at their best.

Support the holy church
and holy temple,

then you can shit on
    whoever you want.

Big business, holy business
the great people cutting
up the profit.
Calculation, conflagration
holy innocents' flagellation.

THE MUSCLES OF ANIMALS
December 5, 1985

Angry dogs, we are angry dogs
vicious cats, we are
            vicious cats.
Hungry gorillas, we are
            starving gorillas

Roll around in death
Rub along decay
of living things

Don't tell me I'm wrong
or I'll bite you.

FIRST SNOW
December 6, 1985

Starving snow falling through its cycle
In the blanket, the tracks of a motorcycle.
Got up "and got myself a beer,"
ate a rat and muscled up a deer.

Tomorrow's dream in vice
and ice and pockets of video dreams
lie scattered in God's tongue
licking our celestial body.
Bowie, Morrison, Jagger, Pres
shifting shoveling tunes on the waves.
Tigers, cougars, leopards, cheetahs
leaving tracks that tempt the follower.

Pray for us o holy fountain
      of human and other life.
Grieve for us in the path.
Rejoice for us on the way
in the sun, in the snow and cold
where we invent some love
from sleep and sleep divine.

HYMN
December 14, 1985

Keep me away
O temptation. Do I sound
bleak and unmodern,
last in an old forest
that has already been burned deeply?
Or gone?   Are the baptisms
of secular relief gone?
  Draw me nearer O
  redemption sensation.

Do I seem like a leper
squeezing his way
        back to civilization
opening up my self
        for a touch? Then
        keep me away.
Do I seem like the
        warrior of Sumeria
or a crusader in the
        immense dustiness
trekking his way through strangeness?

And you, if a stranger gives drink
and bread
in the great rubble of the night
am I nearer to you?
Then keep me away!
Then keep me!
or throw me away to the
howling wilderness of revelation
that brings me closer and closer.

1986

NEW YEAR
January 2, 1986

New day, new find, new food.
Revolutions in the night
        while we asleep,
awaken belief of a newer day.

New love, new kiss, new eyes,
new bodies, new flesh,
finding lost soul's new soul.
New threats new wars new lies.

New generation, new born
new music, new syntax, new spirit
O spirit great spirit
that ties ourselves to old.

New day, new promise
            of transformation bold
descends, ascends
A bird cries in the sky,

a new eternity. . . . . inside.

January 9, 1986

Where are we headed?
into the eyes of lightning
into the claws of darkness
into the claws of lightning
into the eyes of darkness?
Alone, together, misshapen, near perfect;
where are we headed?

One of a million
    one of a billion
        one of a trillion
calmly without grace
softly, beatitudinously, violently,
in the sleep and energy of first spring seeds;
where are we headed?

MELODY FOR FOOD

January 16, 1986

Children going to school
children drinking coffee
children going to work
children getting married
children kissing
children born and children growin'
children hunting, children fighting

Forget the dream, forget the dream
over all it's shining,
the childlike sun.

Children angry at the world,
children happy in thc snow.
In the jungle, rain forest children
climb trees, it is wet.

Children starving children eating
children singing children building
structures low and tall.
Children having babies, nursing children
children growing up
baby children, big children

Forget the dreams, forget the dreams
over all it's shining
the childlike sun

Over all it's shining
     the childlike sun.

MORNING TOUCHED

January 22, 1986

This morning Walt Whitman
walked past me
Ed Poe sat next to me with a coffee
Emmy Dickinson watched
TV with me in amazement
      in detachment
Hart Crane waved to me
from a boat as I hung over a bridge,
Waldo Emerson sat meditating,
pen in hand. Bill Williams was
looking out the window
everything dripping wet
      as I passed.
Hank Thoreau rested in
the fog of a huge wetland.
Wally Stevens, notebook under arm
sad eyes, moved under the cloudy brightness.
H.D. and Gertrude walked
toward me from the railing
of the departing ship,
Langston Hughes sang weeping.
This morning Walt Whitman
walked past me.

MID OCEAN

January 28, 1986

I think I'm fished out
like parts of the green Caribbean,
few fish left. Groping for
the small ones.   They fit
through the netting.   All about
are the same, only now libertarian
forces threaten while earth grows more

than some can eat. Not a breeze
finds a way to uplift the doubt
of some or to fill the empty seas,
or to lift a fallen heart
when all is fished out.

I think I'm fished out like that,
or maybe it's a gathering of dark
for deeper and heavier waters.

LYRIC
January 29, 1986

Should I start you
or should I turn the key
to soft wilderness, hard desolation,
sweet dream face, firm body real,
should I ride you in or should
I wait another wave
to airy childness, earthy mandrakes
in forest goldness hidden deep.

February 4, 1986

White as a deer's tail
White as floods
is the baptism of midwinter.
Holy sun, holy orb
just another planetary phantom
from the reaches of invisibility.

Lazy bodies with hidden knives
stagger on streets
cigarette butts hanging
burning the lips.

O forgotten sorrow,
sullen kisses setting fire
to the white flashes of desire.

Tomorrow night no matter
how much we lie
enveloped in each other
that exaggeration even shrinks to dust
when that reminder enveloping light
envelops you in joy and fight.

RIFLE SHOT
February 10, 1986

What you can't have is what
you can't have
is what you want
when you cannot want
because good times and good love
fly out of you
quicker than an automatic gun
quicker than an automatic
quicker than a gun
quicker than a particle
flies from you when you're dead.

Dream stuff, dream towns, dream schemes
act upon the heart
and wait and dream
till all's gone, all's dissolved,
by crystal dust in space,
quicker than a spirit
when you're dead
quicker than a spirit leaves
the beauty of your face.

WINTER
February 13, 1986

Ask the sun why today
a glow passes over your face
and the ice stretches in the bay
over the cool whiteness of your race.

February winds, late winter warmth
faraway ancestral eyes blind
by deserts, and tundra's growth
that eats up whatever I find.

Ask the sun why the day
flows over every last trace
of struggle in the sacred decay
of love in the human race.

AMOR & PSYCHE
February 14, 1986

Given all the love that's left
in all the world bereft of energy
light and tears,
there still remains the fear
of losing, close to lost,
closer to battlefields in frost.

When lying in each other's arms
and legs enraptured in memory,
there still remains the kiss
like the fires of a candle,
or a forest in seclusion,
or a migration lost for ages.

PORTRAIT PAINTER REALISTIC

March 5, 1986

The girl with the long tumbling wavy light hair
is eating a muffin with a fork,

thinking observing looking
out the window
at the cars passing on the morning avenue
early, earlier than destiny

in contemplation lost,
something like a contemplative
all dressed up in fashion's mystery.
Small lips from the side
smooth cheeks with the lightest of fuzz

not that much like a girl
in some foreign city
looking for beauty
like a man looking for redemption

but still in observation of the world
Not much like that, but still
the eyes in faraway dreams
of a new life and love
with faraway thoughts alone

as she wipes her lips
puts on her coat
goes out through the door
out through the poem
in the freedom of the next morning
when she returns again

STAMPEDING VISUALIZATIONS
March 12, 1986

Clouds at 15 knots cutting
        the rays of the sun,

blocking, not blocking, blocking,

not blocking, not stopping the movement

of a village in the dawn-remains,

or a town in the after-birth or

    a city morning storm before stampede.

Clouds over the brown March meadows

showering sun, filtering sun

over the bodies that walk

and over their spirits ascending
through the veins to
        the cerebral cortex
that explodes with chills of early Spring.

March 13, 1986

Calm me!
I've become like clay

Give me some strength, some milk,

some bread, some

some light for unshed tears

from swerving sin to solid grace

through my fault and no one else's

a trembling fire raging inside.

Calm us, this earth, this heavenly music.

March 19, 1986

A police siren passes in the street

Rain falls for Spring.

The Great Lakes are rising
higher than in recorded history,

but not higher than in recent geologic time

when the shores stretched out beyond.

But we are far from there,
and the Spring birds fly and dart
like the feet of sailors on a merchant ship.

I see the seagulls
feeding on the inland ponds and rivers
circling in the distance, disappearing, appearing.

I hear the buzz of the sun
in perpetual harmonics with the rain
and a sound appearing, disappearing,

and the metallic scent of a bird
squawking in a tree around.

DARKNESS ODE

March 26, 1986

He was in his 70's then
and he told me that 25 years
before then the doctors told him
he had only a year to live.
He was noble all right
and could look into my face
and know I wasn't just right.

I remember I was only 19 or 20,
he used to clean the gym
and stay in the locker room
and talk with me at CCNY.
Sometimes that great gymnast
was there too. We'd talk for hours.

We discussed philosophy and
very profound concepts
for a wiry little white
son of the Mediterranean and
a small little black son of Africa.

He was noble and one of the great men.
I remember him as if he were here
leaning on the dust mop
every word relating to life.

I think it was he
who got me through the first 2 years.
Remember him in the daylight
as he reaffirmed my feeling that there was spirit.

If I could call him back now
and tell him what doctors tell people,
he would probably look very serious
then grin as he did
when he told me what doctors told him.

Can't tell how many souls
there are or how many spirits
flash existence since that time,
or how it is to breathe freely
on a warm morning
or how it is to be busy and smell flowers,

and gas exhaust on highways
and hear birds or planes or wind
or heartbeat in the bed.
O deep and languid day!
O body of water and clay
O compounds of alchemy's dismay!
No! I'm not cracking up!

But the sweat of Spring
is beginning to exude

and the sweat of suffering
continuing in the illusions

that I try to betray. In these buds
that flash birth, from this fire

that burns the body
comes the darkness of eternal light.

THOUGHTS
April 14, 1986

A jet plane takes off from
    Newark International Airport
turning in the sky.
Cold lessons of struggling.
One plane lowering
heading east to LaGuardia Airport
another heading north from Newark,

crossing miles apart in the sky.
Early morning vespers in the garden,
amid flowerings of peach and apple
and trembling fish in the lake,
full as are the smells of shadows of reality.
America bombs Tripoli
far from home, yet near to brother
and children and sisters in the gardens
beneath the flying jets.

An only earth ever changing
amidst the changing stars
forever and ever, creator creating created,
no substance, unsubstanced
non-body, no body
with us in rush of smallness
with thoughts of visitation from angels
and their breath of life and death
that falls on us like pollen,
like a meltdown's nuclear fallout
amid flowering trees and plants,
the animals of the earth
the burns on bodies and organs,
amid the Gods' melodious proliferation
of holy angels, holy angels.

MODERN SORROWS
April 24, 1986

Don't be afraid my light,
tumbling in the darkness of delight,
in the pecho of modern sorrows
covered over by arrows of sight.

Don't languish in the deep furrow
like turned earth in the marrow
of Spring getting ready to sprout
peeking from dirt's first green rows.

Don't be afraid to shout out
whether lost love or feverish bout
imprisons you and freedom explodes
finally (in the heart) the doubt

folds up and the chest unloads
bright arrows of new light.

May 1, 1986

I walked out. It was raining
Went out. Was raining.
Rain, bring oxygen
to the May plantings,
and pray the world be free of
  universal radiation,
and for my brother find peace
so suffering be eased
in this ionic web of nitrogen.
All in divine salvation.

The rain and the rivers
settle in the valleys,
a mixed voice says
"I am the tears of a city,"
it was raining, as I walked
  from the pain,
saw the pain, felt the rivers,
asked the rivers to carry him
through the jungles
to where a holy spring washes
all insidious damnation sublimely.

The plaintive chords of the rain
and the traffic and the air collide.
A perfect harmony.

NOW
May 12, 1986

Last night, the moon was crescent,
but round behind the light
was the full circle and the outline
of a daily nocturnal orb,

since before the first poet or music,
before the first human,
before the first tiny creature's evanescent

light, full shining
in the web of the universe
even though creatures do not absorb
all that is to come. Mystic
and full circled to the crescent,

in the dawn were the remains
of the sacrifice, a new life, a new love
a new dream, a new moon
from the valleys of zero
to the pressing of your human form
pressing against your flesh.

May 21, 1986

Turn me around in your hands, O wind!

until I feel right, sleep right

Turn me, O wind! Burn me, O sun!

in your envelope of hot tears

until I think right, talk right

Burn me, O sun.

Soothe me, O spirit!
in the intestines of creation
until I breathe right, sing right

Soothe me, O spirit

May 28, 1986

I have a bad day today.
I'm having a bad day
Bad as of an angry spirit,
although it's a beautiful day
and I call upon a new baptism,
one that will not drown
but at least hold suffering
under water long enough
for the fugitive spirit to fly.

I have a day today
one that is bombarded
with calcium and flowers of Nueva York
of buildings and stainless steel dreams,
of beasts and hymns
of the setting sun, held
down long enough
in the western eternality
for the fugitive spirit to fly.

Looking at beetles and ants,
that they have life too,
it's a miracle that a virus is not alive,
unless we don't understand
what life is, which we probably don't,
not that we can be sure a rock is alive,
but that it has some spirit
or that some spirit has been given it
by who knows who or what,
and that the reasoning leads only
to a soothing of the spirit
which is afire with mystery of doubt.

Long days of summer,
seem like nothing can bear it
when love tears from your lonely
tongue a few words of grace
or forgiveness, or of bloody days
and blood shed of the innocent,
the martyr's bits of redemption,
freedom for the suffering.

Looking at beetles and ants
our lives though more, are no more than
eternity sucked inward by infinity,
something like the voice of a child heard
on a summer path hidden,
when all you have is taken.

Smoke rises like claws that lock me in
and do not let go except in pains,
like monkeys climbing trees
or guitars connected to power stations
exploding the organs of the body.

Azure sky over the city,
bursts open like the fountain
from which everything still operates.

Phantoms fly from eyes,
music thunders from balls,
the smallest particles in the old universe
are loaded everywhere, in me in you
in the memory of sweating bodies
in the meditating wings of the hawk above
in the crazy packed up butterfly of the mind.

CRESCENT MOON

June 20, 1986

Full desolation, full jokes full battle
against the beauty of body.
Songs, songs of blood and childhood
Revolutionary armies gather
on the fields of graves
more quiet than steel.
O bridges of night, emphatic with guns
O young armies of Ireland, Persia, Troy
from peoples gathered in the night
fire rituals and wine
swooning eyes, morning abdomens
burning emergence through the woods
under the mercenary blade
of the crescent moon.

REPRIEVE

June 26, 1986

Landward flies the night
toward the metropolis of chance.
Showering lights through buildings,
on Park and Fifth, downtown and everywhere.
Beggars sleep while the buildings
and the good guide look over them.

Medicine of wine bottles, and
invisible white powder is lost in wind
while everything is lost in summer night
rolling from the Atlantic.

Vagabond fires start
in enclaves of subterranean crucifixions,
sulphur fills the nostrils
plutonium the bones and meat,
while the cyclotron of subways
pushes through embryo's dark passage
past islands of light and music
through limpid foliage and measured algae.

Landward flies the night
toward luxury and poverty
feast and famine.
It passes like a gentle plague
that doesn't stop off.
It passes by Lancelot's dreams,
ancient Egyptians' doors,
baseball fields and racetracks,
magic nights of love,
the grotto, bordello and den,
the predators of woods and deserts,

until the blinding haunt of day.

July 3, 1986

The purple plant, leaves thick
with hair's texture and shine,
has shot a flower,
pink, purple, fellow feelers
shining in the
magnificent conjunction of two long leaves.
A flower, only a flower of mortality
to conjure up the night's pre-dusk
when chip-chip-chip in flowering voice
tzell-tzell-tzell-tzell-tzell
answers across the branches, throat extended.
    What's this praise, this crazy wine
this evening gale of inner voice,
all-too, all-too, all-too, all-too purple happily
that conjures up the flower that has no sound?

HYMN TO RAIN
July 12, 1986

Again rain on the evolved leaves.
Rain in the jungle forest
where people tend the garden
or hunt the monkey.
Rain where people pound the pavement

and wet trucks rest
after a flashing night.
Rain that dissolves the mount
or fills the valley
or breaks the dam

or wakes the face
washes the hair
stiffens the organ.

Rain that dissolves the dreams
or creates the dreams
in atmospheric phantoms.

O, praise be rain, praise be mist
praise be fish deep and dark,
praise be stirring ocean
and starting wind,
and kinematic waves
in altered motion.

Rain before life, rain before
       death
Praise be rain again, rain again praise!

BAD THOUGHTS
July 15, 1986

On the sleeves of the dark dropped
on our innocent heads is murder,
rape and casual insanity.
But don't look now or it passes
like a wind tied to trees,
where gods of sacrifice knife maidens,
country leaders deny genocide,
or religocide in the dark corners
of golden temples to their one and only god.

Hypocrisy lives well with riches
and the night lives within us
in the grinding sacrificial wheels of destroy.
Cars and planes, electronics
and computers develop dying intelligence
in the twilight disguised as dawn while

squirming through the hole in the wall
is a roach that remembers earth.

I work in a dreamscape of reality. Everything seems to shut down for a split second. The language the feeling seems to exist on that edge of shutdown when suddenly all opens up. It's a tremendous relief. One doesn't worry about success or failure, only the motion of the gods feeding the words, and that freedom, that freedom.

CHARACTERS
July 23, 1986

The woman said, "I saw the royal wedding
this morning." "Yeah, how did she look?"

"Oh her dress was beautiful, gorgeous," said
the woman in her summer knit sweater

and golden blond dried baked hair
and pocketbook of by-gone years

on her way to the factory

to pack some equipment
or sweaters, blouses or socks,

the lady with gossamer hair
and make-up like a web across the face,

an american commoner
and her maids in waiting,

waiting for the passing day

to see again the royal wedding
in the evening summer sunset.

The men, women, in the bars and pubs of eternity
are glimpsing the royal faces

as common as theirs, as noble as theirs,
scars of the heart hidden.

Someone said, "Queen Mother Mary,"

and another said, "Hail Holy Queen
Mother of Mercy."

Our life is hidden in the armies
and lives of our ancestors

riding walking fainting through northern forests
toward a stellar of eternity

hidden in meaning but common in symbol

for an unknown future

bodily lazily settling

to die in some foreign cave
and to emerge in some future unknown eternity.

God bless us all
God bless the Queen
God bless the people dirty and clean
God bless the energy   God bless the trance
God bless the everyday
with no fuss or circumstance.

COME CLEAN

August 1, 1986

Everything upsets me,
sick people suffering,
friends leaving, friends parting.
Even having to tell you this,
having to admit that
I am burning out like the edges
of lava. But I think it is related
to you as I try to understand,
because I am not brilliant
like a nuclear formula.
But I think it is related to you
and only music seems to breathe,
only insects seem to speak.
I do not want to be a fool
who struggles within my own breast forever.

Now the sun is coming out
and the sting within my breast crawling away,
troubled, spiked with insanity

Everything is sighing, even
the trees without the wind that you possess.

COMPLAINT

August 27, 1986

Have no social complaints
have no god complaints
was born a beggar
live a beggar.
I have no complaints.
Have no complaints to the moon,
none to the stars,
none to the astrology of the mind,

none to the liars of religious words,
or to the doom prophets
on the edges of truth.
Have no complaints.

Not to the rich, not to the poor,
not to the powerful, not to
the weak. I only ask for a little grace,
a tear here and there
shed for the brotherhood of man and woman,
not for me.
I have no complaints.

SOMEONE
August 28, 1986

In a dream
someone showed me
   a poem, short
and dynamic! I can't
                  remember
   how it went
but it cleaned me.

STILL LIFE
August 31, 1986

O hydrant, how strange it is
to be mortal flesh and blood
and die off, and be born
and be more moveable than a tree
be gravity fed like all creatures
and sun fed

when at any moment
a volcano erupts poison gas,
an earth movement swallows itself
while cicadas rub sound off
in the sunny stillness,

and fool the continuity of love.

MORNING
September 3, 1986

In one swoop
birds fly off together,
an estimated 120.
Regular little birds
not hawks or eagles
soaring alone above a valley
majestically gliding out
in a horizontal loop
as if on a tether.
The busy flock is empty
like evangelical words
promising the earth's people
that suffering is abolishable
on television's mouth.
In one moment they will be gone
on facades, in trees,
then swoop down fast again
like human destiny
in the peace of a bitter world.

The best time is when the body
below the navel
    is reflexed
and the mechanism of incomprehensibility
rules the soul.

Then, deep and dark thoughts,
sacred feelings beyond the stars
meet in the alchemical brew,

to stir you up and steer you up
the river of a new day.

Song birds
  enter the morning
the pre-dawn
  before the fires,
you know,
  when the night
    floats away
like vapors
  on a lake
or like kisses
  in the woods.
Songs that even nightingales
  didn't know
or even the gods learned
  for their created.
Continuous,
  threaded,
like a cherry pit
  stuck
   in the heart

NUCLEAR DISASTER

September 16, 1986

O fly, disgusting beautiful fly
do you know that the late
September sun through the window
is fooling you,
because the cold wind last night
swept down the eastern seaboard
and froze creatures on the wing.

O fly, it was a surprise,
like an eruption surprises.
Now the morning is calm
I am sweating, the sky is blue
and the proposed existence shuns
revelations that well up
in that space
between the navel and penis.

O dirty fly rubbing your hands
before my hands
catching a sunbeam in your eyes,
if the Ramapo Fault opened up
and swallowed me,
if the comet collided with the planet,
if the mistakes we make
close our eyes forever
       in multiple suffering,
you will probably still
be here next Spring.

September 17, 1986

Does loneliness take over the body
at the time when you are eating out
and after you finish

you realize you are alone
and free, does loneliness
take over freedom?

If a wounded man
comes up to you
his leg torn apart
into and out of your heart
does escape take over?
Do angels take the flesh?
Does anger turn you trembling?

If you be sleeping
on the immense plains,
animals passing you in the night,
lions panting on your chest,
would the land still be beautiful,
soft grasses, rocks and trees,
sands and waters,
creatures fighting and eating,
wet forests, dry deserts,
cities' enclaves, caves,
lovers embracing touching,
comrades of the earth
doing battle in the fields.

Will the earth still be beautiful?
Does loneliness take over the body?

WORLD WAR II
September 23, 1986

Gawayn spread the wager sword
across the land, east, while continents away
in rising-sun-land war spread
thunder of cruelty,
left-hand-sword-holder, Takamoto,

cut freely the head from body of
Island's people, big toe touching ground
hanging by wretched hands
from trees, trees of gum
            with giant leaves.

Back in Europa's lap
Teuton the fires stoked
with coal and gas technology,
base cruelties with obscene rationale,
all deadened feelings, clouded souls,
all clenched bodies
flying through the night
toward Wotan's thunderous eye.

In forest glenn to glenn
to Nippon's tides and rips
brave soldiers, all, of shakened
sexuality and dire smiles
think of beloveds waiting home
in heroic guise,
fooling the mastery of
            hypnotic delusion.

Meanwhile, like other side of shadow
stalk the innocent
phantasmagoria of flesh,
soul mixed with soul of dragon,
gaping hole of childhood,
eyes of hunger vaster and vaster
to the deep repetition of torture
'til pain becomes like light.

In Takamoto's dreams unveiled
the smiles of kamikaze
a wind of ancient salvation
to give a name to suicide.
While Teuton's dreams elevate

with smell of gas and cyanide
the cross of ancient loneliness
into the communion of death.

In dreaming Gawayn's dream
from which awakened living cells
and haunts of his mortality
that all is good, all is bad
continued rains of blood
the march of god's triumphant
patriotism, hypocrisy and bomb. Gawayn
stabbed his own side for love
and bestuck the eyes of greed.

Teuton's blood bloodied tundra grass
far away to bodies blown upon sands and rocks.
Away from home, alone
like nightingale's throaty sounds,
all soldiers cruel and kind
to death or home return.

Gawayn closes eyes again
and dreams the dream
to end all dreaming.
From womb that no one can return,
the light, the moon, the stars
moved further out, moved
further in, in cyclatory creeps,
but Gawayn's eyes do not close. He
enters deep awake
where light and suffering
joy and pain converge like
living cells in all our blood.

Route 3 and lonely
cloudless sky except for
virgin clouds like irregular cocoons,
but in the distant east
an army of wormy clouds
white caterpillars
strung together southward

River's quiet million ripples
generated by north wind

O rivers oceans spurning
O oceans joining oceans
O spark of living motion
in holy ecstasy
Set us free, set us free
like rivers to the sea

MASS
October 5, 1986

A body here covered with
   coal dust (vomited charcoal)
as if a mine cave-in
covered his wretched body,
hands tied to stretcher
to resist that drugged brain
with protuberant forehead bandaged
that wants to carry
the wretched body home
or into the street again.
But his fear and will to get out
and into the world again
in sickness or in health
is greater than the bonds.
No beauty, no pain.

Across is a moaning young man
who hasn't been able to urinate.
A kidney stone, they said.
Suddenly a painful groan
and in his bed
let loose a yellow flow
in exotic release:
poor soul apologized
but made clear
that no control was near,
when it came it came.
Pray that no blood was
in the urine. No specimen.
No beauty, no pain.

No wheelchairs, no help to limpers,
a broken knee that shows no break.
Another with a swollen leg
    dragging behind
No wheelchair, no help
No beauty, no pain.

The signal buzzes
a stretcher pushed in fast
two hands held on the chest
pushed down hard. The pain
The pump of pumps doth stop,
the pump of pumps doth start.
Hail Mary, Hail Nature
Hail Body, Hail Soul
hail master, hail servant
Hail Life, Hail Death
hail tears, hail strength,
No beauty, no pain.

DISCOVERY

October 13, 1986

O bloody days!
O Badlands, O Great Plains!
With wilderness bones
America was discovered
many times in ancient days.
Was not really discovered,
man was there already.
Many nations, many peoples,
many bodies walked the corners
of the continent.
This was the world
but even they
knew that earth was bigger.
Badlands to Great Plains
to southern coasts and western coasts
eastern coasts and desert floods
ancient people in animal skins.
We put our hands inside a dead animal
and found it warm and final
O sunspots, O corona
on the edges of desolate explosions.
O bloody days of tribal blood
The smoke is burning our eyes,
The powder scorching our skin,
The arrow contacting a heated organ
O bloody days!

ANGELIC MEDITATION

October 20, 1986

We're only little creatures
in ancient lands alone,
in cities in mesas in
valley, on sand dune, and mountain
in ancient lands alone.

From Badlands to Great Plains
from La Brea to Montauk to Atlantis.
Arrows, spears, knives, guns
on the edges of double expansion,
still desolate, still lonely and bony
with muscles pulling plows,
corn species development
out of the earth of sand and stones.

Volcanoes nourish worms
that never see light
thriving on darkness, nor see
the warmth of that gracious orb
that easily can destroy us all
in one angelic meditation
in ancient lands alone

WEEK DAY

October 22, 1986

One coffee, milk, no sugar
Two little girls
talking up a storm.
Sun up, shadows long.
One coffee milk no sugar

Trees, rust and yellow.
School days in the galley.
Sails at mast ready to fill,
the ship tilting through reddish trees
One coffee milk no sugar

Money makers hiding trouble
Leaders of countries in a quandary
Spirits' salvation on a tube
Mystical kisses on the navel
One coffee milk no sugar
One coffee milk
                   no sugar

HAND GUN
October 24, 1986

When I was a child
I thought a handgun in a holster
and the lead colored bullets on the belt
was one of the most beautiful things
made by man.
Of course at that time
I didn't consciously know
of the phallic significance or symbol,
but it doesn't really matter.
It's not the object now
but the feeling that accompanied,
which still remains and comes back,
but not for guns and bullets
but for eternity.
It must be the way Sumerians
felt for their Gilgamesh
and Jews for David
and Egyptians for Pharaoh
and anyone for heroes,
a hope of eternity

forever and ever new.
A chance not for the object
but for the soul alone,
it that be possible.
But it's too easy
to love life too much
and all is gone away, alas,
like a shot from
the gun of childhood.

When I was a child
I thought of eternity.

October 25, 1986

Between a rock and a hard place
I looked for love
So unlikely, yet I entered
the cave, secret though it was
nestled in the Ramapos
Appalachian chain, there for centuries

leading further and further in,
so unbridled and endless
without sound without sight,
without division, expected angels,
original powers, leading inward scared,
yet between the rocky walls a warmth.

Days upon days I walked
living only on flowers of darkness
until a junction appeared in the dark,
man-made, drilled and a size
through which I just passed.
Through this I could hear
the faint flow of a river overhead.

A man lay dead at the cloudy entrance
as the small opening opened into
an arcade of tile and concrete.
Another man and woman lay squirming
on the wide platform
above a series of tracks.

A stench of urine suffused
with the exotics of burning leaves,
burning tobacco, burning cocaine and marijuana.
Men with pale foreheads, men with dreadlocks
passed by my caution, my fear,
while lamentations broke everywhere.

Along the tile wall others moved hips and shoulders
while radios on the platform
and drums in the distance
vibrated a bass beat like a giant
beating on the walls of a city.
Lamentations rose from the wretched with babies
in their arms, scavenging along tracks.

Hundreds of feet above, through an opening
the cries of a celebration above descended
to the deaf and dying ears
through an area infused with hydrocarbons
in tubes and containers like an industrial grave
of chemicals and strains
of undreamed, unknown viruses.

Above, the crowd roared through the machinery
The glass of buildings shook from vibrations
originating at the beginning of the world,
but where there was violence originating
God seemed to be calling, and the earth
was crazier above than it was beneath.

O greater light infused by darkness
opening up creation and shaking the world!
O luminous rays waiting in dark
as shadows closed on mountains
and dusk appears on swamps!
O hazy light resurrected from dirt!

But can I receive for myself this grace,
being so unworthy and longing
being so incomplete and frightened
by the level of threshold holding pain?
And people were thrown down from above
my soul led my body back to the beginning.

At the entrance back an angel leaned
all bloody from head to ankles,
his left wing broken and hanging,
his right across his red body.
A woman naked in the clouds
held his broken wing to not collapse.

This body had not been there
when I had entered, I came in free,
and now my only thought was how
would I get by those sensitive wings
that could block me out forever
could close on me and rack me.

But as I approached slowly
the woman grasped the angel
in a winged embrace
and it seemed the feathered angelic
whispered something strange
to the beautiful woman embracing.

And I noticed his arms
were full of needle marks and scars
his eyes in dark brown deceived the blueness they were,

his heart beat wildly under the pumping
while she looked pleadingly at me
as if to say "pray for me, give me freedom,"

and he whispered again to the woman in embrace,
"Don't let him pass without the words"
I stood motionless while, at this,
the woman dropped embrace
and the wing flew out against the rock,
a wing like steel bars, locked out the tunnel.

It was then my hairs erected on all parts of my body.
My penis, my stomach, my heart throbbed
without control, I was enslaved.

November 12, 1986

Am I a fool in the temperate sun
of cool November to keep remembering
the solar winds running
away from the universe as I run?

Baby oh! baby oh!
Captured, captured, bad day
fools day, starvation's trembling
Baby oh, baby oh

Am I a fool in the tempered moon
of wolf November in the dry
spirit footprints following as I follow
a light leaving the universe as I leave?

No baby, No! wishful dreams
like a running back streams
out of the innocent world
No baby! No!

Am I a fool to see the new light
of the family, as I look across
at a stranger's child,
as my sons and daughter like solar wind
shimmer behind these eyes mixed with joy.

O Baby oh!
Eternity again, eternity once.
Baby oh baby.

SUBWAY
November 16, 1986

Hail o train people
in the subterranean veins
of rebirth, sainthood and martyrdom.
Why mix these, o train
when all it does is go
from point to point, and we
see this as a transfiguration
of that old saint carried from
station to station through the Umbrian hills,
his stigmata bleeding on our heads
through the subterranean pains of fate.

November 23, 1986

Old world, there are roads in front
of us and sleep and sleep, forever,
for what makes mixing
where average strains and timeless
rains combat the everyday thirst
of the average human body bursting
the warped sun-beam of dusk,
when all we ask is to be free

of strains, too much, or freedom
to have love and give love as
night drops in on the soul,
and the fire inside burns freely
of spirit, and fights forever, the world
for the newer light   and newer dark.

November 26, 1986

Grind away, trumpet, beat away,
drum, snake away, clarinet;
the sad mystical beat of blues
moaned by the woman
the siren of the inlet to the sea
winds up and out in the rain.

Inseminate each drop
in the dance of fingers, to see
on the hands. Each tooth, each eye,
or sound picked up
in the traffic din. Inseminate the moles
that never see light, the creatures
without hair, the insects without sight.
Inseminate the sun,
and the work spaces of earth.
Grind away, saxophone of the forest,
organ of the underworld, oboe of the sea,
horn of the sad bird song
that ties up the lake in dusk,
but that really does nothing
but squeeze the heart-base until dawn.
Grind away, O Dawn

How could the comet be
the subject of your embrace
when following and following
there's a living case
of wartime, and how bodies groveling
in the swampy mudland, the water

lilies and the drunken gloxinia
blissfully rest between birds
of the meadows and far off place
that lead to me, a race
so far back that hiding
their eyes, the comet hurled closer.

Then war on the meadows, comets
in the universe, and the embrace
on the bloody swamp
is what we had and what we have,
electrified like birds sweeping
between the gunfire and the torch.

BREEZE
November 28, 1986

It's gotta be fast
because the houses pass
too quickly for time.
It's gotta be fast
before it gets past.

It's gonna be true,
sun shining, the blue
patches in the upper sky.
It's gonna be the children
that praise all living sense.

It's gotta be the savage truth
It's gonna be a magic root.
It's gotta be the children
that praise all living tense.

TRAFFIC SONNET
November 30, 1986

Traffic ahead, traffic behind,
the arrows of the geese migration
dart in the clouded sky. Slow, migrant
frozen in eternity, the upper skies of methane
nitrogen, hydrogen, oxygenation
as traffic flows across broad plains, wide rivers,
ridge and valleys.

Traffic bad, tunnels packed, bridges loaded,
ahead, behind, air lanes jammed.
Chemical, industry, processing,
the farmers and shepherds glowing,
while frozen eternity of geese in sky,
migration, sensation, everyday eternity,
binds me to your path

December 7, 1986

Under high tension towers,
under power lines
the crackle of vegetation,
gathering of radio waves pounds
the minimum surf of the hills.

Pure misfortune and mis-luck showers
on the old bent bodies and defines
the hardship of people until regurgitation.
I hear inhuman sounds
and the world does what God wills.

But even with the wild flowers
overgrowing the volcanic mines
the soul's runaway child of agitation
breathes deeply in your mouth, resounds,
as the morning light fills.

December 10, 1986

Hardly a lightning flies overhead,
bands together the silver and gold
in your eyes
like a welder's spark. Then
the hydrogen of surf waters
the oxygen of tides
keeps the ocean breathing
in our ears from hill to hill,
like the kiss of a wild eagle
in death. Morning
comes on like the unstoppable,
like the notes of a singer
in a prison, about to be free.

SPIRIT
December 13, 1986

Is America so different, these
whole two continents where bird feathers
adorned our resurrection into unknowns
better slept upon and crept upon
than all the trails of heroes?

The blade still cuts from inside
like loneliness until a spirit
fuses courage to the light, and
the bodies that claim the silt
will become the soil of continents
ready to be washed into the seas
or to be left on sacred million grounds
sucked up by the sun
into the energy of night.

Like a blade that cuts from inside,
is the way people feel loneliness,
but this is not just lonely
not even inside us or outside,
that cuts us free from disaster
just so we can dream.

BLUES
December 16, 1986

Blues is still blues
night is still night
bad news is still bad news
and when you know
you wake up this morning
walking on glass
in sadness when blues
fill in your insides:
Blues is still blues
to drive the moans away.

DER WANDERER

December 23, 1986

Something overtakes me on the train.
Excavate the universe to brotherhood
of humankind. Sing out!
These last pale morns of paradise
break the blood apart.
      What good is it
    where a harmonic chord
calls to a desolate child, hermetic,
and the clatter around me
is chewing up the earth.
      Something overtakes the trip
   and lone mountains with three sailing birds
recall days of wandering and nights awake.

December 27, 1986

My deepness away from you
is as high as a steel boom
out of the airy sky, clouds overtaking,
looming, and as symphonic
as the ocean shelf through
which the giant steel legs penetrate,
fossils, shells, sand, volcanic ash,
and as angular as the collapse
in violent storm toppling
and sucking all with it
into the cold deep waters.

December 29, 1986

What is a year ending?
It's not a time or a space
or a dream or a sexual penetration
that changed the course of cellular growth.
What blossoms there does not
      blossom here, but can
fly on the wind for decades
and come to life with rain.

Political battles still churn.
Worlds still threaten.
Mystery lingers over every breath every atom
Ten centuries from now a man still feels.

December 30, 1986

Overpayment, underpayment, Florida lakes,
Georgia pines, it's cold up north.
The frog in the wind, the searching bird,
in exile, making ends meet,
the storms of freedom challenged.
Robbery, murder, fraud, inequity
in the cellular growth of poverty,
subliminal in the market place of greed.

New payments, old payments
Computer overflow, data overrun,
sexual advances in the moonlight,
overpayment, underpayment.

OBSERVATION
December 31, 1986

> A jet grinds slowly
> toward the airport.
> Wings bent back as if gliding in.
> A blue heron takes off from marshland.
> Mars is almost in conjunction with Venus.
> Jupiter will glide in the heavens.
> A plane will crash, two trains
> will collide. The universe is burning
> in the cold cosmos.

December 31, 1986

> It is cold, it is cloudy,
> seagulls scattered against clouds.
> It is windy down here.
> Today is a day of celebration.
> A sadness pounds into me,
> because my son
> is so far away
> even though the telephone was invented.

1987

January 10, 1987

> Consecrate the birds,
> consecrate the dogs,
> concentrate on love in the bogs and woods.
> Eat the holy tree, eat the holy body.
> Break the sunny rhythm.
> Hard cold facts.

Static in the bosom
Consecrate the food that they don't eat
consecrate the love that they don't feel
Harder colder facts. Hammered in.
Static in the breast.

WINTER SONNET
January 10, 1987

Summertime is in the shimmer
of the road here beneath
the empty shadows
of hinterlands, mountains, ridges,
ring of mountains with moons
overlooking the old village,
brooding on the deaf countenance
of insects in the dirt.

Springtime is in the shelter
of the tree
by which we're embraced
from where the blood dries
from the hanging golden face
in the hours of embrace

HYMN
January 12, 1987

Out of illusions, out of delusions,
under the body, under the baby,
try to detain it, try to refrain it.
Golden farmers in the plains,
northern desert in the veins,
sitting home, flying away,
all illusions make you pay.

A CHILD STORY

January 15, 1987

> From the golden steps of sunlight
> he was lifted into a cave
> and drifted to immortality
> A child like you and I
> like Horus born of undefiled Isis
> like   lain in a cave for our redemption
> in the equinox of mid-winter,
> in the faith of a revived and eternal sun
> in the midst of all the deaths

January 17, 1987

> I saw a red-tailed hawk
> flying inland today. My son
> pointed him out flying around the tree tops
> in our town over the highway
> resting in the branches
> of the highest trees, then disappearing.
>
> O hawk of our inner brain and vision
> powerful as a microbe invading life,
> beautiful as a comet in the night
> subtle as the weak force
> curving the universe left,
>
> painful as the spark that gives us life.

MOTHER & FATHER (SIMPLE)
January 17, 1987

It's a simple trip
from a town in New Jersey
to a borough in New York City
from Sparta to Crete
from Capri to Naples
from Messina to Reggio

It's a simple trip
only birth and death, tears and laughs,
first sex first love
first mistakes, first manhood,
first sports, first studies
pack the luggage of the trip.

It's a simple trip.
Shut down the mind!
get into today and move!
the now, the ever present
eternal moment, or just stop
the hypnotic trances of memory!

It's a simple trip.

HOTLINE FOR YOUTH
January 29, 1987

You're so messed up in the thoughts,
today where fewer than few sparks
lighten up the dark, but
love yourself, my loves, love
yourself. Sing a few sad laments,
don't be afraid, weep, hold yourself up,
as if a crystal were to form the eyeless night.

Talk to you, whisper to you, hold you,
there, sing to me, I sing to you.

As if snow could cleanse,
it is snowing as reckless as it is,
until a little destroyed
we're born each day,
but on everyone's face
is an immense love of life
as if springtime were
waiting in the corner for your lips.

Fall, snow! settle into the earthquakes,
the volcanoes, the tornadoes,
look how our faces . . . . .

SUBWAY WALKMAN
January 31, 1987

Riding, galloping, here to there,
the plane flies through the drafts
as a subway train slides through
like old coach shakes through the towns
on journey after journey.
The piano, the impromptu
     of all nocturnal smells,
of melody powerful and sweet,
unrelenting, now key change
     now mode embrace,
a stab wound in the heart
unravished as a bullet passing train
as a peak of lights disappear
as a subterfuge fades the music.

TODAY'S BENEDICTION

February 2, 1987

I'm really sad because I've done nothing right,
or I should ask, what do I mean,
nothing right? Sometimes trying
is trying and lying is the word, but
like that bird taking a snow bath
I'm not daunted. So, I went overboard.
Is not showing love and attention sometimes
that big a mistake? Yes! I guess it is.
You must dwell on sins
until the nitrogen forms in the brain
and the bends overtake you,
and you ascend from the deep
in resurrection plain and simple
to find yourself afloat in benediction.

February 3, 1987

It's the quiet that we
suck out of the noise.
The morning carries Carbon 14
a relative waste jackknifed
in the middle of the universe.
O brook, o river, o baptism,
falling in the hands of moneyseekers.
It's the hermit that we must feel
in the multitudes. O woods
O forests, o river!
It's the quiet to extract
  from the wind.

Tundra and deer, liberty and fear
Sunshine is blinding.
Stopping at a shrine way atop mountain.
Snow has fallen, feet swollen, soul
a'floating in the sky.
Don't know why, don't know why.

SEARCH
February 5, 1987

It's the eye looking at the self
in the wind looking at the eye
that the young man
really tries to carry with him.
The universe and the fly
both looking in your cells
with music like a raptor
plunging down   a sun ray,
rising again   without the prey.

BIRD
February 6, 1987

Awaken, body! free of spirits, suffering,
and other things.
Through the windows the western light
grey and white,
like a locust-storm just clearing,
bites the eyes gently,
from where no sound starts
and no sound ends,
awakens the body, begins!

SUN

February 10, 1987

> A garbage truck across the road
> turns into the traffic, the avenue
> a burst of solar   blindness.
> It is the birthday   of the universe.

NOTES ON THE 20TH CENTURY SCIENTIST

February 10, 1987

> How dumb for scientists
> to say the atomic explosion
> was 20 times brighter than the sun,
> forgetting what distance does
> to brightness. What explosion
> can be understood
> in the heat of the sun
> or any dim remote star?
>
> A garbage collector knows more
> about the universe and change
> than the formularized brain
> of the physicist, taut and narrow
> bent on a religious type destruction
> that is a biblical deific model of fate.
>
> God help us

February 13, 1987

> "Crazy nut," the girls said. They're
> excited about a horror movie that frightened
> them last night. Girls, chubby
> and sweet, still unaware of most dangers,

in their catholic dress with
their sonic breasts resounding.
See that man reading the newspaper
held one inch from his eyes?
He's almost blind, his eyes like vapor
on a hot night liquefy the words,
but he still stares the holy,
the holy information of every day. In the garden
is the holy desert
where the dreamer weaves melodies
through the wind. Crazy wind of sanity.

SUBLIMATION
February 18, 1987

Held, hold, holding without
which my love is gone.
Meld, molt, melting in
your arms without a trace.
Felt, fold, fooling as
the morning takes my place,
like snows to vapors gone.

UNSEEN SONNET
February 22, 1987

A squirrel jumps a tree
from one branch to the other
upside down hanging on,
flipping up: the sun is shining.
Speckled birds rise up in pairs
searching ground in patches of snow,
one branch to the other.

I think of my mistakes
and travel along the wires
of my heart, strings that carry
information, electrification, vibration

to the power base of the soul.

A YOUNG COUPLE
February 23, 1987

A wet and heavy weight, like snow
presses on me when I think
of the people of an easeful world.
That young couple, so much in love,
yawning like tulips in sun.
What are we doing?

The silence is like free weights
resting on me, immense flow
running through the holy system,
heavenly eyes, heavenly skin
that stirs the pain away.

February 24, 1987

Morning breaks
the vigil of the night.
The two centurions
weapons hanging
over their shoulders
drop their steps forward
like a tired embrace.

Samson and Delilah
stir in the shadows.
Tristan and Iseult sigh
the second sleep.
Morning breaks
no rooster crows
no star compares with birth.

OK
February 24, 1987

What comes, comes for you
to make it different. It's OK
to dream, okay for you
in blind faith and deaf hope
to keep your body up straight,
and your mind
        like a paleolithic's vision
uses its own electricity
of the nerves and soul.
It's OK to have purity
even if it's only
for a second or two.
It's OK to dream. OK to love

CAT OF ETERNITY
February 25, 1987

About 2 feet from the curb, in the street
a cat was crouched. From afar I thought
it was sniffing, but as I got closer
I knew. It was looking down at the ground,
looking at eternity, breathing,
its head down like a disappointment.
It was only a cat,

dirty, black and white, solid
as a wooden beam, not underfed.
Cars swerving left. I picked it up,
this lump of breath.
What is the noble truth of death? Blindness
turned inward to endless seas
as the struggle ebbs far away.

MEDITATION

March 4, 1987

As if bitten by a snake
I sit here while the news spews
forth a venomous distaste pervading air.
All misfortunes dangers hazards of this
20th century betrayed, horrors of fate.
Big nations, small nations, bitter viperous
    people with centuries old apocalyptics,
fooling with the brink of frail humanity.
The same people kissing freedom
embrace injustice and fear.
Ah! the snake
is too innocent here.
Feel the way through dark,
and tears. Don't touch the slime
on the walls of phony faith.

March 9, 1987

The multitudes betray the fallen city. The glass
of night, the lights irridescent
of some distended disease, effervescent
in the locked body of humanity.
Sometimes the soul like lethal gas
is lost in the streets, enters a sewer

into evil buildings of
architects of destruction.
With corruption
big hands take from little:
the day of tumescence is here.

IRISH ENTRY
March 17, 1987

All bark, no whiskey. The Irish
fill streets with jigs and songs
of ancient rhyme. No matter,
all passes, all sinks
to happiness in the root. Fallen
scenes of flying birds. Heavy
heartbeats on a Spring day carried over
from Canadian lakes to Cambrian hills.

O to be free in the fields again,
to wander aimlessly from begin
to end, to sing up something new.
O to be free in the hills right now,
and feel the snake upon thy brow
be driven from the
colors of its beautiful skin.

A CALL
March 18, 1987

"Things will change, I'll see you later
You can handle it, take my word"
A mother's cry on the phone,
"I'll see you later," a mother's call to son,
"You'll see, things will change,"
overheard love on a telephone,

"have a nice day, don't worry."
Dressed, puffing away, short hair.
Sorrow in the work force, worry
from the feet to the teeth.
"God bless the child," sang Billie Holiday,
gods help the child! to look out
and see the blue sky and seagulls circling
in the wind, gods help the child
in hidden rooms with dark imaginings
O angels drop in, ignite spirits!
keep company until the trance disintegrates.

March 24, 1987

Slowly my love,
the day is just beginning.
Strongly my children,
the arms are just entwining.

Quietly my brothers,
the bombs are just exploding.
Softly my sisters,
the earth is just eroding.

Slowly my sweat,
the sun is only dripping.
Coldly my dream,
the light is just beginning.

AN OLD TESTAMENT
March 24, 1987

Need time to fill the mind as oceans fill
with all the shit and flotsam
of the age. Sly rats on television

think they report the truth,
evangelists scaring the feces
out of human perpetual sinners.
With tears in our eyes
retelling a tragic bitterness
turned sweet by the power
of self hypnosis sparked by them
through the fictitious words attributed
to you know who. The blasphemers
of the unknowable universe,
fake, that they through the lie
have the way to eternal truth.
Need time to empty my mind
of people who can't take a joke.

RAIN DRIVEN
March 31, 1987

O one of little turmoil
along the boulevard of beauty,
in the cavern of felicity.
Help as the rain drips
before this cavernous entrance,
and the dark edges away
into the mist of morning
where the quiet and lonely
melt away as the glow of fires
casts new shadows upon the rockface.
After we have eaten
the rain beats down the leaves
and the dark moves further
from the flesh's soft body . . . . .
Before the hunt begins.

KOYAANISQATSI
April 8, 1987

A dog walks the master
among the big trees of the little city,
a dog walks his master in sun.
The trot of the wolf
walks inside the dog. Happiness
lights its eyes aslant with anxiety.

A building collapses while
an explosion blows the night
apart. A master takes a slave,
a monk converts an Inca
in the breathless night of America.
Scientific language breaks apart

in the saliva of the mouth.

TO A DOGWOOD TREE
April 29, 1987

A dogwood tree
with beautiful buds spaced and
formed as no other tree,
its blossoms spread out
like a northeast woodland forest.
Not like a canopy of overhead flowering
but like a meadow in the sky.
O dogwood   O beautiful eyes.
Rain hits sand,
rocks shoot from volcanoes
ghosts of burning deserts
steam the earth of dusty sorrow.
O dogwood tree, blossoms and branches,
even an embrace would do

that we might borrow.
O dogwood   O beautiful eyes,
that we might borrow.

BEGINNER METHOD

May 4, 1987

Stand with feet apart
Hold the bat up and back
Hips level, knees bent
Keep eyes level, head straight
Watch ball, keep eyes on ball.

Concentrate
Weight slightly shifted to back leg
Keep eyes on ball
Snap or swing bat at ball
with level, slightly upward motion
holding onto bat with both hands
shifting weight slightly forward.
Follow swing through,
holding onto bat with both hands.
When ball is hit at split second
let the body do what feels right for you.

May 18, 1987

The morning is warm. A fan whirling
the air. The calm force of tiredness
shows in everyone's body
chewing, languidly talking.
What chemicals have we forgotten?

The air blows cold
down the northern corridor
the ink freezes in my fingers
no electronics can soothe love.
What chemicals have we forgotten?

KIN PAIN
June 18, 1987

Walk quietly into the confusion,
all murky and acid.
Ascend lovingly into the marshes
until you breathe no more.
Walk quietly into the fusion
of love and kindred pain.

SPARK
July 15, 1987

The bus is screaming on. It is early,
before the grass dries. The birds have
taken their first rest.
They were mad awhile ago.
No one is going to work yet
except the darkies along the rivers
of industry. The cotton is rotting on the vine,
the bus is streaming through the air
like Hermes to Odysseus. O wings,
O breeze, O never changing, O, always,
O vegetation of the night,
and quiet visits of mutation
that spark the fire, baby spark,
that starts the flare-up of light.

July 27, 1987

Dark inside me every day
I am nothing to be
or see, or hear, compared
to what I am not here.
Because what I am, I am not,
and what I am not   I disappear
like light through dark:
Dark inside me every day.

July 28, 1987

Take away the hours of creation,
everything is stinking of elation.
Take away my blood
and my hands   and my heart
make me eat the dark of your negation.
Take away the space from all expansion
Take my eyes and nose and ears
I'll still feel it all:
The shrug of salvation,
on the shoulders of youth

August 5, 1987

Tunnels are closed.
No one can go anywhere.
A tiredness breaks over our heads.
The Hudson is flowing full
while hookers are stepping fast
to the river, to the sea,
hookers are shining slippery
in the dreamscape of City

O holy mass, o holy waters
O holy woman, man, and rain,
the tunnels are closed,
there is no way to freedom,
no one can go   no one can stay

PERPETUAL
September 16, 1987

Tank cleaning, Getty, sandwiches to go,
Ice cream, cold drinks
Oak trees in a row, school bus,
94¢ 3 eggs, toast and home's
keys and cars, ties and shirts, skirts
and sweaters. Food luncheonette,
windows, sulfates
of your tears exchanged
in an empty lot of sorrow, a lucky bet,
hardware and lumber, orders to takeout,
behind the face morning creeps,
keep right, no turn, one way
the blue jay, the blue sky,
the beautiful oily of the crow,
keep right, no turn   one way, just go.

October 26, 1987

Somewhere between a missile
and a charging rhinoceros
the heart breaks open the dark nest
of the city.   Heart for heart,
word for word, the crescent moon
of October 26, 1987, lights the steel work
of the icy bridge as
it opens to receive the wounds
of pandemonium and fever.

But youth still rolls on
thinking of love and kisses
and icy sheets made warm,
still sauntering wildly to nowhere,
where sighs and whispers
blow apart loneliness and sorrow
in the great suffering that melts away.

October–November 1987

Million dreams, billion nights,
    trillion souls that
    hide in the eyes

November 3 & 11, 1987

My arms are heavy and I feel
the trucks passing at speeds
that vibrate my head as if I were
in a tank hit by artillery.
My dreams are heavy tonight and a fear
grips me like drowning
in a coastal storm.
An internal loss, an imbalance,
    but I still love you

Going from stability to fractured dreams
as though living were without a body.
The heaviness is a specter in the chest,
a difficult breath in a smoky fire,
    but I still love you

A storm is coming. Then tonight another.
To oversleep. To knock on the door
To wear gloves in this cold.

All night long   all night long
A fly still walks the table, and ice melts.
A storm is coming. The body perspires.
    But I still love you.

November 24, 1987

Too many times there is
solar warnings in the kiss.
Already taken is the land,
ocean, shore, that whole band
fighting the tides that lift the sand.
Too many times there is no kiss.

November 25, 1987

Resurrect, reserve, resound. Winter ice
is always there. Striations, scratched
down the mountain faces, winds
like torches of burning oil, acetylene
frozen deep in the woods.

DECEMBER

December 1, 1987

The trees have no more leaves
except the pin oak, still hanging on
except the evergreens, pines, spruce,
green as shadows behind
the pin oak's brown dead leaves.

Thank the gods for life
within the sleep or wake of breath.
When jungles disappear
and oxygen becomes the fight
all people grope for light.

When angels despair,
eyes close like concrete
and the world starts to secrete,
then thank the gods for fire
that warms and destroys

Then thank the gods, thank the gods for love.

STARVATION
December 6, 1987

For the new crusaders tired and dusty
from the trek across the Dardanelles
felt diseased and lost
abandoned and tricked
by the Holy of the Empire.
Empire upon empire
death upon death
Lord upon Lord
the holy children wept.
While an ailanthus tree crushes
its way between 2 close buildings
the space between an alley and a dream.
Saints martyred
find their way through dead forests
Holy bridges span the straits
bound for the change
and the chance to begin another life.
A drunken crusader, lost

for the past years,
abandoned his children, his woman,
winds along the street
looking for wine, the harvest
and the abandoned salvation.
The taxes in the land
drive him further away, no sword
no word, no control while wine fills veins.
He must get off and sleep.

The garbage of the city speaks,
"You are all eternal"
The answer comes,
"We are all abandoned
we are abandoned eternal."
Charge the sudden dream with breath
The armor tears down
the muscles of the lofty body
now worn and skeletal, starved
of food, love, and the home.
Cruelty, plots, destruction of innocent souls
and the body of the city weeps.
The seasons end.
We must get off and sleep.

Sleep forever in a divine swoon
that ends the hope of gods. Thin
in the dirt of the deserts, death
like a kiss upon the abdomen.
Suffering takes place in gold
as well as excrement,
and so the journey ends
and poison begins its hold
on limpid flesh, the rattles shake
ugliness chortles in joy
The song of death perspires in
the Warsaw of the eyes.
Good tidings good food good holyday, goodbye.

The boat that leaves Golgotha
is in the Charon of dreams.
They must get off and sleep

Hidden underground in a frame
    of relics and love.
Come on down, come on deep.
    The pigeon, the dove, the owl
cross over a boulder in the mud.
    O carrion, o carrion
thy gentle swollen tune
    just promise me and promise me
the world in total ruin

The streets were empty as ice
young and old wailing:
pleasure never goes too far.
Treasures in heaven or hell.
The cities fade, the meadows reek
    O carrion, o carrion
thy gentle swollen sight
just promise me, and promise me
the world in total light

1988

All the stars will be gone,
there is enough emptiness in space
to absorb all dust of stars,
while you and I speak under voice
of birth, sleep, mist
in the hour of the street.

Nobody is loitering, O sensual eyes
just see or connect the dreamers
and as our generation's blood spills,
the water of night is flooding us.
Nobody's holding anybody's wrist
nobody's humming nobody's singing
in the hour of the street.

IRISH ENTRY
February 4, 1988

Looking at the crow on roof
now on top the wire
wet soaked in January heavy rain,
heavy traffic at crossroad
soaked with desire
in a cottage by an Ireland lake.
Three crows together
in the thunderous rain,
a cat's wide head, swaying,
soaking in rainfall,
in a cottage by a lake in Ireland.
Two crows, one picking its feet,
the other eating something big.
One crow in the integration of cries
by a lake in Ireland in a cottage in the rain,
by a lake, in a loch
in a moment locked up,
mindless, faceless, bottomed out
without motion, speed, or sound
in the bottom of the lake of
grief and dreams splintered
by the rising sun

March 7, 1988

Swamps and people live in a lake
risen from a volcano
An island bolted from fire
appears out of the sea like
A memory appearing in the shadow
of dark yearnings.
Who can appear to me?

March 17, 1988

Turn the screw, bang the nail,
grind the stone,
in absolute fragmentation.
There's making a poem
there's poverty—
There's holding in your arms
something you love,
there's childhood
that comes jumping at you
like a bird's syntactical song
on the first Spring morning

March 29, 1988

8:27, have a language, that bundles
against the cold wind
against a hungry trestle
vibrating the stormy mind
of loneliness nestled
in tomorrow's prisons
of substances, visions
muddied in substantial poverty.

When you can choke off the under-
development of love
the wonder of settlement
in the dust and sand
the Egypt of loneliness
and the kiss of everything,
then you'll believe
the spear that burns the heart
the volcano in the bowels
the poverty in the street
where love chokes you back

A man listens to music next to me, and
a woman next to him listens
to music, and a woman reads next to her.
Two men talk, one a white boy
the other a black white bearded man
describing the stops along the
tracks. Sweet descriptions and voices
of holy mankind, holy rites
along the route to Troy.

But where is the warrior and where
is the guide, O Hermes
in the drafty Spring moonlight
where wind shakes apart tears
that soldiers keep to themselves
even in the music of the trees that set
them free along the holy ring of stars
in the destruction of the world

March 1988

Happy heart that sows the breeze
with seeds & pollen gods freeze
to keep motivation
for love's regeneration
What I mean is that every
particle of life is a reverie
a dream where death takes over

March 1988

Song birds enter the morning
the pre-dawn before the fires
you know, when the night
                    floats away
like vapor on a lake,
or like kisses in the woods.

Songs that even God didn't know,
or even the gods learned
                    from their created.
Continuous, threaded, like a
            cherry was stuck in
the throat

March 1988

When I think of all these fuckin' hours
lost in weeping over nothing
and of my own broken wings
that screw up my soul
to the septic rhythms in the head.
How could I be tough to turn down

my own humility
and not to follow, say, Pushkin to
   his death?

O what a rotten fuck
to not have the seasons or heaven
or errors of unknown elements
breathing down my neck
and being thankful for that.
No one sees me. I am just here,
my foot a decoy for compassion
my sympathies and despairs for
   another generation to find.
And if in the dichotomy of a
     missing world

a cough awakes the night
you'll find I'm not asleep

March 1988

When a spirit comes to me
  and frightens
and the weight on my chest
  turns butterflies into desert lands
and rivers flow through
     arms to heart
shepherds and farmers sit to drink
my isolated soul,
but not because I'm away
from you or may never see again
  the drunken night
    or shaking star's illusion
  that distance is not time
  and time not space
  but the spirit comes to me

INDEXES

Index of Titles

1984, 425

Above Clouds Above, 397
After Image, 332
After the Rain, 141
Alive, 410
All at Once, 453
Alone Swollen, 225
Amor & Psyche, 475
Amphibian, The, 379
Angelic Meditation, 503
Another World, 226
Apocalypse, 238
Apollo in the Night, 299
Apology, 232
Apology, 353
April Already, 344
Asia, 361
Assimilation (in the Streets of This City), 345
Aurora, 356
Autumn Break, 166
Autumn Torches, 414
Autumn-Time, Wind and the Planet Pluto, 129
Awareness, 238

Bad Ass, 235
Bad Thoughts, 489
Barbaric, 263
Basic Heart, 254
Before It Is Destroyed, 154
Beginner Method, 533
Beyond Phony, 241
Bird, 523
Birth Day, 226
Birth in the Dunes, 317
Bloodsucker, 229
Blues, 514
BMX, 444
Body Jet, 337
Body of Earth, 270
Body Weight, 311
Book of Wild Flowers, The, 138
Both Close by Me, Both, 162
Breeze, 511
Bright Sun, 259
Broken, 236

Brook, 328
Builders (Large Moon Rise), 382
But, 252

Call, A, 529
Can't Sleep, 314
Car, The, 240
Cardinal Conjunction, 309
Cat of Eternity, 527
Catskills, The, 263
Caught in the Swamp, 141
Cave Man's Dream, A, 253
Celebration, 10
Century Sonnet, 433
Chains of Mountains, 20
Characters, 490
Child Story, A, 519
City, 391
City Scape, 374
City, The, 458
Cold Night Alone, 289
Come Clean, 492
Comet Returns, The, 466
Complaint, 492
Concealed Wound, 324
Conception, 290
Continuum, 250
Contrast, 17
Cool Breeze, 144
Cooling Galaxy, 273
Courage, 439
Crazy Death, 323
Crazy in the Night, 349
Crescent Moon, 486
Cross Fire, 260
Cuando Amenecer El Sol, 243

Dangerous Journey, 234
Dangers of the Journey to the Happy Land, 135
Darkness Ode, 479
Data, 165
Dawn Hunt, 309
Dead Sea Scrolls, 407
December, 538
Der Wanderer, 515
Descending the Slope, 5

Dinosaurs of Pain, 18
Dirt, 360
Dirty Benediction, 412
Dirty Snow, 330
Disasters, 248
Discovery, 502
Dominica, 368
Don't Break It, 136
Double Blind Concerto (for Epictetus), 374
Doubts, 154
Down, 167
Dragons and Dungeons, 455
Dream Ode, 459
Drunk on the Brain, 265
Drunken Winter, 132
Dusk, 142

Earth, 229
Earth So Beautiful, 367
Earthquake, 293
Elegy, 412
End, 131
End of the World, 248
Escape to Atlantis, 268
Espacio, 340
Experience, 230

Fable, 235
Fault (Penance), 388
Feast of Visions, 5
Fever, 318
Fill and Illumined, 150
Final Dimensions, 331
Fire of Myself, 270
First Snow, 468
Fits of Dawn, 39
Flight, 252
Floating Gardens, 6
Floods, 156
Fly, 171
Football, 166
Footing, 249
Forecast, 445
Forest Dreams, 369
Forest Wetness, The, 251
Forgive, 390
Freedom, 233
Freedom, 434
Frozen Lookout, 18
Full Bloom, 322
Funny Day, 128

Futura, 237
Future Landscape, 247

Generations of Clouds, 272
Geological Hymn, 262
Ghost of Spring, 256
Glass and Steel Structures, 325
Gods in Me, The, 246
Good Friday, 315
Grand Jury, 393
Gravity Awakening, 319
Great Plains, 306
Green Lake Is Awake, The, 172
Grow, 170
Guitar Ode, 375

Hand Gun, 504
Happiness in the Trees, 137
Hard Energy, 242
Hard or Soft, 239
Haunting Ghosts, 340
Heart Feels the Water, 142
Hermit Gambler, 409
Hidden Bird, 450
Hills, 287
His Universe Eyes, 12
Ho Ho Ho Caribou, 145
Holy, 347
Hospital, 434
Hotel, 231
Hotline for Youth, 520
Hungry, 429
Hunting, 245
Hymn, 468, 518
Hymn to Earth, 312
Hymn to Rain, 488

I Like to Collapse, 167
If I Can't, 250
If You Loved Me, 427
Ignition of Dawn, 311
Ignorance (Strong), 446
Illuminant before Dawn, 295
Imaginary Styx, 247
In Full View of Sappho, 22
In My Crib, 135
In the Desert, 124
In the Grass, 145
Incantation, 436
Indian Song, 394
Indian Suffering, 126

Infinite Thunder, 256
Inland, 295
Inside, 241
Inside Story, 267
Instantaneous Takes Time, 291
Interior of the Poem, 215
Internal Rays, 237
Invisible Autumn, 9
Irish Entry, 529
Irish Entry, 542
Is It Impossible to Know Where the Impulse
    Has Originated? 132
It Is Morning, 141
It's Only Glue, 380

Jet Resurrection, 395
Job, 240
Just at the Beginning of Summer, 341

Kin Pain, 534
Koyaanisqatsi, 532
Kyrie Eleison, 313

Lament #1 for Poland, 357
Lament #2 for Lebanon, 360
Lament #3 for Bayreuth, 389
Lament #4 for Ethiopia, 422
Lament #5 for Lebanon and Israel, 450
Last Song, A, 261
Late Birds, 296
Layout, 236
Legacy (Going Back), 398
Lethal Sonnet, 451
Libera Me, 415
Life of Freedom, 3
Life Sentence, 454
Lighthouse, 142
Lighting Up, 240
Lights of Childhood, 8
Linear Ballad, 377
Litanical, 466
Live Today, 227
Lonely in the Park, 166
Long Sonnet, 372
Longer Trip, 308
Lost Words, 3
Love Eyes, 338
Love Song, 427
Lyric, 473

Macro, 238
Mad Angels, 457

Manure, 253
Marginal Existence, 249
Marketeers Entwined, 464
Mass, 500
May, 143
Mayhem, 349
Meadowlands, 319
Meditation, 528
Melody for Food, 471
Metaphorical Desert, 9
Mid Ocean, 472
Middle of Winter (off the Hudson), 362
Migratory Noon, 17
Milky Ways, 290
Millenium Dust, 328
Mistake, 232
Mixture, 236
Modern Sorrows, 481
Montauk, 329
Mood, 317
Morning, 494
Morning Insults, 289
Morning Touched, 472
Morning Vespers, 440
Mother & Father (Simple), 520
Mother Land, 396
Motion, 243
Mountains, 172
Muscles of Animals, The, 467

Narrative Night, 447
Negative Mountain Peak, 255
New Realism, 314
New World, The, 326
New Year, 469
Night Birds, 307
Night Flash, 386
Night Ride, 346
Night Strokes, 443
Night Wander, 288
No Help, 233
No More People, 327
Noise Outside, 150
Non-spatial, 251
Not a Baby, 133
Not Afraid of the Dark, 271
Not One, 235
Not Really Punishment, 322
Note from St. Francis, 24
Notes on the 20th Century Scientist, 524
Nothing, 155

Notoriety—Academy Awards, 441
Now, 483
Nuclear Disaster, 496
Nude Madness, 322

O Heart Uncovered, 11
O Moon, 225
Observation, 517
Ocean, 144
Ocean Body, 325
Ode, 458
Ode Song, 456
OK, 527
Old Friend Hung, 246
Old Testament, An, 530
One, 457
Orchard, 169
Over Music, 370

Pages of Storms, 429
Pain Songs, 12
Park Thoughts, 324
Pass Me By, 242
Passion for the Sky, 157
Passivation, 151
Pastoral, 21
People's Republic, 462
Perched, 228
Perpetual, 536
Perpetual Life, 298
Piece of Glass, A, 423
Planet Sonnet, 389
Plant Is Growing, The, 130
Polar Flower, 168
Portrait Painter Realistic, 476
Positive Disintegration, 356
Pre-Christian, 406
Pregnant, I Come, 161
Projection, 292
Promontory, 228
Pumping Iron, 437

Question Haunting, 226

Railway Box (Deo Te Salve), 335
Railway Stop, A, 306
Rain & Wolves Inhabit Me, 452
Rain, 123
Rain Driven, 531
Rain Forest Ode, 366
Rampant God, 229

REAL, 463
Reality Printed, 249
Reborn, 237
Red Sun, 149
Reggae Mine, 438
Release, 394
Reprieve, 487
Requiem, 343
Resting, 21
Reversals, 321
Rhythm, 266
Rifle Shot, 474
Rising Sound, 239
Risk, 171
Ritual, 254
River Flooded, 250
Road of Trials, 158
Rocket, The, 273
Romance of Awakening, 8
Rte 3 into N.Y., 341
Runs Me Over, 252

Sacred and Profane, 310
Savage Nocturne, 261
Scope, 342
Sculpture, 157
Sea Level, 109
Search, 523
Serenade No. 1, 401
Shifting Lives, 318
Signals, 352
Silent, 404
Simple Creation I, 406
Simple Creation II, 407
Skies, 132
Sleep in Park, 4
Sleeping by the Rocks, 264
Sleeping One, 244
Someone, 493
Song of Autumn, A, 127
Sonnet, 419, 449
Soul in Migration, 167
Space Out, 231
Spark, 534
Spell of Eternity, 23
Spiral, 262
Spirit, 513
Spirit Matter, 384
Spirit Mercury, The, 265
Spring, 137
Spring Breeze, 244

Spring in This World of Poor Mutts, 163
Spring of Work Storm, 128
Spring Rise, 392
Stampeding Visualizations, 477
Star Song, 293
Starting Up Again, 19
Starvation, 539
Stay, 419
Still Life, 493
Stolen Away, 19
Storm Breaking Over, 286
Story in Winter, A, 130
Street Journal, 431
Street Wise Romantic, 421
Struggling, 170
Stupor, 243
Sub-Scape, 351
Sublimation, 525
Subway, 509
Subway Walkman, 521
Summer Lightning, 297
Sun, 524
Sunburn, 377
Sunset, 361
Supplication, 354
Survival, 269

Tensions, 319
Thanksgiving Day, 420
That's Where It Is!, 292
The Hellgate, 185
This Land, 245
Thoughts, 480
Tidelands, 330
Time on Earth, 291
To a Dogwood Tree, 532
To Open Regions, 320
To Seed, 253
To the Death of a Poet, 371
Today's Benediction, 522
Today's Night, 264
Tones, 385
Tongues, 347
Toxic Wastes, 413
Traffic Sonnet, 512

Transmigration Solo, 21
Travelin' Blue Highway, 461
Tripod, 166
Trouble, 230

Unable to Move, 242
Unemployment, 321
Unfinished, 432
Unfinished Sonnet, 329
Unseen Sonnet, 525

Verses of the Soul Suffering to See God, 364
Vision, 227
Voice on My Birthday, 294
Volcano Tears, 259

War, 403
Warmth, 127
Water: How Weather Feels the Cotton
    Hotels, 25
Waves Apart, 273
Week Day, 503
Wet Sand, 260
What It's Like, 339
When the First Tree Blossoms, 151
White Dwarf, 266
White Fish in Reeds, 123
White Sky, 20
Why God Should Know the Gods, 402
Wild Provoke of the Endurance Sky, 134
Wind Is Blowing West, The, 125
Winds of the Comet, 268
Winds of the Comet, The, 255
Winter, 475
Winter Song, 150
Winter Sonnet, 518
Within, 234
Women, The, 7
Woods, 411
Words from a Young Father (Leaving Body),
    343
World War II, 497
Worse Enemy, 234

Young Couple, A, 526

Index of First Lines

7:53, 36 degrees, 341
8:27, have a language, that bundles, 543
9:01, 440

A body here covered with, 500
A coyote's song, 314
A dog disappears, 127
A dog walks the master, 532
A dogwood tree, 532
A fight with her today, 249
A garbage truck across the road, 524
A guitar plays the light of afternoon, 375
A jet grinds slowly, 517
A jet plane takes off from, 480
A little girl, 402
A man is sleeping, 456
A man listens to music next to me, and, 544
A man off a subway, 380
A man with bloody lips, 345
A novel can't be as strong, 235
A piece of metal, 270
A poem is like a cat sleeping, 454
A police siren passes in the street, 478
A sore of love, 166
A squirrel jumps a tree, 525
A wet and heavy weight, like snow, 526
A wind comes down the station, 404
About 2 feet from the curb, in the street, 527
Again rain on the evolved leaves, 488
Ah shit! 401
All bark, no whiskey. The Irish, 529
All I got left is the car, 240
All I will amount to: knowing, 137
All the stars will be gone, 541
All these future, 227
All this summer fun, 142
All winter the, 385
Allergy of, 74
Alone, more than alone, 236
Alternate side of the street parking, 429
Am I a fool in the temperate sun, 508
Am I supposed to, 231
Angels are falling, 237
Angry dogs, we are angry dogs, 467
Anti-stars far away, 262
April here already! 344
"Are you an eland?" Yes! Yes! 103

As I open the, 254
As if bitten by a snake, 528
As if I had inhaled, 459
As if snow could cleanse, 521
Ask the sun why today, 475
At dawn whatever light, 228
At night when you are off, 264
Autumn is very wild though, 135
Awaken, body! free of spirits, suffering, 523

Back; gone country around, 12
Be uncovered! 134
Before it is destroyed, 154
Before the dusk grows deeper, 142
Being of sound body & sound mind, 187
Being with you, 273
Between a rock and a hard place, 505
Bicycles pass, 243
Big man is no more here, 371
Bird on the chimney, 347
Blue Ocean, 397
Blues is still blues, 514
Bodies bathing in the river, 368
Bread! Get your bread, 464
Break it all down! 229

Calculation mitigation, 466
Calm me! 477
Can we look through, 12
Cars pass me by, 242
Chained to this gang he looks around, 357
Children going to school, 471
Clean Cutting breeze, 244
Close my eyes, 295
Close to you, 291
Closer and closer to the ground, 452
Clouds at 15 knots cutting, 477
Clouds below like spit, 367
Cold and the cranes, 17
Come and go see over there, 162
Come on sit next to me, 346
Consecrate the birds, 517
"Crazy nut," the girls said. They're, 524
Cruelty, love, derangement, 260

Dark inside me every day, 535
Death is a seed, 253

December! end! 293
Dirt on shoes, 360
Do a little job, 386
Do you think, 261
Does loneliness take over the body, 496
Domination in creation, 455
Don't be afraid my light, 481
Down near "The river, 128
Dried up and dogged, 432
Dry leaves, light trees, 460
'Du bist in meinen Blut,' 438

Earth is only scraping, 327
Eros is lying next to us, 412
Everything is out of me, 353
Everything is part of me, 226
Everything upsets me, 492
Existential, Existential, 241
Eyes are swollen, 289
Eyes like god's insects, 244
Eyes without light, 288

Fantasy grips me, 239
Feeding on solitude, 311
Fireworks dot the sky, 352
Fish is swimming near top, 133
Flies are eating, 318
Floating emotions, 404
Foliage on the snow, 361
For complex reasons, 453
For the new crusaders tired and dusty, 539
For want of words, 366
For who can human back? 166
Forgive me, 390
From the golden steps of sunlight, 519
From what lost age are you? 335
Full desolation, full jokes full battle, 486

Gawayn spread the wager sword, 497
Given all the love that's left, 475
God created his image, 150
Grace and lust, lust and grace, 374
Gradually, the wind, 236
Green is the night, 317
Grind away, trumpet, beat away, 510

Hail o train people, 509
Happy heart that sows the breeze, 424, 545
Hardly a lightning flies overhead, 513
Have I been beaten by love, 287
Have no social complaints, 492

He played with a toy they bought, 136
He was in his 70's then, 479
He was walking down a street, 393
Heightened in passion, 407
Held, hold, holding without, 525
Here I am, 240
Here I am, right here, 226
Here I am without you, 272
Here in the grass, 145
Here's a traveler in the womb, 383
Hidden underground in a frame, 541
High is the dark clouds, 141
Hold me, 123
Hold me light, hold me tight, 371
Houses, garages, dogs, people, 374
How can anyone on the steam of light, 427
How can I disconnect, 418
How can I get away from here, kid? 128
How can I give you freedom? 232
How can we destroy earth? 229
How could the comet be, 511
How do people feel, 19
How dumb for scientists, 524
How long has it been, 246
How many sights, 167

I am lost, 143
I am not able to move, 448
I am paralysed, 240
I am so alone on, 291
I am trying to decide to go swimming, 125
I can always go back, 396
I can't live, 245
I can't live blossoming drunk, 138
I can't repeat OM, OM, 313
I climbed to the top of Blackhead Mountain,
    263
I come to you, 161
I don't feel it, 322
I fight and fight, 170, 289
I find myself without a guide, 196
I found out, 308
I have a bad day today, 484
I hear the music from below, 380
I hold her hand held, 264
I kiss your lips, 163
I know, 261
I know the tops of these trees, 394
I lean on my bus, 417
I live, but not inside myself, 364
I love life, I really, 253

I need a cliff I need zero, 5
I open my mouth, 422
I paid you off, 144
I ride home, 150
I salute you, 382
I saw a red-tailed hawk, 519
I see worlds passing by, 252
I sit here, it is 4 AM, 314
I talk to you plainly, 440
I think I'm fished out, 472
I try to lighten myself with, 263
I wake up, 210
I wake up, it's morning, 339
I walked out. It was raining, 482
I want to throw away, 331
I wish a spider, 338
I work in a dreamscape of reality, 490
I'm a blank, 259
I'm not weeping and weeping, 433
I'm really sad because I've done nothing
    right, 522
I'm tired, 150
I'm torn apart by light, 226
I've been around, 230
Ideas are just ideas, 252
If I left, 408
If I lived here, 295
If I went to a medicine man, 158
In a dream, 493
In one day everything's green, 346
In one swoop, 494
In the middle of Autumn, 419
In the night, 144
In the southwest. The eagle falls, 132
In the world today, 24
In this cooling air, 328
In this space, 340
Inside the cold rain, 392
Inspired to conquer, 388
Instead it's that one damn spot, 5
Is America so different, these, 513
Is beauty lost forever, 449
It is cold, it is cloudy, 517
It is made up of (in our latitude), 171
It only takes a machine, 363
It was night. It turned day, 458
It's a simple trip, 520
It's almost summer, 445
It's gotta be fast, 511
It's here in whatever shoots come up, 17
It's the eye looking at the self, 523

It's the last day of, 425
It's the quiet that we, 522
It's time America, 229
It's windy. . . . . the rain is over, 309

Just lain at cover, 51

Keep me away, 468

Landward flies the night, 487
Last night I went to a bar, 315
Last night my eyes, 286
Last night, the moon was crescent, 483
Laughter filters through the clash of dishes,
    451
Leaped at the caribou, 145
Legs are cold, 18
Let your imagination, 432
Let's face it, 463
Let's get going, 436
Life penetrates, 241
Lift the weights off us, 437
Like a dinosaur licking a tiger, 267
Like a pig of iron, 420
Like a punch in the face, 427
Like a spear afterwards, 129
Like the growth, 254
Loneliness is so feared, 238
Look, ah, dry, 126
Look at the trees shake! 130
Looking at beetles and ants, 485
Looking at the crow on roof, 542
Love has swollen, 225

Man is blood, 384
March 30th and the air, 297
ME NO CARE, 273
Million dreams, billion nights, 537
Minor eruptions in the air, 407
Monday morning in the Americas, 414
Moons of the wind, 377
Morning breaks, 526
Morning ground, 8
Morning shadows, 341
Mothers and fathers, 386
Motion is spirit, 247
Mountains meet hills, back, 458
My arms are heavy and I feel, 537
My breath is gone, 343
My deepness away from you, 515
My eyes hurt, 354

My hair is black, my eyes are black, 217
My head falls on the dirt, 412
My head is swollen, 349
My intellect seems to breathe, 426
My screams, 238

Need time to fill the mind as oceans fill, 530
New day, new find, new food, 469
News continues, 377
No formulas for storm clouds, 457
No more footing, 249
Nobody can get inside me, 332
Noise cells Root barks Piss grass, 3
NOT KNOWING, 321
Nothing exists that does not empty, 155

O anaerobic delights, 356
O ancient Rivers, 405
O beautiful one rising therefore, 204
O bloody days! 502
O clouds above these trees, 324
O fly, disgusting beautiful fly, 496
O gong of wept, 96
O great world that trains me! that loses my,
    151
O height dispersed and head, 137
O hydrant, how strange it is, 493
O if only I could, 347
O Loneliness, 231
O lost world in found continent! 268
O moon, 225
O night of dreams, 447
O one of little turmoil, 531
O Real Spirit! 255
O sacred women going, 20
O waters of April and Winter, 389
O webs inside me, 330
O wild navel, 318
O world without light, 420
Oak oak! like like, 132
Oh bum! 21
Oh young of this world! 398
Old Atlantis, 237
Old world, there are roads in front, 509
On a line reading "Friday Reporters Only," 321
On a night in a distant country, 448
On the desert, 237
On the sleeves of the dark dropped, 489
One by one. The city, 131
One coffee, milk, no sugar, 503
One corner is enough, 3

One lone sea gull, 319
Only a few song birds are out, 319
Open body singing in the trees, 389
Orchard sweet, 169
Orpheus is in my bowels, 246
Out of illusions, out of delusions, 518
Out the window of the clouds, 293
Overpayment, underpayment, Florida lakes,
    516

Pain penetrates, it penetrates deeply, 324
Perched here, 228
Poor animal, his dead tail waving, 413
Poverty needs us in, 168
Radical frozen light, 439
Rain cycle, hold my brains, 380
Rain is not surrounded by sleep like a drum,
    123
Raise the limit, 409
Reach out to the people, 462
Regular quality. Drowsy in the sun, 21
Reporting noise on the west front, 446
Resurrect, reserve, resound. Winter ice, 538
Riding, galloping, here to there, 521
Rising from the river, a mist, 362
Route 3 and lonely, 500

Sacrifice love and record position, 227
Sailing Sailing, 6
Saturday night I buy a soda, 167
Save the morning, 466
Seagulls are in from the sea, 428
See the black bird, 21
She is not wearing, 111
Should I start you, 473
Since this tripod of despair is, 166
Sleep quietly under the snow, 329
Slowly my love, 530
Smoke rises like claws that lock me in, 486
Snow fall like April, 151
So many leaves on trees, 372
So much bad luck, 330
So much that I see, O night, 443
Solid States abound in us, 391
Someday, this moment, 250
Something overtakes me on the train, 515
Sometimes, 320
Sometimes when I sit here, 252
Somewhere between a missile, 536
Song birds, 495
Song birds enter the morning, 450, 545

Songs of the track fly all around, 444
Speeding with me, 234
Stand with feet apart, 533
Staring on the ground, 423
Stars are created, 407
Starting from nothing, 239
Starving snow falling through its cycle, 468
Stay Pure, bright wind, 419
Stop Going! 351
Storm over the land is over, 370
Stretched out in the street, 234
Summer's on the other side, 245
Summertime is in the shimmer, 518
Sunny day with ice, 388
Surrounded, I feel the clouds, 379
Swallow me in all particles, 385
Swamps and people live in a lake, 543
Sweat is pouring, 243
Sweaty hands no memory, 441
Sweet sun that makes the trees, 406

Take away the hours of creation, 535
Take my mouth, 250
Taking me away. . . . , 351
Talk of energy. Mayan sub-flower, 135
Talking outside in the light, 292
Tank cleaning, Getty, sandwiches to go, 536
Thank the gods for life, 539
That should what I habitute, 42
The agonies of fortune, 236
The beach is so windy, 292
The best time is when the body, 495
The blade days, 9
The brook curves to the left, 312
The building's shadow, 242
The bus is screaming on. It is early, 534
The city is up now, 310
The clouds are panting, 20
The dogs are barking, 157
The dying are all over, 434
The economy is good for some, 431
The first August day is over, 376
The first snow, 325
The fish are staying here, 142
The Formula is regained for the ghosts, 340
The ghost of Spring, 256
The girl with the long tumbling wavy light
    hair, 476
The hawks float over us, 411
The helmets, there all alone, 166
The lights are on, 171

The look of the end, 248
The migration flaps, 409
The Mississippi floods, 248
The more along you are the more, 154
The morning is warm. A fan whirling, 533
The multitudes betray the fallen city. The
    glass, 528
The music is played. Play, 10
The night gets lonely, 348
The notes that I hear, 322
The ocean like an open butterfly, 325
The pains flip me around, 290
The pains of children, 400
The Phoenicians are waiting, 450
The police from all over, 415
The purple plant, leaves thick, 488
The rain falls, 167
The rain floods, 156
The river below has tiny whirlpools, 343
The sand is washed from eroded rocks, 319
The shit of the dunes, 317
The soap is wet from the storm, 141
The spread of suffering, 328
The squirrel leaping frightens, 387
The stars are created, 406
The stars fall the same, 395
The steel mill is burning, 434
The stone is hard, 394
The streets against their stomachs, 442
The streets are empty and still, 421
The sun disappears behind hills, 298
The sun is blinding! 273
The sun is in the sky, 259
The sun is shining, 349
The sun on my body, 242
The surface of the mountain flows, 172
The thunder is dirty, 265
The trees have no more leaves, 538
The universe is volatile, 299
The unsteady flow, 309
The waves keep coming, 410
The wind like glass, 251
The winds of the comet, 255
The winds of the comet are quiet, 268
The wine is gone, 262
The woman said, "I saw the royal wedding,
    490
The womb can, 172
The woodwind light, 27
There are no dinosaurs, 18
There is magical, 253

There is no pleasure, yet there is, 429
There is no way, 454
There is not one honest, 235
There will always, 234
There's nothing to love in this, 127
These, my understanding green, 4
They have the corner, 7
They roam through & through, 452
"Things will change, I'll see you later, 529
This is not the place I want to be, 435
This is the second day without anyone, 260
This is the top, 265
This morning I could, 233
This morning I know there's a dawn, 323
This morning Walt Whitman, 472
Thou son of a great woman, 41
Three nazis turned to swans, 457
Thunder on the shore, 369
Tie me down, 323
Tie one on, tie it on, 353
Tile floor, open glass, 430
To indicate is to, 165
To the salt, 266
Today the arrows of, 124
Tomorrow night before the winds blow
    down, 360
Too late, 141
Too many times there is, 538
Toy for the raking gully, 99
Traffic ahead, traffic behind, 512
Trees light up, 251
Try my gate, 235
Tundra and deer, liberty and fear, 523
Tunnels are closed, 535
Turn me around in your hands, O wind! 483
Turn the screw, bang the nail, 543
Two students kiss goodbye, 306

Under high tension towers, 512

Vacant, annulled, disabled, 342
Volcano mud covering exquisite bodies, 463

Walk quietly into the confusion, 534
We are going the park, 170
We are going to the park, 23
We lived in province snow range, 11
We're only little creatures, 503
weep Ah giraffe scordial and unseen, 85

Weeping at the crude greatness, 337
Went a travelin' long time ago, 461
What a beautiful storm! 256
What am I gonna do, 19
What bothers me most running, 132
What comes, comes for you, 527
What do we do with, 9
What holds this together? 290
What I give you tomorrow, 271
What I miss most is, 270
What is a year ending? 516
What landscape should I stalk, 266
What no one else was no, 130
What, no one here? No one, 306
What obsolete! what lift! 63
What says it is gone, 247
What shame! 250
What you can't have is what, 474
Whatever sound it is, 311
When a spirit comes to me and frightens, 433
When a spirit comes to me, 546
When did it change? 238
When I button my fly, 232
When I think of all these fuckin' hours, 545
When I was a child, 504
When you can choke off the under-, 544
Where am I now? 401
Where are we headed? 470
Where are you? 329
Where have I got time, 373
Where is love? 233
While the animals rest, 307
White as a deer's tail, 473
Who is out tonight? 296
Who put me together, 356
Who says you, 243
Who's there? 326
Why are we, 22
Why do I follow you, 361
With wings reached out, 269
Without you, 249
Women have gotten so tall, 230

You are near me. The night, 157
You can't take me with a look, 149
You light like a flashlight, 8
You to me, 438
You're so messed up in the thoughts, 520
Your song, 294